Ever Wonder Why?

EVER WONDER WHY?

and Other Controversial Essays

Thomas Sowell

HOOVER INSTITUTION PRESS
Stanford University   Stanford, California

The Hoover Institution on War, Revolution and Peace, founded at Stanford University in 1919 by Herbert Hoover, who went on to become the thirty-first president of the United States, is an interdisciplinary research center for advanced study on domestic and international affairs. The views expressed in its publications are entirely those of the authors and do not necessarily reflect the views of the staff, officers, or Board of Overseers of the Hoover Institution.

www.hoover.org

Hoover Institution Press Publication No. 548
Hoover Institution at Leland Stanford Junior University,
Stanford, California 94305

First printing, 2006
23 22 21 20 19   14 13 12 11 10 9 8 7

Manufactured in the United States of America
The paper used in this publication meets the minimum requirements of
American National Standard for Information Sciences—Permanence
of Paper for Printed Library Materials, ANSI Z39.48–1992. ∞

Library of Congress Cataloging-in-Publication Data
is available from the Library of Congress
ISBN 978-0-8179-4752-1 (pbk. : alk. paper)
ISBN 978-0-8179-4753-8 (epub)
ISBN 978-0-8179-4757-6 (mobi)
ISBN 978-0-8179-4758-3 (PDF)

Half the harm that is done in this world is due to people who want to feel important. They don't mean to do harm—but the harm does not interest them. Or they do not see it, or they justify it because they are absorbed in the endless struggle to think well of themselves.

T. S. Eliot

Contents

PART III: LEGAL ISSUES

PART IV: POLITICAL ISSUES

PART V: SOCIAL ISSUES

PART VI: EDUCATION ISSUES

PART VII: RACIAL ISSUES

PART VIII: RANDOM THOUGHTS

Preface

Many explanations are given for the events of our time and the events in history. One of the most common explanations is that various external circumstances led or forced people to do this or that, and one of the most overlooked explanations is that various *internal* drives led them to do the things they did, including things that made no sense in terms of the external circumstances. One of these internal drives—especially the desire "to feel important," in T.S. Eliot's words—fits many notions and actions that would be hard to explain otherwise.

The desire of individuals and groups to puff themselves up by imposing their vision on other people is a recurring theme in the culture wars discussed in the first section of the essays that follow. Such attempts at self-aggrandizement in the name of noble-sounding crusades are too often called "idealism" rather than the narrow ego trip that it is.

Right after the section containing essays on culture war issues comes the largest section in this book, on economic issues. The reason for so many essays on economics is not just the importance of the subject itself but also the utter confusion that reigns among the general public, and even among the intelligentsia, over very basic principles of economics—and even very basic words, like "wages," "taxes," or the "national debt."

The great Supreme Court Justice Oliver Wendell Holmes said that we need education in the obvious more than exploration of the obscure. It is especially important to explain economics so plainly that it becomes obvious because so many in politics and the media have created so much confusion in the process of spinning issues to fit their own agendas. Those who want a complete introduction to the subject can read my *Basic Economics* but the essays here simply try to clarify particular misconceptions on particular issues.

A wide range of legal, social, racial, and educational issues are dealt with in the other sections of this book. All of these essays first appeared as syndicated columns carried in newspapers across the country. As such, they had to be readable and concise, and they often dealt with issues that were in the news. However, from the large number of these columns written over the past few years I have selected for publication here those columns which deal with issues of continuing relevance and interest.

While I take responsibility for all the conclusions reached in these essays, I must also acknowledge the work of others that made these writings possible. First of all, there is my research assistant, Na Liu, whose insights as well as diligence have enabled me to discuss the wide range of topics covered in these columns with a background of knowledge to draw on. She has been very ably assisted by the dedicated work of Elizabeth Costa. All this is made possible by the Hoover Institution at Stanford University, where we are all employed and which has generously supported our research. Finally, I must acknowledge the contribution of Karen Duryea, my editor at Creators Syndicate, who has caught many a typographical or grammatical error in my columns, as well as inadvertent misstatements, saving me from public embarrassment.

While many serious issues are discussed in these pages,

sometimes there is also a little humor, without which it would be hard to face many of life's realities.

Thomas Sowell
Hoover Institution
Stanford University

PART I

THE CULTURE WARS

Ever Wonder Why?

When you have seen scenes of poverty and squalor in many Third World countries, either in person or in pictures, have you ever wondered why we in America have been spared such a fate?

When you have learned of the bitter oppressions that so many people have suffered under, in despotic countries around the world, have you ever wondered why Americans have been spared?

Have scenes of government-sponsored carnage and lethal mob violence in countries like Rwanda or in the Balkans ever made you wonder why such horrifying scenes are not found on the streets of America?

Nothing is easier than to take for granted what we are used to, and to imagine that it is more or less natural, so that it requires no explanation. Instead, many Americans demand explanations of why things are not even better and express indignation that they are not.

Some people think the issue is whether the glass is half empty or half full. More fundamentally, the question is whether the glass started out empty or started out full.

Those who are constantly looking for the "root causes" of poverty, of crime, and of other national and international problems, act as if prosperity and law-abiding behavior were so natural that it is their absence which has to be explained. But a casual glance around the world today, or back through history, would dispel any notion that good things just happen naturally, much less inevitably.

The United States of America is the exception, not the rule. Once we realize that America is an exception, we might even have a sense of gratitude for having been born here, even if gratitude has become un-cool in many quarters. At the very least, we might develop some concern for seeing that whatever has made this country better off is not lost or discarded—or eroded away, bit by bit, until it is gone.

Those among us who are constantly rhapsodizing about "change" in vague and general terms seem to have no fear that a blank check for change can be a huge risk in a world where so many other countries that are different are also far worse off.

Chirping about "change" may produce a giddy sense of excitement or of personal exaltation but, as usual, the devil is in the details. Even despotic countries that have embraced sweeping changes have often found that these were changes for the worse.

The czars in Russia, the shah of Iran, the Batista regime in Cuba, were all despotic. But they look like sweethearts compared to the regimes that followed. For example, the czars never executed as many people in half a century as Stalin did in one day.

Even the best countries must make changes and the United States has made many economic, social, and political changes for the better. But that is wholly different from making "change" a mantra.

To be for or against "change" in general is childish. Everything depends on the specifics. To be for generic "change" is to say that what we have is so bad that any change is likely to be for the better.

Such a pose may make some people feel superior to others who find much that is worth preserving in our values, traditions and institutions. The status quo is never sacrosanct but its very existence proves that it is viable, as seductive theoretical alternatives may not turn out to be.

Most Americans take our values, traditions and institutions so much for granted that they find it hard to realize how much all these things are under constant attack in our schools, our colleges, and in much of the press, the movies and literature.

There is a culture war going on within the United States—and in fact, within Western civilization as a whole—which may ultimately have as much to do with our survival, or failure to survive, as the war on terrorism.

There are all sorts of financial, ideological, and psychic rewards for undermining American society and its values. Unless some of us realize the existence of this culture war, and the high stakes in it, we can lose what cost those Americans before us so much to win and preserve.

Animal Rites

If you think there is a limit to how much childishness there is among Californians, you may want to reconsider—especially for Californians in academic communities.

Recently a mountain lion was discovered up in a tree in Palo Alto, a residential community adjacent to Stanford University. This was at about the time of day when a nearby school was getting ready to let out. There had already been an incident of a horse being found mauled by some animal on Stanford land, and some thought it might have been a mountain lion that did it.

Fearing that the mountain lion might find one of the local school children a tempting target, the police shot and killed the animal. Outrage against the police erupted up and down the San Francisco peninsula and as far away as Marin County, on the other side of the Golden Gate Bridge, more than 30 miles away.

According to the *San Francisco Chronicle*, "The police agency has been flooded with outraged calls and e-mails from people inflamed by TV news videotape of the lion lolling peacefully in a tree just before an officer shot it to death with a high-powered rifle."

Yes, the mountain lion was sitting peacefully. That is what cats do before they pounce—usually very swiftly.

Second-guessers always have easy alternatives. One protester against "the murdering of such a beautiful creature" said that it "easily could have been removed from the premises and relocated" and that the "dirty blood-thirsty bastards" who killed it should be ashamed of themselves.

The protester offered no helpful hints on how you "easily" remove a mountain lion from a tree—and certainly did not volunteer to demonstrate how to do it in person the next time the police find a mountain lion up a tree in a residential neighborhood.

Animal rights advocates said the police could have given the mountain lion "a chance" by attempting to tranquilize it while it was up in the tree, and save shooting as a last resort if it turned aggressive.

A makeshift shrine has been erected on the spot where the mountain lion died. Flowers, cards and photos have been placed around it.

This is an academic community where indignation is a way of life. Those engaged in moral exhibitionism have no time for mundane realities.

The police, of course, have to deal with mundane realities all the time. Not long before this episode, the police had tried to capture three mountain lion cubs by shooting them with tranquilizers. They missed on two out of three tries with one cub.

What if the police had shot a tranquilizer gun at the adult mountain lion in the tree and missed? Would they have had a chance to get off a second shot at a swiftly moving target before he pounced on one of the hundreds of children that were soon to be leaving school near him?

Moral exhibitionists never make allowance for the police missing, whether with tranquilizers shot at mountain lions or bullets fired at a criminal. The perpetually indignant are forever wondering why it took so many shots.

It would never occur to people with academic degrees

and professorships that they are both ignorant and incompetent in vast areas of human life, much less that they should keep that in mind before they vent their emotions and wax self-righteous.

Degrees show that you have knowledge in some special area. Too often they embolden people to pontificate on a wide range of other subjects where they don't know what they are talking about.

The fact that academics are overwhelmingly of the political left is perfectly consistent with their assumption that third parties—especially third parties like themselves—should be controlling the decisions of other people who have first-hand knowledge and experience.

The cops probably haven't read Chaucer and don't know what existentialism is. But they may know what danger is.

Some Palo Alto parents of small children living near where the mountain lion was killed said that the police did the right thing. There are still some pockets of sanity, even in Palo Alto.

"Us" or "Them"?

A reader recently sent me an e-mail about a woman he had met and fallen for. Apparently the attraction was mutual—until one fateful day the subject of the environment came up.

She was absolutely opposed to any drilling for oil in Alaska, on grounds of what harm she said it would do to the environment.

He argued that, since oil was going to be drilled for somewhere in the world anyway, was it not better to drill where there were environmental laws to provide at least some kinds of safeguards, rather than in countries where there were none?

That was the end of a beautiful relationship.

Environmentalist true believers don't think in terms of trade-offs and cost-benefit analysis. There are things that are sacred to them. Trying to get them to compromise on those things would be like trying to convince a Muslim to eat pork, if it was only twice a week.

Compromise and tolerance are not the hallmarks of true believers. What they believe in goes to the heart of what they are. As far as true believers are concerned, you are either one of Us or one of Them.

The man apparently thought that it was just a question of which policy would produce which results. But many issues that look on the surface like they are just about which alternative would best serve the general public are really about being one of Us or one of Them—and this woman was not about to become one of Them.

Many crusades of the political left have been misunderstood by people who do not realize that these crusades are about establishing the identity and the superiority of the crusaders.

T.S. Eliot understood this more than half a century ago when he wrote: "Half the harm that is done in this world is due to people who want to feel important. They don't mean to do harm—but the harm does not interest them. Or they do not see it, or they justify it because they are absorbed in the endless struggle to think well of themselves."

In this case, the man thought he was asking the woman to accept a certain policy as the lesser of two evils, when in fact he was asking her to give up her sense of being one of the morally anointed.

This is not unique to our times or to environmentalists. Back during the 1930s, in the years leading up to World War II, one of the fashionable self-indulgences of the left in Britain was to argue that the British should disarm "as an example to others" in order to serve the interests of peace.

When economist Roy Harrod asked one of his friends whether she thought that disarming Britain would cause Hitler to disarm, her reply was: "Oh, Roy, have you lost all your idealism?"

In other words, it was not really about which policy would produce what results. It was about personal identification with lofty goals and kindred souls.

The ostensible goal of peace was window-dressing. Ultimately it was not a question whether arming or disarming Britain was more likely to deter Hitler. It was a question of which policy would best establish the moral superiority of the anointed and solidify their identification with one another.

"Peace" movements are not judged by the empirical test of how often they actually produce peace or how often their disarmament tempts an aggressor into war. It is not an empirical question. It is an article of faith and a badge of identity.

Yasser Arafat was awarded the Nobel Prize for peace—not for actually producing peace but for being part of what was called "the peace process" in the Middle East, based on fashionable notions that were common bonds among members of what are called "peace movements" around the world.

Meanwhile, nobody suggested awarding a Nobel Prize for peace to Ronald Reagan, just because he brought the nuclear dangers of a decades-long cold war to an end. He did it the opposite way from how members of "peace movements" thought it should be done.

Reagan beefed up the military and entered into an "arms race" that he knew would bankrupt the Soviet Union if they didn't back off, even though arms races are anathema to members of "peace movements."

The fact that events proved him right was no excuse, as far as members of "peace movements" were concerned. As far as they were concerned, he was not one of Us. He was one of Them.

Twisted History

One of the reasons our children do not measure up academically to children in other countries is that so much time is spent in American classrooms twisting our history for ideological purposes.

"How would you feel if you were a Native American who saw the European invaders taking away your land?" is the kind of question our children are likely to be confronted with in our schools. It is a classic example of trying to look at the past with the assumptions—and the ignorance—of the present.

One of the things we take for granted today is that it is wrong to take other people's land by force. Neither American Indians nor the European invaders believed that.

Both took other people's land by force—as did Asians, Africans, Arabs, Polynesians, and others. The Indians no doubt regretted losing so many battles. But that is wholly different from saying that they thought battles were the wrong way to settle the question of who would control the land.

Today's child cannot possibly put himself or herself in the mindset of Indians centuries ago, without infinitely more knowledge of history than our schools have ever taught.

Nor is understanding history the purpose of such questions. The purpose is to score points against Western society. In short, propaganda has replaced education as the goal of too many "educators."

Schools are not the only institutions that twist history to score ideological points. "Never Forget That They Owned Lots of Slaves" is the huge headline across the front page of the *New York Times*' book review section in its December 14, 2004 issue. Inside was an indictment of George Washington and Thomas Jefferson.

Of all the tragic facts about the history of slavery, the most astonishing to an American today is that, although slavery was a worldwide institution for thousands of years, nowhere in the world was slavery a controversial issue prior to the 18th century.

People of every race and color were enslaved—and enslaved others. White people were still being bought and sold as slaves in the Ottoman Empire, decades after American blacks were freed.

Everyone hated the idea of being a slave but few had any qualms about enslaving others. Slavery was just not an issue, not even among intellectuals, much less among political leaders, until the 18th century—and then it was an issue only in Western civilization.

Among those who turned against slavery in the 18th century were George Washington, Thomas Jefferson, Patrick Henry and other American leaders. You could research all of 18th century Africa or Asia or the Middle East without finding any comparable rejection of slavery there.

But who is singled out for scathing criticism today? American leaders of the 18th century.

Deciding that slavery was wrong was much easier than deciding what to do with millions of people from another continent, of another race, and without any historical preparation for living as free citizens in a society like that of the United States, where they were 20 percent of the total population.

It is clear from the private correspondence of Washington, Jefferson, and many others that their moral rejection of slavery was unambiguous, but the practical question of what to do now had them baffled. That would remain so for more than half a century.

In 1862, a ship carrying slaves from Africa to Cuba, in violation of a ban on the international slave trade, was captured on the high seas by the U.S. Navy. The crew were imprisoned and the captain was hanged in the United States—despite the fact that slavery itself was still legal at the time in Africa, in Cuba, and in the United States.

What does this tell us? That enslaving people was considered an abomination but what to do with millions of people who were already enslaved was not equally clear.

That question was finally answered by a war in which one life was lost for every six people freed. Maybe that was the only answer. But don't pretend today that it was an easy answer—or that those who grappled with the dilemma in the 18th century were some special villains, when most leaders and most people around the world at that time saw nothing wrong with slavery.

Incidentally, the September 2004 issue of *National Geographic* had an article about the millions of people still enslaved around the world right now. But where was the moral indignation about that?

Explaining to the Grand Kids

These of us who are optimists believe that someday sanity will return to our society. Our media, our officials—perhaps even our schools and colleges—will begin to talk sense. Those of you who are young may live to see it.

But there is a down side to sanity. Once there is a whole generation raised to think—to examine evidence and use logic—you are going to be confronted with a need to explain to your grandchildren how our generation could have done the things we did. You don't want your grand kids to think that your whole generation was crazy.

"Grandpa," they will say, "today we were reading in history—"

"History?"

"Yes, Grandpa. There's a subject in school called history."

"Well, we didn't have that back in my day. We had social studies or current events or multiculturalism. But we didn't have this thing you call history."

"Well, history is about what happened in the past, Grandpa—like back when you were young."

"I'll be darned."

"Anyway, we learned in history today that back in your times, people who refused to work were supported by people who did work. Is that true, Grandpa?"

"Well, yes, we were compassionate to the poor and the downtrodden, like the homeless and such."

"Why were people homeless, Grandpa?"

"They didn't have enough money to buy houses or rent apartments."

"Were you homeless, Grandpa?"

"No. I had a regular job and used part of my salary to pay the rent."

"Why didn't the homeless do that?"

"Well, it is hard to explain. They had a different kind of lifestyle, they sort of dropped out of society. They lived a more laid back kind of way."

"Took drugs?"

"Yeah, drugs, alcohol, stuff like that."

"And you gave them money that you had worked for, Grandpa?"

"Well, not so much personally, but I paid taxes and the government gave money to the homeless, provided places for them to sleep, and so forth."

"But you voted for the government, Grandpa."

"Yeah, most of the time."

"If the voters didn't want their money spent this way, the elected officials wouldn't have done it."

"You sure do a lot of thinking things out, honey."

"That's called logic. They teach that in school too."

"Logic? I heard something about it vaguely, but we didn't have time for it in school when I was young. We had to express our feelings about things like trees and animal rights and being non-judgmental."

"You weren't supposed to have judgment, Grandpa?"

"Well, if you were judgmental, that might hurt someone else's self-esteem."

"So you couldn't tell the homeless to go get a job like you had, because it would hurt their self-esteem?"

"Exactly. It would be cultural imperialism—and that

would be wrong because one culture is just as good as another."

"But, Grandpa, in our history class we learned that people from all over the world were trying desperately to get into the United States—some paying to get smuggled in from Mexico or Asia, some trying to cross the Caribbean in leaky boats and drowning."

"Why, yes, that happened."

"But, if all cultures were equal, why were these people risking their lives trying to go from one culture to another?"

"I never really thought about that, honey. Gee, they must be working you pretty hard in school, to have you doing all this thinking."

"Aren't people supposed to think, Grandpa?"

"I suppose it's all right for those who like it. I don't want to be judgmental."

Human Livestock

An old television special featured great boxing matches of the past, including a video of a match between legendary light-heavyweight champion Archie Moore and a young Canadian fighter named Yvon Durelle. In that fight, each man was knocked down four times. Since Archie Moore was also among those serving as commentators on the program, someone asked him if he knew that this was a great boxing match while he was fighting it.

"Yes!" he replied emphatically. At the time, he had said to himself: "This is the kind of fight that any fighter would love to be in—a knockdown, drag-out—and emerge the winner."

Overcoming adversity is one of our great desires and one of our great sources of pride. But it is something that our anointed deep thinkers strive to eliminate from our lives, through everything from grade inflation to the welfare state.

The anointed want to eliminate stress, challenge, striving, and competition. They want the necessities of life to be supplied as "rights"—which is to say, at the taxpayers' expense, without anyone's being forced to work for those necessities, except of course the taxpayers.

Nothing is to be earned. "Self-esteem" is to be dispensed to school children as largess from the teacher. Adults are to have their medical care and other necessities dispensed as largess from the government. People are to be mixed and matched by race and sex and whatever else the anointed want to take into account, in order to present whatever kind of picture the anointed think should be presented.

This is a vision of human beings as livestock to be fed by the government and herded and tended by the anointed. All the things that make us human beings are to be removed from our lives and we are to live as denatured creatures controlled and directed by our betters.

Those things that help human beings be independent and self-reliant—whether automobiles, guns, the free market, or vouchers—provoke instant hostility from the anointed.

Automobiles enable you to come and go as you wish, without so much as a "by your leave" to your betters. The very idea that other people will go where they want, live where they want, how they want, and send their children to whatever schools they choose, is galling to the anointed, for it denies the very specialness that is at the heart of their picture of themselves.

Guns are completely inappropriate for the kind of sheep-like people the anointed envision or the orderly, prepackaged world in which they are to live. When you are in mortal danger, you are supposed to dial 911, so that the police can arrive on the scene some time later, identify your body, and file reports in triplicate.

The free market is a daily assault on the vision of the anointed. Just think of all those millions of people out there buying whatever they want, whenever they want, whether or not the anointed think it is good for them.

Think of those people earning whatever incomes they happen to get from producing goods or services for other people, at prices resulting from supply and demand, with the anointed cut out of the loop entirely and standing on the sidelines in helpless frustration, unable to impose their particular vision of "social justice."

The welfare state is not really about the welfare of the masses. It is about the egos of the elites.

One of the most dangerous things about the welfare state is that it breaks the connection between what people have produced and what they consume, at least in many people's minds. For the society as a whole, that connection remains as fixed as ever, but the welfare state makes it possible for individuals to think of money or goods as just arbitrary dispensations.

Thus those who have less can feel a grievance against "society" and are less inhibited about stealing or vandalizing. And the very concept of gratitude or obligation disappears— even the obligation of common decency out of respect for other people. The next time you see a bum leaving drug needles in a park where children play or urinating in the street, you are seeing your tax dollars at work and the end result of the vision of the anointed.

The Wright Stuff

One of the greatest inventions of the 20th century—indeed, one of the landmark inventions in the history of the human race—was the work of a couple of young men who had never gone to college and who were just bicycle mechanics in Dayton, Ohio.

That part of the United States is often referred to disdainfully as "flyover country" because it is part of America that the east coast and west coast elites fly over on their way to what they consider more important places. But they are able to fly over it only because of those mechanics in Dayton.

The Wright brothers' first airplane flight was only about 120 feet—roughly the distance from home plate to second base—and not as long as the wingspan of a 747. But it began one of the longest journeys ever taken by the human race, and that journey is not over yet, as we soar farther into space.

Man had dreamed of flying for centuries and others were hard at work on the project in various places around the world when the Wright brothers finally got their plane off the ground on December 17, 1903. It didn't matter how long or how short the flight was. What mattered was that they showed that it could be done.

Alas, Orville and Wilbur Wright are today pigeon-holed as "dead white males" whom we are supposed to ignore, if not deplore. Had either of them been a woman, or black or any of a number of other specially singled out groups, this hundredth anniversary of their flight would be a national holiday, with an orgy of parades and speeches across the length and breadth of the country.

Recently, a reporter for a well-known magazine phoned me to check on some facts about famous people who talked late and whom I had mentioned in my book, *The Einstein Syndrome*. Her editor wanted to know why there was not more "diversity" among the people I cited. Almost all of them were men, for example, and white men at that.

The vast majority of people who talk late are boys and I had no control over that. In a predominantly white society, it should not be surprising that famous men who talked late were mostly white. No doubt in China most would be Chinese.

The reporter seemed somewhat relieved when I pointed out that the distinguished mathematician Julia Robinson and famed 19th century concert pianist Clara Schumann were among the women discussed in my book. Ramanujan, a self-taught mathematical genius from India, came to my attention right after the book went into print, but the reporter seemed happy to be able to add his name to the list of famous late-talkers.

This mania for "diversity" has spread far and wide. When I looked through my nieces' high school math book, I saw many pictures of noted mathematicians but—judging by those pictures—you would never dream that anything worth noting had ever been done in mathematics by any white males.

This petty-minded falsification of history is less disturbing than the indoctrination-minded "educators" who are twisting reality to fit their vision. Those who cannot tell the difference between education and brainwashing do not belong in our schools.

History is what happened, not what we wish had happened or what a theory says should have happened. One of the reasons for the great value of history is that it allows us to check our current beliefs against hard facts from around the world and across the centuries.

But history cannot be a reality check for today's fashionable visions when history is itself shaped by those visions. When that happens, we are sealing ourselves up in a closed world of assumptions.

There is no evidence that the Wright brothers intended the airplane to be flown, or ridden in, only by white people. Many of the great breakthroughs in science and technology were gifts to the whole human race. Those whose efforts created these breakthroughs were exalted because of their contributions to mankind, not to their particular tribe or sex.

In trying to cheapen those people as "dead white males" we only cheapen ourselves and do nothing to promote similar achievements by people of every description. When the Wright brothers rose off the ground, we all rose off the ground.

The Legacy of Eric Hoffer

The twentieth anniversary of the death of Eric Hoffer passed with very little notice of one of the most incisive thinkers of his time—a man whose writings continue to have great relevance to our times.

How many people today even know of this remarkable man with no formal schooling, who spent his life in manual labor—most of it as a longshoreman—and who wrote some of the most insightful commentary on our society and trends in the world?

You need only read one of his classics like *The True Believer: Thoughts on the Nature of Mass Movements* to realize that you are seeing the work of an intellectual giant.

Having spent several years in blindness when most other children were in school, Hoffer could only do manual labor after he recovered his eyesight, but he was determined to educate himself. He began by looking for a big book with small print to take with him as he set out on a job as a migratory farm worker.

The book that turned out to fill this bill—based on size and words—was the essays of Montaigne. Over the years, he read many landmark books, including Hitler's *Mein Kampf.* If ever there was a walking advertisement for the Great Books approach to education, it was Eric Hoffer.

Among Hoffer's insights about mass movements was that they are an outlet for people whose individual significance is meager in the eyes of the world and—more important—in their own eyes. He pointed out that the leaders of the

Nazi movement were men whose artistic and intellectual aspirations were wholly frustrated.

Hoffer said: "The less justified a man is in claiming excellence for his own self, the more ready he is to claim all excellence for his nation, his religion, his race or his holy cause."

People who are fulfilled in their own lives and careers are not the ones attracted to mass movements: "A man is likely to mind his own business when it is worth minding," Hoffer said. "When it is not, he takes his mind off his own meaningless affairs by minding other people's business."

What Hoffer was describing was the political busybody, the zealot for a cause—the "true believer," who filled the ranks of ideological movements that created the totalitarian tyrannies of the 20th century.

In a comment very relevant to the later disintegration of the Soviet bloc in Eastern Europe and the fall of Communism in the Soviet Union itself, he observed that totalitarian governments' "moment of greatest danger is when they begin to reform, that is to say, when they begin to show liberal tendencies."

Mikhail Gorbachev's place in history was secured by his failure to understand that and his willingness to believe that a decent and humane Communist society was possible. But, once the people in Eastern Europe no longer had to fear tanks or the gulags, the statues of Lenin and Stalin began being toppled from their pedestals, like the governments they represented.

Contrary to the prevailing assumptions of his time, Eric Hoffer did not believe that revolutionary movements were based on the sufferings of the downtrodden. "Where people toil from sunrise to sunset for a bare living, they nurse no grievances and dream no dreams," he said. He had spent years living among such people and being one of them.

Hoffer's insights may help explain something that many of us have found very puzzling—the offspring of wealthy families spending their lives and their inherited money backing radical movements. He said: "Unlimited opportunities can be as potent a cause of frustration as a paucity or lack of opportunities."

What can people with inherited fortunes do that is at all commensurate with their unlimited opportunities, much less what their parents or grandparents did to create the fortune in the first place, starting from far fewer opportunities?

Like the frustrated artists and failed intellectuals who turn to mass movements for fulfillment, rich heirs cannot win the game of comparison of individual achievements. So they must change the game. As zealots for radical movements, they often attack the very things that made their own good fortune possible, as well as undermining the freedom and well-being of other people.

One-Uppers versus Survival

Among the many commemorations of the September 11th anniversary, the one at Berkeley was unique. The American flag was banned because it might offend people from other countries. "The Star Spangled Banner" was banned because it was considered too militaristic, while "God Bless America" was not regarded as an acceptable substitute because God is politically incorrect in Berkeley.

This might all be just an incidental sidelight on the silliness of Berkeley, except that such attitudes are far more widespread among academics, the literati, and the glitterati. Too often such attitudes are based on nothing more substantial than a desire to be part of the self-anointed elite who are one-up on everyone else.

Being one-up is so important to some people that it colors the way they see every issue and can even override concern for their own safety in a world of international terrorism. One of the ways of being one-up is to jump on the bandwagon of the latest fads, like being non-judgmental or supporting multiculturalism and deconstruction. These clever sophistries are the self-indulgences of sheltered and comfortable people.

Does anyone suffering the agonies of some terrible disease question whether what he is experiencing is real or just a matter of "perceptions" that are "socially constructed"? Does a mother whose child has died in her arms question whether that is of any greater significance than swatting a mosquito? Do people who risk their lives trying to escape from some brutal dictatorship and reach American soil regard all cultures as "equally valid"?

People can define things inside their own heads any way they want to. It is only when they pretend to be talking about things outside their heads, in the real world, that they spread intellectual confusion and social chaos. Many a foolish policy is based on trying to make the real world match the picture inside someone's head.

Since all people and all cultures are equal—inside the heads of the one-uppers—any disparities in the real world are seen as injustices to be corrected. Therefore, if a high school punishes more black males than Asian females for misconduct, then apparently that school must be racist and should be sued.

Differences in income, mortality rates, unemployment, and innumerable other things are all automatically suspect as evils of society, because different groups cannot possibly be behaving differently, since they are equal inside the heads of the one-uppers. Countries that are poor cannot possibly be less productive, but must have been "exploited" somehow.

People who think this way are especially dangerous when we are facing mortal perils, such as international terrorism. Since there is moral equivalence inside their heads, their conclusion is that we must have done something wrong to make terrorists hate us.

It will never occur to such people that the kind of envy and resentments which they themselves promote incessantly may be behind the hatred from those who are lagging far behind the progress of the West, and who can achieve significance only by destruction.

We cannot do anything about what is inside other people's heads—except let it stay there and not get inside ours. But getting inside our heads, and especially inside the heads of our children, is the compelling urge of those who want to make the real world outside match their inner vision.

Why? Because theirs is a very self-flattering vision, which establishes them as morally one-up on the rest of us. Going against the common sense of ordinary people is the key to their self-exaltation, whether they are favoring criminals over victims, animals over humans, or other countries over America.

In a long war against terrorism, where we may have to both suffer and inflict terrible devastation, unity and resolve are the keys to enduring and prevailing. One-uppers are the last thing we need. They are enemies within, who can be the most dangerous kinds of enemies.

If they are so preoccupied with flattering their own vanity that they do not understand that their own survival is at stake, so be it. But the tragedy is that millions of other people's survival is also at stake.

The Equality Dogma

A statement in this column that black students usually do not perform as well in school as white students or Asian American students brought fierce objections. Some people seemed to think that this was a personal opinion—or even an immoral remark.

It never seemed to occur to them that this was a verifiable fact, shown by innumerable studies over the years by many scholars of various races. As John Adams said, more than two centuries ago: "Facts are stubborn things, and whatever may be our wishes, our inclinations, or the dictates of our passions, they cannot alter the state of facts and evidence."

More is involved than a confusion between facts and opinions. The reigning dogma of our time is equality—and anything that seems to go against that dogma creates an automatic response, much like the conditioned responses of Pavlov's dog.

When discussing equality, we must at least be clear in our own minds as to what we mean: Equality of *what?* Performance? Potential? Treatment? Humanity? Too often, fervor for the word serves as a substitute for clarity as to its meaning.

It is an undeniable fact that different groups have different performances across a whole spectrum of activities. Does anyone seriously believe that whites usually play basketball just as well as blacks? Is anyone surprised when

Asian American youngsters walk off with science prizes, year after year?

When it comes to performance, huge disparities are the rule rather than the exception. And performance is what pays off.

Those who are politically correct may try to claim that these disparities are all "stereotypes" or "perceptions" but hard data show the best selling beers in America to be those created by people of German ancestry. It is the same story on the other side of the world, where China's famed Tsingtao beer was also created by Germans. And Germans have been leading beer brewers in Europe, Australia, and South America.

What upsets some people is the inference that performance differences reflect innate differences in potential. But there are huge differences in all the things that turn potential into performance.

Back in the early 19th century, a Russian official reported that even the poorest Jews there somehow managed to have books in their homes and "their entire population studies," while books were virtually unknown among most of the surrounding population.

When C-SPAN's Brian Lamb asked author Abigail Thernstrom why Jews scored so high on mental tests, she replied: "They have been preparing for them for a thousand years."

A recent study by the United Nations shows that publications per capita in Europe today are at least ten times as numerous as in the Arab countries or in Africa. How could equal potential lead to equal performance when there are such great disparities in the intervening factors?

The fact that some societies have long educated both girls and boys, while others have not bothered to educate most girls, means that some societies have thrown away half their inborn talents and abilities. How could the performances of such societies not be different?

Recognizing the equal humanity of all peoples, and a need to treat everyone with decency and compassion, is very different from insisting on a dogma that their performances are all equal.

It is not just politically correct people but government agencies and the highest courts in the land that dogmatize against any recognition of differences in performances among groups. Statistical differences in outcomes automatically fall under suspicion of discrimination, as if the groups themselves could not possibly be any different in behavior or performance.

Any school that disciplines black boys much more frequently than Asian American girls can be risking a federal lawsuit, as if there could not possibly be any differences in behavior among the children themselves. Employers can be judged guilty of discrimination, even if no one can find a single person who was discriminated against, if their hiring and promotions data show differences among ethnic groups or between women and men.

The biggest losers from these dogmatic notions are people who very much need to change their behavior, but from whom that crucial knowledge is withheld by their "leaders" and "friends."

The Inequality Dogma

This is truly the age of dogma when it comes to differences between groups. Some will blindly deny that intergroup differences in performances are anything other than "stereotypes," "perceptions," or "discrimination."

At the other end of the spectrum, the dogma is that mental differences especially, whether among individuals or groups, are innate in the genes. Reaction against this view is so strong in some places that it can literally be a federal case if schools give IQ tests to black children.

Both these opposing views go back for centuries. Back in the 18th century, Adam Smith said that the difference between porters and philosophers was due to education and suggested that there are fewer innate differences among human beings than among dogs.

On the other side, an Islamic scholar of the 10th century noted that Europeans grow more pale the farther north you go and also that the "farther they are to the north the more stupid, gross, and brutish they are."

This correlation between skin color and mental ability would of course be anathema to the politically correct today—and the question as to whether it was true or false would never get off the ground. But what were the facts, as of the 10th century?

Since antiquity, Mediterranean Europe—especially at the eastern end—had been far more advanced than northern Europe in technology, organization, literacy and all the things that make for a more advanced society. The fact that this has all changed in the centuries since then does not mean that this 10th century scholar was not correct in what he said when he said it.

At the very least, he was there and we were not.

Unfortunately, facts have played a very subordinate role in much discussion of differences among groups, races, nations, and civilizations—whether among those arguing for innate equality or for innate inequality.

In the early 20th century, many believers in innate inequality presented what may have seemed like a logically airtight argument that our national IQ was in danger of declining over time, because people with low IQs usually had more children than people with high IQs. The eugenics movement and the birth control movement sought to counter this trend by reducing the number of children born to low IQ people.

The logical airtightness of this argument turned out to be its greatest vulnerability when confronted with hard facts. Extensive research by Professor James R. Flynn, an American expatriate in New Zealand, has shown that in fact whole nations have had their performances on mental tests rise by substantial amounts over the years.

This should never have happened if IQ tests measured innate ability, predetermined by genes. Yet Professor Flynn's work, widely recognized among scholars, showed more than a dozen countries where whole generations answered more IQ questions correctly than their parents or grandparents had.

Because IQ tests by definition have an average score of 100, the standards keep getting changed. In other words, if the average person answers 42 questions correctly on a given IQ test at a given time, then 42 correct answers will be counted as an IQ of 100.

A generation later, if the average person answers 53 questions correctly on that same test, then 53 correct answers will be defined as an IQ of 100. What this means is that there was nothing to indicate how much IQ test results were improving until Professor Flynn went all the way back to the original raw scores and discovered how much they had risen over the generations.

The time is long overdue to let facts be acknowledged as facts, whatever our differing philosophies or hopes may be. The preponderance of evidence is that northern Europeans were not nearly as advanced as southern Europeans in the 10th century. If there had been IQ tests given then, the northerners would undoubtedly have come in a poor second.

By the time real IQ tests had been developed and given in early 20th century America, immigrants from northern Europe scored higher than immigrants from southern Europe, many of the latter having IQs similar to those of American blacks. We don't need to fight the tests. We need to change the reality.

Equality, Inequality, and Fate

One of the confusions that plagues discussions of equality and inequality is a confusion between the vagaries of fate and the sins of man. There are plenty of both but they need to be sharply distinguished from one another.

The plain fact that there are large differences among individuals in incomes, occupations and whole ways of life dependent upon these things has been widely seen as "unfair," especially when the accident of birth has had much to do with these large economic and social differences.

Life is unfair. There is no point denying it. Indeed, it is hard even to imagine how life could possibly be fair, given all the innumerable factors that go into individual success or failure—and how these factors vary greatly from one person to another, one group to another, and one nation or civilization to another.

Whatever the potentialities with which anyone enters the world, the development of those potentialities into specific skills and abilities depends on each individual's parents, schools, peers and the surrounding culture and its values. These are never the same for everyone.

Eskimos no doubt have all the intelligence required to grow pineapples but they are unlikely to have the experience to do so. Nor are Hawaiians likely to know how to hunt seals in the Arctic. Children who grow up in homes where sports are discussed constantly, but science is not, are unlikely to have the same goals or careers as children who grow up in homes where the reverse is true.

None of this is really anyone's fault, not even that universal scapegoat, "society." These are simply the vagaries of fate.

For thousands of years, the whole Western Hemisphere had no opportunity to develop in the same way as Europe or Asia, because horses and oxen enabled Europeans and Asians to build their agriculture and their transport around these beasts of burden—neither of which existed in the Western Hemisphere until they were brought here by European invaders.

Whole ways of life had to be different on this half of the planet from what they were on the vast Eurasian land mass. Whose fault was that?

Some ethnic groups have an average age that is a decade older than the average age of others, and whole countries like Germany and Italy have average ages that are two decades older than the average age in Afghanistan or Yemen.

Is that a level playing field? No! It is an unfair advantage to those with more experience and the increased capabilities that come with experience.

Other differences are due to the sins of man—discrimination, conquest, slavery and more. Yet, whatever the sources of the differences among people, those differences are huge and the economic consequences are huge.

None of this is hard to understand in itself. But much of it gets confused and twisted by the rhetoric, the visions and the crusades of the intelligentsia, politicians, mush heads and hot heads.

Even our courts of law are ready to consider different distributions of groups in employment as evidence that the employer discriminated, since it is apparently beyond the pale to consider that the groups themselves may differ, whether in quantifiable ways like age or in intangible ways like attitudes.

So deeply ingrained is this egalitarian dogma that different rates of passing tests from one group to another are taken as evidence that something is wrong with the tests. Different rates of promotion at work or in school are taken as virtual proof that the employer or the school is doing something wrong.

Best-selling author Shelby Steele has argued persuasively that whites are afraid of being considered racists and blacks are afraid of being considered innately inferior—and that both do many foolish and counterproductive things as a result. Such attitudes apply even beyond racial issues.

A nation's laws and policies need to serve more serious purposes than allowing people to escape their psychological hangups. The time is overdue for these laws and policies to be based on realities and geared toward consequences.

Hiroshima

Every August, there are some Americans who insist on wringing their hands over the dropping of the atomic bomb on Hiroshima on August 6, 1945, so it was perhaps inevitable that such people would have an orgy of wallowing in guilt on the 60th anniversary of that tragic day. *Time* magazine has page after page of photographs of people scarred by the radiation, as if General Sherman had not already said long ago that war is hell.

Winston Churchill once spoke of the secrets of the atom, "hitherto mercifully withheld from man." We can all lament that this terrible power of mass destruction has been revealed to the world and fear its ominous consequences for us all, including our children and grandchildren. But that is wholly different from saying that a great moral evil was committed when the first atomic bombs were dropped on Hiroshima and Nagasaki.

What was new about these bombs was the technology, not the morality. More people were killed with ordinary bombs in German cities or in Tokyo. Vastly more people were killed with ordinary bullets and cannon on the Russian front. Morality is about what you do to people, not the technology you use.

The guilt-mongers have twisted the facts of history beyond recognition in order to say that it was unnecessary to drop those atomic bombs. Japan was going to lose the war anyway, they say. What they don't say is—at what price in American lives? Or even in Japanese lives?

Much of the self-righteous nonsense that abounds on so many subjects cannot stand up to three questions: (1) Compared to what? (2) At what cost? and (3) What are the hard facts?

The alternative to the atomic bombs was an invasion of Japan, which was already being planned, and those plans included casualty estimates even more staggering than the deaths that have left a sea of crosses in American cemeteries at Normandy and elsewhere. "Revisionist" historians have come up with casualty estimates a small fraction of what the American and British military leaders responsible for planning the invasion of Japan had come up with.

Who are we to believe, those who had personally experienced the horrors of the war in the Pacific, and who had a lifetime of military experience, or leftist historians hot to find something else to blame America for?

During the island-hopping war in the Pacific, it was not uncommon for thousands of Japanese troops to fight to the death on an island, while the number captured were a few dozen. Even some Japanese soldiers too badly wounded to stand would lie where they fell until an American medical corpsman approached to treat their wounds—and then they would set off a grenade to kill them both.

In the air the same spirit led the kamikaze pilots to deliberately crash their planes into American ships and bombers.

Japan's plans for defense against invasion involved mobilizing the civilian population, including women and children, for the same suicidal battle tactics. That invasion could have been the greatest bloodbath in history.

No mass killing, especially of civilians, can leave any humane person happy. But compared to what? Compared to killing many times more Japanese and seeing many times more Americans die?

We might have gotten a negotiated peace if we had dropped the "unconditional surrender" demand. But at what cost? Seeing a militaristic Japan arise again in a few years, this time armed with nuclear weapons that they would not have hesitated for one minute to drop on Americans?

As it was, the unconditional surrender of Japan enabled General Douglas MacArthur to engineer one of the great historic transformations of a nation from militarism to pacifism, to the relief of hundreds of millions of their neighbors, who had suffered horribly at the hands of their Japanese conquerors.

The facts may deprive the revisionists of their platform for lashing out at America and for the ego trip of moral preening but, fear not, they will find or manufacture other occasions for that. The rest of us need to understand what irresponsible frauds they are—and how the stakes are too high to let the 4th estate succeed as a 5th column undermining the society on which our children and grandchildren's security will depend.

The Tyranny of Visions

At long last there is some reconsideration of the child molestation hysteria that has sent innocent people to jail for long terms behind bars, often with zero evidence and with testimony from children who have been heavily pressured or manipulated by "experts."

Genuine child molesters certainly belong behind bars and a case could be made that they should never be allowed out again. But that is wholly different from saying that an unsubstantiated allegation should be automatically believed in a court of law.

The *New York Times Magazine* in its September 19, 2004 issue had a long article featuring one of the children who made false accusations against a man who spent 15 years in prison as a result. The supposed victim now says that all of it was a lie. Why did he lie? Because "experts" leaned on him to say what they wanted him to say and he was just a kid at the time.

Were those "experts" trying to frame this particular man? Probably not. More likely, they just had a set of preconceptions about the world—a vision—that made them believe that the accused man was guilty, so they saw their duty as getting the kid to testify in a way that would get a conviction.

CBS News probably didn't set out to frame President Bush with a forged document about his National Guard service. More likely, the story they heard fit their vision of the world so strongly that they believed it—and brushed aside any witness or expert who told them something different.

Visions are powerful things. For some people, visions make facts unnecessary and can even override facts to the contrary.

In the years leading up to the Bolshevik revolution in Russia, Lenin developed a whole vision of the world of the past, the present, and the future. Although he spoke in the name of the workers, he never bothered to ask what actual flesh-and-blood workers thought. In his years of exile before returning to lead a revolution, he never bothered to go where workers lived or worked.

Lenin was just the first of the great vision-driven dictators of the 20th century. Like Hitler and Mao after him, Lenin was prepared to sacrifice the lives of millions of human beings on the altar to his vision.

Even in democratic nations, there are people who can impose their vision on other people, with no consequences for being wrong and no requirement that they prove themselves right.

Social workers have for years tried to stop white couples from adopting orphans from minority groups because that goes against their vision. They don't need a speck of evidence to back up their preconceptions.

Many minority children have been ripped out of the only home they have ever known by social workers who have sent them off to live among strangers, or a whole succession of strangers in foster homes, simply because a vision says that this is better than having them grow up with a white couple who have raised them from infancy.

Everyone has visions but everyone is not in a position to indulge those visions, or to impose them on other people, without suffering any consequences for being wrong. Even the biggest businesses can find themselves looking red ink in the face if their idea of what the public wants turns out to be different from what the public will buy.

Federal judges, however, pay no price for being wrong, even if the costs to others—sometimes the whole society—turn out to be catastrophic. When murder rates skyrocketed after 1960s judges started conjuring up new "rights" out of thin air for criminals, there were no consequences for those judges, who had lifetime appointments and were not likely to be living in high-crime neighborhoods.

The political left has long favored putting more and more decisions in the hands of people who pay no price for being wrong—not only judges but zoning boards, environmental commissions and, internationally, the United Nations and the World Court. This is a vision of the wise and the virtuous imposing their wisdom and virtue on the lesser people who make up the rest of humanity.

Egalitarians are often in the vanguard of those seeking to promote this most dangerous of all inequalities—the inequality of unaccountable power in the service of a vision.

The Tyranny of Visions: Part II

Some people think of California as a place where many kooky ideas originate. It is that but there is more to it than that.

California has long had more than its fair share of busybodies with a vision of the world in which it is necessary for them to force other people to do Good Things. That is not just a vision of the world, it is a vision of themselves—a very flattering vision that they are not likely to give up for anything so mundane as facts or logic.

One of the latest examples is a recent ruling by one of the many busybody commissions in California that people who build houses, or just remodel their homes, will in the future have to have more fluorescent lights and even install motion sensors to control lights—all in the name of saving energy.

Motion sensors? Yes. If you are in a room where motion sensors control the lights, sitting still for a while will cause the lights to go off automatically.

The idea of the anointed busybodies is that we lesser people often leave the lights on when we walk out of a room, thereby wasting energy. The answer, as in so many other cases, is to impose their superior wisdom and virtue by forcing us to do a Good Thing—in this case install motion sensors to turn out the lights automatically when there is no one moving in the room.

If you are one of those people who just likes to sit still and think for a while, or perhaps listen to music or watch television, look for the lights to start going off if you are in California—and get used to having to wave your arms or shake your legs in order to get them to come back on again. But it's a Good Thing.

The world is full of Good Things, which is why there are so many laws and regulations increasingly intruding into our lives and restricting what we can do, even in our own homes. The vision of imposing Good Things means an ever-growing petty tyranny.

In some countries, where such visions are more sweeping, the tyranny is far from petty. Around the world and for thousands of years, human beings have not been able to leave other human beings alone.

Just think of all the centuries in which Christians tried to force Jews to change their religion or Muslims tried to force other people to adopt Islam. Was there nothing better to do with all that time and energy except persecute people for having different beliefs?

Some people obviously thought it was a Good Thing to have other people believe what they believed or to unify the country with one religion. Like today's busybodies, they seldom stopped to consider the cost of the Good Thing they wanted done.

Whole economies have been ruined by expelling productive minorities who happened to have a different religion or belonged to a different race. After Spain expelled the Moriscoes in the 16th century, one of the religious leaders who had advocated their expulsion asked: "Who will make our shoes now?"

That would have been a very good question to ask *before* expelling the Moriscoes. Similar questions might well have been asked before France's persecution of the Huguenots led them to flee in the 17th century, taking many productive enterprises from France with them. Twentieth century examples are too numerous to cite.

Good Things have costs, often costs out of all proportion to whatever good they might do. But notions like trade-offs and diminishing returns seldom deter zealots, whose own egos are served by their zealotry in imposing their vision, however costly or counterproductive it may be for others.

The whole environmental extremist movement is based on doing Good Things, in utter disregard of costs or diminishing returns.

The idea that DDT might leave residues with harmful effects on the eggs of some birds was enough to set off a worldwide environmental crusade to ban the use of that insecticide. The resurgence of malaria after that ban has cost millions of human lives.

Green zealots are not about to reconsider, on this or a whole range of other issues. Their vision triumphed, their superior wisdom and virtue were affirmed, and that is what it is ultimately all about. To admit, even to themselves, that their ego trips have cost other people their lives would be too much.

The Tyranny of Visions: Part III

Nowhere is the tyranny of visions more absolute than with issues involving safety. Attempts to talk about costs, trade-offs or diminishing returns are only likely to provoke safety zealots to respond with something like, "If it saves just one human life, it is worth it!"

That immediately establishes the safety zealot as being on a higher moral plane than those who stoop to consider crass materialistic costs. And being morally one-up is what a great deal of zealotry is all about.

The vision of zealots is not just a vision of the world. It is a vision of themselves as special people in that world. The down side is that such a heavy ego investment makes reconsideration of the issues highly unlikely. Ego trumps mundane facts or dry logic.

If the recent hurricanes that have swept across the Caribbean and Florida prove anything, it should be that wealth saves many human lives. Deaths from hurricane Jeanne in the Caribbean have been in the thousands while the death toll in Florida was less than a dozen.

The difference is that Florida is far more affluent. Houses there can be built to withstand more stress. Ambulances can rush more people more quickly to better equipped medical facilities. It has been estimated that more than 95 percent of the deaths from natural disasters worldwide occur in the poorer countries.

How does this affect safety issues?

Safety laws and regulations all have costs—not just

money outlays but other restrictions that reduce the rate of production of wealth. If wealth is itself one of the biggest lifesavers, costly safety devices cannot automatically be considered justified "if it saves just one human life" when the wealth it forfeits could have saved many lives.

Everything depends on the particular safety rule or device. Some save many lives at small costs and others save few, if any, lives at huge costs.

Diminishing returns matter as well, though these are seldom taken into account by safety zealots.

Many dangerous impurities can be removed from water or air at costs that virtually everyone will agree are worth it. But there is no such thing as "pure water" or "pure air," so the only real question is how far you want to go in removing impurities—and at what cost.

Impurities that are deadly at high concentrations can become harmless at sufficiently low concentrations. In extremely minute traces, even arsenic has been found to have beneficial effects. But the vision of "pure water" keeps zealots pushing for removing ever more minute traces of ever more questionable impurities, regardless of how much more it costs or how little good it does—if any.

Alcohol takes huge numbers of lives every year, whether in automobile accidents, liver disease or innumerable foolish risks taken while "under the influence." Yet studies show that a very moderate daily intake of alcohol reduces hypertension and the incidence of dementia. Everything depends on how much.

Trade-offs and diminishing returns are not the stuff from which heady visions and dramatic crusades are made. For that you need goals to be reached "at all costs" and a clash between heroes and villains. This appeals to the young and to those who remain adolescents all their lives.

The realities of life force most of us to grow up, whether we want to or not. But for people protected from realities by being born rich, or by having lifetime tenure as academics or federal judges, maturity is optional.

Many of the most extreme safety and environmental crusaders are rich busybodies or academics and their students, and they are often helped by judges whose rulings allow them to violate other people's rights while pursuing their own vision.

The "thousand natural shocks that flesh is heir to" have become a thousand reasons for lawsuits against those who produce anything that is not "safe."

Nothing is categorically safe. But few things are as dangerous as those who are pursuing a safety vision that ministers to their egos, with the costs being paid by others.

The Immigration Taboo

Immigration has joined the long list of subjects on which it is taboo to talk sense in plain English. At the heart of much confusion about immigration is the notion that we "need" immigrants—legal or illegal—to do work that Americans won't do.

What we "need" depends on what it costs and what we are willing to pay. If I were a billionaire, I might "need" my own private jet. But I can remember a time when my family didn't even "need" electricity.

Leaving prices out of the picture is probably the source of more fallacies in economics than any other single misconception. At current wages for low-level jobs and current levels of welfare, there are indeed many jobs that Americans will not take.

The fact that immigrants—and especially illegal immigrants—will take those jobs is the very reason the wage levels will not rise enough to attract Americans.

This is not rocket science. It is elementary supply and demand. Yet we continue to hear about the "need" for immigrants to do jobs that Americans will not do—even though these are all jobs that Americans have done for generations before mass illegal immigration became a way of life.

There is more to this issue than economics. The same mindless substitution of rhetoric for thinking that prevails on economic issues also prevails on other aspects of immigration.

Bombings in London, Madrid and the 9/11 terrorist attacks here are all part of the high price being paid today for decades of importing human time bombs from the Arab world. That in turn has been the fruit of an unwillingness to filter out people according to the countries they come from.

That squeamishness is still with us today, as shown by all the hand-wringing about "profiling" Middle Eastern airline passengers.

No doubt most Middle Eastern airline passengers are not carrying any weapons or any bombs—and wouldn't be, even if there were no airport security to go through. But it is also true that most of the time you will not be harmed by playing Russian roulette.

Europeans and Americans have for decades been playing Russian roulette with their loose immigration policies. The intelligentsia have told us that it would be wrong, and even racist, to set limits based on where the immigrants come from.

There are thousands of Americans who might still be alive if we had banned immigration from Saudi Arabia—and perhaps that might be more important than the rhetoric of the intelligentsia.

In that rhetoric, all differences between peoples are magically transformed into mere "stereotypes" and "perceptions." This blithely ignores hard data showing, for example, that people who come here from some countries are ten times more likely to go on welfare than people from some other countries.

The media and the intelligentsia love to say that most immigrants, from whatever group, are good people. But what "most" people from a given country are like is irrelevant.

If 85 percent of group A are fine people and 95 percent

of group B are fine people, that means you are going to be importing three times as many undesirables when you let in people from Group A.

Citizen-of-the-world types are resistant to the idea of tightening our borders, and especially resistant to the idea of making a distinction between people from different countries. But the real problem is not their self-righteous fetishes but the fact that they have intimidated so many other people into silence.

In the current climate of political correctness it is taboo even to mention facts that go against the rosy picture of immigrants—for example, the fact that Russia and Nigeria are always listed among the most corrupt countries on earth, and that Russian and Nigerian immigrants in the United States have already established patterns of crime well known to law enforcement but kept from the public by the mainstream media.

Self-preservation used to be called the first law of nature. But today self-preservation has been superseded by a need to preserve the prevailing rhetoric and visions. Immigration is just one of the things we can no longer discuss rationally as a result.

The Left Monopoly

Recently Albert Hunt's last column for the *Wall Street Journal* mentioned how he was recruited by the late and great Robert L. Bartley, who made that newspaper's editorial page unsurpassed in quality. What made the hiring of Albert Hunt especially significant was that Bartley was a staunch conservative in the Reagan tradition, while Hunt is a standard issue liberal.

It was precisely for that reason that Bartley wanted Hunt to write for the *Wall Street Journal,* so that readers would be sure to get more than one side of the issues discussed.

Many years ago, when I was teaching economics at UCLA, we likewise had a staunchly conservative department. We were sometimes called the west coast branch of the University of Chicago, because so many of us had studied under Milton Friedman and other leaders of "the Chicago school" of economists.

Like Bob Bartley, we wanted our students to see more than one way of looking at economics. One young, liberal-minded economist was regarded by some as a possible permanent member of the department, to add variety.

He never really measured up to our expectations, but he was probably kept on longer than he would have been if he had been a conservative economist, because of hopes that he would turn out to be better than he did.

Even though the word "diversity" has become a mantra on the left, there is no such drive for intellectual diversity in bastions of the left, such as academia or the mainstream media.

In recent years, the liberal media have at least added some token conservatives, but our colleges and universities are content with whole departments consisting solely of people ranging from the left to the far left. In academia, "diversity" in practice too often means simply white leftists, black leftists, female leftists and Hispanic leftists.

Perhaps it was the remarkable popularity of conservative talk radio and the meteoric rise of the Fox News channel that led liberal TV networks to begin adding some conservatives to their lineups. No such competitive pressures operate in academia.

There are a few good small conservative colleges like Hillsdale or Grove City, but Ivy League schools have no conservative rivals of comparable size and prominence, and neither do most state universities. A student can spend four years at many colleges and universities and graduate with no real awareness of any other viewpoints than those on the left.

College and university faculties do not simply happen to be leftist. Too often ideological questions are asked at faculty job interviews and ideological litmus tests are applied in hiring. One reason for the prominence of conservative think tanks is that so many top scholars who are not leftists do not find a home in academia and go to work for think tanks instead.

Not even visiting speakers with a conservative viewpoint are tolerated on many campuses. It seems incredible that there would be fears that a one-hour lecture would undo years of indoctrination. But perhaps it is just sheer intolerance that creates hostility to anyone expressing ideas contrary to the prevailing notions of the left.

Students often report that their professors react against them for stating a viewpoint different from the prevailing orthodoxy of the left. They can be ridiculed in class discussions or given low grades on exams.

Dartmouth College has been carrying on a running battle with the conservative student newspaper, the *Dartmouth Review,* from the moment it was founded many years ago. On some campuses, conservative student newspapers are seized and destroyed by leftist students or even burned publicly, with little or no effort by the college administration to maintain freedom of speech.

A student at Lewis College in Colorado was actually kicked by a professor for wearing a sweatshirt proclaiming his Republican views. This happened at a birthday party, of all places, and the professor has been quoted as saying that her only regret was that her kick was not "harder and higher."

The American Council of Trustees and Alumni, which monitors campus intolerance, is trying to get some action taken against that professor. Good luck.

I Beg to Disagree

My assistant sorts the incoming mail into various categories, such as "critical mail," "fan mail," etc. But the so-called critical mail is seldom critical. It may be bombastic or vituperative or full of pop psychology, but it seldom presents a critical argument based on facts or logic.

Too many people today act as if no one can honestly disagree with them. If you have a difference of opinion with them, you are considered to be not merely in error but in sin. You are a racist, a homophobe or whatever the villain of the day happens to be.

Disagreements are inevitable whenever there are human beings but we seem to be in an era when the art of disagreeing is vanishing. That is a huge loss because out of disagreements have often come deeper understandings than either side had before confronting each other's arguments.

Even wacko ideas have led to progress, when dealt with critically, in terms of logic and evidence. Astrology led to astronomy. The medieval notion of turning lead into gold—alchemy—led to chemistry, from which have come everything from a wide range of industrial products and consumer goods to more productive agriculture and life-saving drugs.

Where an argument starts is far less important than where it finishes because the logic and evidence in between is crucial. Unfortunately, our educational system is not only failing to teach critical thinking, it is often itself a source of confused rhetoric and emotional venting in place of systematic reasoning.

It is hard to think of a stronger argument for teaching people to examine arguments critically than the tragic history of 20th century totalitarianism and its horrors in peace and war. Dictators often gained total power over a whole nation by their ability to arouse emotions and evade thought.

Watch old newsreels of Hitler and see the adoring and enraptured look on the faces in his audience. Then read what he said and see if it makes any sense whatever. Yet he convinced others—and himself—that he had a great message and a great mission.

The same could be said of Lenin, of Mao, of Pol Pot, and of countless other despots, large and small, who brought devastation to the people they ruled. It is not even necessary to look solely at government leaders. Cult leader Jim Jones used the same ability to sway people's emotions and numb their brains to lead them ultimately to mass deaths in his Guiana compound.

Instead of trying to propagandize children to hug trees and recycle garbage, our schools would be put to better use teaching them how to analyze and test what is said by people who advocate tree-hugging, recycling, and innumerable other causes across the political spectrum.

The point is not to teach them correct conclusions but to teach them to be able to use their own minds to analyze the issues that will come up in the years ahead, which may have nothing to do with recycling or any of the other issues of our time.

Rational disagreement can be not only useful but stimulating. Many years ago, when my friend and colleague Walter Williams and I worked on the same research project, he and I kept up a running debate on the reasons why blacks excelled in some sports and were virtually non-existent in others.

Walter was convinced that the reasons were physical while I thought the reasons were social and economic. Walter would show me articles on physiology from scholarly journals, using them as explanations of why blacks had so many top basketball players and few, if any, swimming champions.

We never settled that issue but it provided lively debates and we may both have learned something.

I even met my wife as a result of a disagreement. She read something of mine that she disagreed with and told a mutual friend. He in turn suggested that we get together for lunch and hash out our differences.

Although we have now been married more than 20 years, we have still not completely settled our differences over that issue. But when we met our attention turned to other things. There are a lot of reasons to be able to have rational discussions about things on which people disagree.

4th Estate or 5th Column?

There are still people in the mainstream media who profess bewilderment that they are accused of being biased. But you need to look no further than reporting on the war in Iraq to see the bias staring you in the face, day after day, on the front page of the *New York Times* and in much of the rest of the media.

If a battle ends with Americans killing a hundred guerrillas and terrorists, while sustaining ten fatalities, that is an American victory. But not in the mainstream media. The headline is more likely to read: "Ten More Americans Killed in Iraq Today."

This kind of journalism can turn victory into defeat in print or on TV. Kept up long enough, it can even end up with real defeat, when support for the war collapses at home and abroad.

One of the biggest American victories during the Second World War was called "the great Marianas turkey shoot" because American fighter pilots shot down more than 340 Japanese planes over the Marianas islands while losing just 30 American planes. But what if our current reporting practices had been used back then?

The story, as printed and broadcast, could have been: "Today eighteen American pilots were killed and five more severely wounded, as the Japanese blasted more than two dozen American planes out of the sky." A steady diet of that kind of one-sided reporting and our whole war effort against Japan might have collapsed.

Whether the one-sided reporting of the war in Vietnam was a factor in the American defeat there used to be a matter of controversy. But, in recent years, high officials of the Communist government of Vietnam have themselves admitted that they lost the war on the battlefields but won it in the U.S. media and on the streets of America, where political pressures from the anti-war movement threw away the victory for which thousands of American lives had been sacrificed.

Too many in the media today regard the reporting of the Vietnam war as one of their greatest triumphs. It certainly showed the power of the media—but also its irresponsibility. Some in the media today seem determined to recapture those glory days by the way they report on events in the Iraq war.

First, there is the mainstream media's almost exclusive focus on American casualties in Iraq, with little or no attention to the often much larger casualties inflicted on the guerrillas and terrorists from inside and outside Iraq.

Since terrorists are pouring into Iraq in response to calls from international terrorist networks, the number of those who are killed is especially important, for these are people who will no longer be around to launch more attacks on American soil. Iraq has become a magnet for enemies of the United States, a place where they can be killed wholesale, thousands of miles away.

With all the turmoil and bloodshed in Iraq, both military and civilian people returning from that country are increasingly expressing amazement at the difference between what they have seen with their own eyes and the far worse, one-sided picture that the media presents to the public here.

Our media cannot even call terrorists "terrorists," but

instead give these cutthroats the bland name, "insurgents." You might think that these were like the underground fighters in Nazi-occupied Europe during World War II.

The most obvious difference is that the underground in Europe did not go around targeting innocent civilians. As for the Nazis, they tried to deny the atrocities they committed. But today the "insurgents" in Iraq are proud of their barbarism, videotape it, and publicize it—often with the help of the Western media.

Real insurgents want to get the occupying power out of their country. But the fastest way to get Americans out of Iraq would be to do the opposite of what these "insurgents" are doing. Just by letting peace and order return, those who want to see American troops gone would speed their departure.

The United States has voluntarily pulled out of conquered territory all around the world, including neighboring Kuwait during the first Gulf war. But the real goal of the guerrillas and terrorists is to prevent democracy from arising in the Middle East.

Still, much of the Western media even cannot call a spade a spade. The Fourth Estate sometimes seems more like a Fifth Column.

PART II

ECONOMIC ISSUES

Why Economists Are
Not Popular

One of the many reasons why economists are unpopular is that they keep reminding people that things have costs, that there is no free lunch. People already know that—but they like to forget it when there is something they have their hearts set on.

Economists don't have to say anything when people are buying things at a shopping mall or at an automobile dealership. The price tags convey the situation in unmistakable terms. It is when people are voting for nice-sounding things which politicians have dreamed up that economists are likely to point out that the costs ignored by politicians are going to have to be paid, one way or another—and that you have to weigh those costs against whatever benefits you expect.

Who wants to put on green eye shades and start adding up the numbers when someone grandly proclaims, "access to health care for all" or "clean air" or "saving the environment"? Economists are strictly party-poopers at times like these. They are often gate crashers too, since usually nobody asked them how much these things would cost or even thought about these issues in such terms.

Some of the more persistent or insensitive economists may even raise questions about the goals themselves. How much health care at the taxpayers' expense? In Britain, a 12-year-old girl was given breast implants. That much health care?

Meanwhile, Britain's skyrocketing medical costs of taking

care of things that people would never have spent their own money to take care of forced cutbacks and delays in more urgently needed medical treatments. One woman's cancer operation was postponed so many times by the British health service that, by the time the system could take her, the disease was now too far gone for medical help—and she died.

Economists could have told anyone in advance that making things "free" causes excessive use by some, leaving less for others with more urgent needs that have to remain unsatisfied. Rent control, for example, has led to more housing being occupied by some, who would not have paid the market price for as large an apartment as they live in, while others cannot find any housing that they can afford in the city, and have to live far away and commute to work.

Clean air? There is no such thing and never has been. There is only air with varying degrees of impurities, varying amounts of which can be removed at varying costs.

Removing the kinds of things that choke our lungs or otherwise threaten our health is usually not that expensive. But science is becoming capable of detecting ever more minute traces of impurities with ever more insignificant consequences. Yet where is the politician who is going to resist calls for removing more impurities in the name of "clean air"?

Who is going to resist calls to "save the environment"? Only an economist is likely to ask, "Save it from what or from whom—and at what price?"

Bumper stickers in and around Redwood City, California, long proclaimed: "Save Pete's Harbor." What did that even mean? In practice, it meant letting one set of people use it as a marina and preventing other people from replacing the marina with housing.

When the Constitution of the United States says that the government owes "equal protection" to all its citizens, why should the government intervene on behalf of one set of contending citizens against another, much less call that "saving" the environment? People have been bidding against one another for the same resources for centuries. Why replace that process with politicians' control? The 20th century was a virtual laboratory test of political control of economic activities—and it was such a dismal failure that even socialists and communists began abandoning that way of doing things by the 1990s.

Even when you don't realize that you are bidding against other people, you are. When you drive into a filling station and fill up your tank with gasoline, you are bidding against people who want petroleum in the form of heating oil, plastics, or Vaseline.

Lunches don't get free just because you don't see the prices on the menu. And economists don't get popular by reminding people of that.

Housing Hurdles

A new study shows that you need an income of about $104,000 to buy an average home on the San Francisco peninsula with a 20 percent down payment. Since the average price of a home in this area is more than half a million dollars, the 20 percent down payment itself would be more than $100,000.

These aren't mansions we are talking about. Often they are little nondescript houses packed pretty close together.

Who can afford to buy a home in such an area? Not many. California is among the states with the lowest rates of home ownership. Moreover, many of those who do own homes in coastal California bought them long ago, before the state's home prices went sky high in the wake of severe building restrictions promoted by environmental extremists.

Things are not much better when it comes to renting. A calculation of how many hours someone making the minimum wage would have to work to pay the rent on a one-bedroom apartment in this general area showed that, in San Jose, a minimum-wage worker would have to work 168 hours just to pay the rent.

At 40 hours a week, that means working the whole month to pay rent, with nothing left over for frills like food and clothing. Tell this to someone on the Left Coast and the answer will come back immediately: Raise the minimum wage!

If people cannot afford even a one-bedroom apartment while making minimum wages, they certainly cannot afford it when they are unemployed—and minimum wage laws have a track record around the world of increasing the unemployment rate.

Many people are so struck by California's outrageous housing prices that they do not realize that money is just one of the costs of the innumerable restrictions and requirements imposed on anyone who wants to build anything in those parts of California where environmental zealots are dominant—which includes most of the coast and the whole San Francisco Bay area.

Whether costs take the form of money or of long commutes, highway congestion and the deaths that inevitably result, the fundamental problem is that few people stop to think through the consequences of turning fashionable notions into laws.

Among the many restrictions on building in those parts of California dominated by environmental zealots are restrictions on the height of buildings. Some people think that it is enough to say that they don't want California to start looking like Manhattan.

But what if we stop and think through the consequences of height restrictions? First of all, rents are going to have to be higher, but that is just the beginning.

Why are rents going to have to be higher? Because two five story buildings take up twice as much land as one ten-story building housing the same total number of people.

In a state like California, where the cost of land is often higher than the cost of what is built on the land, using twice as much land per apartment means that rents are going to have to be much higher—perhaps twice as high or more—to cover the additional costs created by height restrictions.

With more land being required to house the same number of people, this also means that the whole metropolitan area is going to have to be larger than it would be if it could expand upward instead of just outward. More people are going to have to commute to work.

Those who impose height restrictions can ignore such things. A few blithe words about not wanting their community to look like Manhattan are usually about all the thought they give to the subject. It would never occur to them to ask the real question: How much don't you want it to look like Manhattan? How high a price are you prepared to pay?

A doubling of rent and 3 additional highway fatalities a year? A tripling of rents and 10 additional highway fatalities a year?

Whatever the answer, the point is that height restrictions are not a free lunch—whether the costs are measured in money or in lives. A lot of people who cannot afford it are paying heavily for the ego trips of environmental zealots.

The "Cost" of Medical Care

If you ask most people about the cost of medical care, they may tell you how much they have to pay per visit to their doctor's office or the monthly bill for their prescription drugs. But these are not the costs of medical care. These are the prices paid.

The difference between prices and costs is not just a fine distinction made by economists. Prices are what pay for costs—and if they do not pay enough to cover the costs, then centuries of history in countries around the world show that the supply is going to decline in quantity or quality, or both. In the case of medical care, the supply is a matter of life and death.

The average medical student graduates with a debt of more than $100,000. The cost per doctor of running an office is more than $100 an hour. The average cost of developing a new pharmaceutical drug is $800 million. These are among the costs of medical care.

When politicians talk about "bringing down the cost of medical care," they are not talking about reducing any of these costs by one cent. They are talking about forcing prices down through one scheme or another.

All the existing efforts to control the rising expenses of medical care—whether by government, insurance companies, or health maintenance organizations—are about holding down the amount of money they have to pay out, not about reducing any of the real costs.

Many of the same politicians who are gung ho for

imposing price controls on prescription drugs, or for importing Canadian price controls by importing American medicines from Canada, have not the slightest interest in stopping frivolous lawsuits against doctors, hospitals, or drug companies—which are huge costs.

Price control zealots likewise seldom have any interest in reducing the amount of federal requirements for getting a drug approved for sale to the public—a process that can easily drag on for a decade or more, costing millions of dollars, and also costing the lives of those who die while waiting for the drug to be approved by bureaucrats at the Food and Drug Administration.

For political purposes, what "bringing down the cost of medical care" means is some quick fix that will win votes at the next election, regardless of what the repercussions are thereafter.

What are those repercussions?

If the bureaucratic hassles that doctors have to go through make their huge investment in time and money going to medical school not seem worthwhile, some can retire early and some can take jobs no longer involving treating patients. Either way, the supply of medical care can begin to decline, even in the short run.

In the long run, medical school may no longer look like such a good investment to many in the younger generation. Britain, which has had government-run medical care for more than half a century, has to import doctors from the Third World, where medical school standards are lower.

So long as there are warm bodies with "M.D." after their names, there is no decline in supply, as far as politicians are concerned. Only the patients will find out, the hard way, what declining quality means.

No law passed by more than 500 members of Congress is

going to be simple or even consistent. There are already 125,000 pages of Medicare regulations. "Universal health care" can only mean more.

I saw a vivid example of what bureaucratic medical care meant back in 1959, when I had a summer job at the headquarters of the U.S. Public Health Service in Washington. Around 5 o'clock one afternoon, a man had a heart attack on the street near our office.

He was taken to the nurse's room and was asked if he were a federal employee. If he was, he could be sent to the large, modern medical facility right there in the Public Health Service headquarters. But he was not a government employee, so an ambulance was summoned from a local hospital.

By the time this ambulance made its way through miles of downtown Washington rush-hour traffic, the man was dead. He died waiting for a doctor, in a building full of doctors. That is what bureaucracy means.

Making a government-run medical care system mandatory—"universal" is the pretty word for mandatory—means that we will all have no choice but to be caught up in that bureaucratic maze.

Subsidies Are All Wet

For years we have been hearing about a water shortage in the western states. To most people, that might suggest that there just is not enough water for all the people in those states. But, when an economist hears the word "shortage," it has an entirely different meaning.

What specifically is a shortage? It is a situation where you are willing to pay the price but simply cannot find as much as you want. To an economist, the question is: Why doesn't the price rise then? If it did, some people would demand less and others would supply more until supply and demand balanced.

Put differently, a shortage is a sign that somebody is keeping the price artificially lower than it would be if supply and demand were allowed to operate freely. That is precisely why there is a water shortage in the western states.

Even in California's dry Central Valley, less than 10 percent of the water available from federal water projects is used by cities and industries. The vast majority of it is used by farmers, who pay a fraction of what urban users pay, thanks to federal price fixing.

Like everything that is made artificially cheap, water is used lavishly, including the growing of crops like cotton that require huge amounts of water. It is one thing to grow cotton in Southern states with abundant rainfall. It is something else to grow it out in a California desert with water supplied largely at the taxpayers' expense.

The long-term contracts under which this ridiculous

arrangement goes on expire this year, so theoretically these contracts could be renegotiated so that everyone who uses water supplied by federal water projects has to pay his own way and cover the costs of the operation. Alas, this is an election year, so you can bet the rent money that no such thing is going to happen.

A Department of the Interior spokesman explains it this way: "We don't think it is a good idea for California or the nation to adopt punitive pricing proposals that might have the effect of driving more agriculture out of existence."

Isn't that a lovely thought? Apparently the only people toward whom the government can be "punitive" are the taxpayers.

We live in what is often called a profit system but, as Milton Friedman explained long ago, it is really a profit-and-loss system. The losses are just as important as the profits, though not nearly as popular.

Running up losses because you are using resources that are more valuable somewhere else is precisely what forces you to stop the waste. If you are too stubborn to stop, then you will get stopped by bankruptcy.

In other words, some enterprises should be forced out of existence, however much that might shock the delicate sensibilities of the Department of the Interior during an election year.

As for agriculture, we have been running chronic agricultural surpluses for more than half a century and scrambling to find some way to store it, export it or just plain give it away. So many other countries have the same problem that we might be able to eat heartily—and remain overweight—even if we stopped farming entirely and bought up their agricultural surpluses instead.

Things are never going to get to that point. But it

illustrates how fraudulent it is for the government, the environmentalists or farm lobbies to try to scare us with the specter of losing agricultural land.

Incidentally, these same kinds of policies can be found halfway around the world in India, where government-subsidized water is used so lavishly that the water table is falling in the Punjab. Similar incentives produce similar results in various times and places.

Nobody is going to risk losing the farm vote during an election year. However, even though rationality is not likely to triumph when government water contracts are renewed this year, it should be possible to put limits on the insanity.

First of all, the contracts could be set for much shorter periods, to limit how much longer the damage goes on. And they could be set to expire in an odd-numbered year, when there are no federal elections.

A Taxing Experience

When liberals in the media or in politics start being alarmed about the national debt, it means just one thing: They want higher taxes. The thought of reducing spending would never cross their minds.

As we are endlessly reminded, the federal government's debt has reached record levels during the Bush administration. That enables the liberal media to use their favorite word—"crisis"—and adds urgency to doing their favorite thing, raising taxes.

Since we have a larger population than ever and a larger national income than ever, it should hardly be surprising that we also have a larger national debt than ever. But what does it mean?

Donald Trump probably has a bigger debt than I do—and less reason to worry about it. Debt means nothing unless you compare it to your income or wealth.

How does our national debt today compare to our national income? As a percentage of the national income, the privately held national debt today is lower than it was a decade ago, during the Clinton administration, when liberals did not seem at all panicked as they seem today.

If someone were to produce a political dictionary, "crisis" would be defined as a desire to pass a law and "national debt" would be defined as a desire to raise taxes. And the two in combination would mean a desire to discredit the existing administration.

If it seems that raising taxes is the only way to reduce the national debt, at least when so much spending is mandated by "entitlement" programs, that only shows the need for an economic dictionary. "Taxes" is one of those treacherous words with more than one meaning, enabling politicians to shift back and forth between meanings when they talk.

Unless spending is reduced, then of course more tax revenues are necessary in order to reduce a deficit or bring down a debt. But tax revenues and tax rates are two different things, even though the same word—"taxes"—is used to refer to both.

What "tax cuts" cut is the tax rate. But tax revenues can rise, fall, or stay the same when tax rates are cut. Everything depends on what happens to income.

Tax revenues rose after the Kennedy tax cuts of the 1960s and the Reagan tax cuts of the 1980s because incomes rose. Incomes are likewise rising during the Bush administration today.

If Congress can just reduce the rate of increase in spending, rising tax revenues can reduce the deficit and eventually eliminate it. But of course that will not give liberals an excuse to raise tax rates or even to denounce "tax cuts for the rich."

There was a time when the purpose of taxes was to pay for the inevitable costs of government. To the political left, however, taxes have long been seen as a way to redistribute income and finance other social experiments based on liberal ideology.

Given that agenda, it is hardly surprising that some of the biggest spending liberals can go into hysterics over the national debt, especially when that debt exists under a conservative administration of the opposite party.

This does not mean that nothing needs to be done about the national debt or about our tax system. A lot could be done about both—but it would not be what liberals want done.

Promoting the growth of the national economy would be one of the fastest and best ways of reducing the national debt. We could, for example, stop letting little bands of self-righteous activists stifle the building of homes or businesses under "open space" laws and stop the drilling of oil off-shore, on-shore, or elsewhere.

As for taxes, we could stop taxing productivity and start taxing consumption. After all, productivity is what makes a society more prosperous.

Despite political use of the envy factor to cause resentment of people whose high productivity earns high incomes, someone who is adding to the total wealth of this country is not depriving you of anything. But someone who is consuming the nation's wealth without contributing anything to it, is costing you and everyone else who is carrying his share of the load. Yet our tax system penalizes those who are producing wealth in order to subsidize those who are only consuming it.

Tax reform is overdue, national debt or no national debt.

Profits without Honor

Profits are certainly without honor among the intelligentsia. The very word produces negative reactions, even from people who cannot give you a single reason why money carrying that label is worse than money called by other names.

Many professional athletes and entertainers earn salaries higher than what the vast majority of business owners earn as profits, yet there is no moral indignation from those who are in the business of moral indignation.

Some claim not to be against profits, as such, but against "obscene profits." Yet they offer no clue as to how we are to tell obscene profits from R-rated profits or PG-13 profits.

One of the supposedly damning charges against pharmaceutical companies is that they earn those famous obscene profits. The figure of 18 percent is thrown around and may even be accurate, for all I know. But it doesn't make enough difference to bother checking it out.

The unspoken assumption—and fallacy—is that high profits mean high prices. But, back in the heyday of the A & P grocery chain, its profit rate never fell below 20 percent for a whole decade—and it was at that time the pre-eminent grocery chain in the country precisely because of its low prices and high quality.

Then, as conditions changed, other grocery chains found ways to operate at lower costs, enabling them to charge even lower prices than A & P, taking away its customers.

It has been estimated that a supermarket today makes a

clear profit of about a penny on a dollar of sales. If that sounds pretty skimpy, remember that it is collecting that penny on every dollar at several cash registers simultaneously and, in many cases, around the clock.

When a supermarket sells out its entire contents in about two weeks, that means that the dollar on which it made a penny of profit in the first half of January comes back for them to make another penny in the second half of January. By the end of the year, that dollar has come back 25 times and earned 26 cents.

Does that mean that the supermarket is making a 26 percent rate of profit? Not at all. The rate of profit on sales differs from the rate of profit on investment, which is what really counts.

The point here is that the relationship between prices and the rate of return on investment can be very tenuous. Small grocery stores, with slower turnover, can be struggling to survive while charging higher prices than those in a prospering supermarket.

Why have both local and national governments in recent years begun having many of their traditional functions, from garbage collection to running prisons, done by private companies? Because these private, profit-making companies can usually get the job done cheaper and better.

If profits were just extra costs arbitrarily added on to the costs of production, then non-profit institutions or whole countries that operated without profit, such as the Soviet Union, would have had lower costs. Almost invariably, however, enterprises that operate without the incentive of profit have had higher costs, not lower costs.

It was not a free-market think tank, but Soviet economists, who pointed out that Soviet industry used far more inputs to produce a given output than did market economies like Germany, Japan or the United States. Economically illiterate people—which, unfortunately includes much of the intelligentsia—have never understood the role of profit as an incentive to keep costs down.

To the economically illiterate, if some company makes a million dollars in profit, this means that their products cost a million dollars more than they would have cost without profits. It never occurs to such people that these products might cost several million dollars more to produce if they were produced by enterprises operating without the incentives to be efficient created by the prospect of profits and the fear of losses.

If "obscene profits" are what cause pharmaceutical drugs to cost so much, why haven't socialist countries set up their own government-owned pharmaceutical enterprises to produce drugs more cheaply? Why don't non-profit organizations here do that?

It is because rhetoric is cheap but creating drugs is not. Recent estimates are that it costs $800 million per new drug. That is why drug prices are so high. But needless suffering and premature deaths are even higher costs.

Profits without Honor: Part II

Those who rail against profits and "greed" seldom stop to think through what they are saying, much less go check the facts.

Most of the great American fortunes—Rockefeller, Ford, Carnegie, etc.—came from finding more efficient ways to produce a product or service at a lower cost, so that it could be sold at a lower price and attract more customers. If making a fortune represents greed, then greed is what drives prices down.

None of this matters to people who have been conditioned to respond to the word "profit" automatically, much as Pavlov's dog was conditioned to respond to certain sounds.

"Never speak to me of profit," India's legendary leader Pandit Nehru once said to that country's leading industrialist. "It's a dirty word." Policies based on that attitude cost millions of Indians a better life for decades, by stifling India's businesses.

Indian businesses flourished around the world—except in India. Only after India's severe restrictions on business were lifted in the past dozen years has its economic growth taken off, creating rising incomes, employment and tax revenues. This poverty-stricken country could have had all those things 40 years earlier, except for a prejudice against a word.

Unthinking prejudices and suspicions about profits are often matched by unthinking gullibility about "non-profit" organizations. No matter what money may be called, both individuals and organizations must have it in order to survive.

Businesses get their money from those who buy their goods and services. Non-profit organizations are crucially dependent on money from other people—either voluntary donations, tax money from the government, or money extracted from businesses through lawsuits.

Where there is a product or service of widely recognized value, such as education or medical care, schools and hospitals can attract donations on that basis. But there are other non-profit organizations which can survive only by inspiring fears and anger that bring in donations.

For these kinds of non-profit organizations, the sky is always falling or we are threatened with seeing the last few patches of unspoiled land paved over for shopping malls, virtually everything is "unsafe," we are running out of natural resources, and air and water are becoming dangerously polluted.

Facts do no make a dent in these claims. No matter how much data show air and water pollution to be far less than in the past, that only a small fraction of the land of this country is paved over, or that there are far more known reserves of natural resources today than there were half a century ago, or that life expectancy is increasing despite innumerable "dangers" proclaimed by hysteria-mongers, the media continue to take these people seriously because non-profit is equated with unbiased.

The media treat "consumer advocates," for example, as if they had some expertise, rather than propaganda skills. But there are no qualifications whatever required to become a "consumer advocate." Nor is there any test whatever for whether a "public interest" law firm in fact serves the public interest, rather than filling its own coffers with damage awards or advancing its own ideological agenda with harassing lawsuits.

Unlike profit-seeking businesses, which must keep down costs in order to survive, many of the costs created by non-profit organizations fall entirely on others. Those others include not only their donors but also those who pay in many ways for the government-imposed restrictions created at the urging of non-profit crusaders.

These costs include sky-high housing prices in places where non-profit organizations can get state and local governments to forbid, restrict or harass anyone seeking to build homes or apartments. Frivolous lawsuits by "public-interest" law firms drive up prices with huge damage awards against businesses, doctors, and others.

The biggest costs may be paid by people needing medical care in places where expensive malpractice insurance, brought on by frivolous lawsuits, has driven doctors away.

These are very high prices to pay for a halo around words like "non-profit," "public interest" or "consumer advocate."

Two Earthquakes

Within a week of each other, two earthquakes struck on opposite sides of the world—an earthquake measuring 6.5 on the Richter scale in California and a 6.6 earthquake in Iran. But, however similar the earthquakes, the human costs were enormously different.

The deaths in Iran have been counted in the tens of thousands. In California, the deaths did not reach double digits. Why the difference? In one word, wealth.

Wealth enables homes, buildings and other structures to be built to withstand greater stresses. Wealth permits the creation of modern transportation that can quickly carry injured people to medical facilities. It enables those facilities to be equipped with more advanced medical apparatus and supplies, and amply staffed with highly trained doctors and support staff.

Those who disdain wealth as crass materialism need to understand that wealth is one of the biggest life-saving factors in the world. As an economist in India has pointed out, "95% of deaths from natural hazards occur in poor countries."

You can also see the effect of wealth by looking at the same country at different times. The biggest hurricane to hit the United States was hurricane Andrew in 1992 but it took fewer than 50 lives. Yet another hurricane, back in 1900, took at least 6,000 lives in Galveston.

The difference was that the United States was a much richer country in 1992. It had earlier warning from more advanced weather tracking equipment. It had better roads and more cars in which to evacuate an area before a hurricane strikes, as well as more and better equipment for digging victims out of debris, and better medical treatment available for those who needed it.

Those who preen themselves on their "compassion" for the poor, and who disdain wealth, are being inconsistent, if not hypocritical. Wealth is the only thing that can prevent poverty. However, if you are not trying to prevent poverty but to exploit it for political purposes, that is another story.

There is another side to the story of these two earthquakes and their consequences. It gives the lie to the dogma being propagandized incessantly, from the schools to the media, that one culture is just as good as another.

It is just as good to lose tens of thousands of lives as not to? What hogwash! It is just as good to lack modern medicine, modern transportation, and modern industry as it is to have them? Who is kidding whom?

This dogmatism prevails at home as well as internationally. Cultures that lead to most children being born to single mothers are just as good as cultures where children grow up with two parents—if you believe the dogma.

Facts say the opposite. Whether it is education, crime, or poverty, there are huge differences between single-parent families and two-parent families.

Even race doesn't make as much difference in outcomes. The poverty rate among black married couples is in single digits. The infant mortality rate among black married women with only a high school diploma is lower than the infant mortality rate among white unmarried women who have been to college.

None of this makes a dent in those who promote the big

lie that one culture is just as good as another. What does it even mean to say that? Does it mean that facts fit the dogma? Or does it just mean that they choose to use words in a certain way? It may not make any difference in their theories, but only in the real world.

None of this means that one culture is better than another for all purposes. The cheap vulgarity and brutal ugliness of so much of our media is a legitimate complaint at home and abroad. The sheer silliness of our fad-ridden public schools is a national disgrace.

By the same token, cultures that are less advanced in some ways often have contributions to make in other ways. We all take different things from different cultures to create our own personal lifestyles. We need to stop pretending that it makes no difference when all the facts show that it makes a huge difference, from poverty to matters of life and death.

Peter Bauer (1915–2002)

The death of Peter Bauer cannot pass unmarked. He was one of those people to whom we all owe a great debt, whether we realize it or not. He insisted on talking sense, even when dangerous nonsense was at the height of its popularity.

In the last two decades of his life, he was Lord Bauer, courtesy of British Prime Minister Margaret Thatcher. For most of his career, however, he was Professor Peter Bauer of the London School of Economics. His specialty was the economics of under-developed countries.

The dominant orthodoxy in development economics was that Third World countries were trapped in a vicious cycle of poverty that could be broken only by massive foreign aid from the more prosperous industrial nations of the world. This was in keeping with a more general vision on the left that people were essentially divided into three categories— the heartless, the helpless, and wonderful people like themselves, who would rescue the helpless by playing Lady Bountiful with the taxpayers' money.

Peter Bauer never bought any part of that vision. He had too much respect for people in the Third World, where he had lived for years, to think of them as helpless. "Before 1886," he pointed out, "there was not one cocoa tree in British West Africa. By the 1930s, there were millions of acres under cocoa there, all owned and operated by Africans." He rejected "condescension toward the ordinary people" of the Third World and "the classification of groups as helpless."

Third World people were just as capable of responding to the incentives of a market economy as anyone else, according to Professor Bauer, despite development economists like Gunnar Myrdal who depicted them as needing government planning imposed on them to get ahead. Development economists' hostility to the market and "contempt for ordinary people" were to Bauer "only two sides of the same coin."

If poverty was a trap from which there was no escape, Bauer declared, we would all still be living in the stone age, since all countries were once as poor as Third World nations are today.

Peter Bauer considered it arbitrary and self-serving to call international transfers of money to Third World governments "foreign aid." Whether it was an aid or a hindrance was an empirical question. Sometimes it could turn out to be simply "transferring money from poor people in rich countries to rich people in poor countries."

Bauer likewise rejected "overpopulation" as a cause of Third World poverty, even though that was also one of the key dogmas of development economics. Like so much else that derived from the liberal-left vision of the world, "overpopulation" theories served as justifications for running other people's lives.

Peter Bauer pointed out that many Third World countries were much more thinly populated than such prosperous industrial nations as Japan, which has ten times the population density of sub-Saharan Africa. Moreover, some Third World countries had ample fertile land, much of it lying unused, and often also had valuable natural resources, such as were lacking in Japan.

The later research of Hernando de Soto, published in his book *The Mystery of Capital*, added still more evidence that supported Peter Bauer's thesis that Third World people were capable of creating wealth, even if their governments followed economically counterproductive policies that held them back.

For decades on end, Peter Bauer stood virtually alone in opposing the prevailing dogmas of development economists. They in turn dismissed him as someone far outside the mainstream. But, with the passing years and the repeated and catastrophic failures of policies and programs based on the theories of development economics, the orthodoxy began to erode and finally to collapse.

At the end of his life, Peter Bauer was in the mainstream—not because he had moved but because the mainstream had now moved over to where he had been all along. It is a painful reflection on those who award Nobel Prizes that Gunnar Myrdal received one and Peter Bauer did not. Yet, on the eve of his death, Lord Bauer was awarded the Milton Friedman prize, worth half a million dollars, for his work.

Peter Bauer's career should be an inspiration to all those who fight an uphill battle against prevailing orthodoxies.

Journalists and Economics

A recent front-page story in the *Wall Street Journal* told of rising hunger and malnutrition amid chronic agricultural surpluses in India. India is now exporting wheat, and even donating some to Afghanistan, while malnutrition is a growing problem within India itself.

This situation is both paradoxical and tragic, but what is also remarkable is that the long article about it omits the one key word that explains such a painful paradox: Price.

There can be a surplus of any given thing at any given time. But a chronic surplus of the same thing, year after year, means that somebody is preventing the price from falling. Otherwise the excess supply would drive down the price, leading producers to produce less—and consumers to consume more—until the surplus was gone.

What is happening in India is that the government is keeping the price of wheat and some other agricultural produce from falling. That is exactly what the government of the United States has been doing for more than half a century, leading to chronic agricultural surpluses here as well. Nor are India and the United States the only countries with such policies, leading to such results.

Although Americans are wrestling with obesity while Indians are suffering malnutrition, the economic principle is the same—and that principle is totally ignored by the reporters writing this story for the *Wall Street Journal.*

There is no special need to single out the *Wall Street Journal* for this criticism, except that when economic illiteracy shows up in one of the highest quality publications in the country that shows one of the great deficiencies of journalists in general.

One of the many jobs offered to me over the years, to my wife's astonishment, was a job as dean of a school of journalism. While I was not about to give up my own research and writing, in order to get tangled up in campus politics, the offer made me think about what a school of journalism ought to be teaching people whose jobs will be to inform the public.

They first and foremost ought to know what they are talking about, which requires a solid grounding in history, statistics, science—and economics. Since journalists are reporting on so many things with economic implications, they should have at least a year of introductory economics.

People with a basic knowledge of economics would understand that words like "surplus" and "shortage" imply another word that may not be mentioned explicitly: Price. And chronic surpluses or chronic shortages imply price controls.

Conversely, price controls imply chronic surpluses or shortages—depending on whether price controls keep prices from falling to the level they would reach under supply and demand or keep them from rising to that level.

Controls that keep prices from falling to the level they would reach in response to supply and demand include not only agricultural price supports like those in India but also minimum wage laws, which are equally common in countries around the world. Just as an artificially high price for wheat set by the government leads to a chronic surplus of wheat, so an artificially high price for labor set by the government leads to a surplus of labor—better known as unemployment.

Since all workers are not the same, this unemployment is concentrated among the less skilled and less experienced workers. Many of them are simply priced out of a job.

In the United States, for example, the highest unemployment rates are almost invariably among black teenagers. But this was not always the case.

Although the federal minimum wage law was passed in 1938, wartime inflation during the Second World War meant that the minimum wage law had no major effect until a new round of increases in the minimum wage level began in 1950. Unemployment rates among black teenagers before then were a fraction of what they are today—and no higher than among white teenagers.

The time is long overdue for schools of journalism to start teaching economics. It would eliminate much of the nonsense and hysteria in the media, and with it perhaps some of the demagoguery in politics.

Stock Crash Aftermath

What can be even worse than a stock market crash—including the great crash of 1929—are politicians rushing in to fix things. At one time, it was widely assumed that the 1929 crash led directly to the Great Depression that lasted throughout the decade of the 1930s. Now more and more people who have studied that era have come to the conclusion that what the government did to help was itself one of the biggest reasons why the depression went so deep and lasted so long.

Even a liberal economist like John Kenneth Galbraith described the actions of the Federal Reserve in response to the 1929 crash as "shockingly incompetent." Neither Republican President Herbert Hoover nor his Democratic successor, Franklin D. Roosevelt had a clue about economics or a policy that made any sense.

Both sought to keep prices—including wages—up, despite the fact that the money supply had declined by one third. How was the country supposed to buy all the output at existing prices, and employ all the workers at existing wages, when there was so much less money?

One of Herbert Hoover's biographers said aptly that he was a great man but not a great president. Anyone who doubts his greatness should study the history of his massive program to feed starving people in Europe during and after the First World War.

Most people would have raised the money first and then bought the food, but Hoover realized that people would be dying while he was raising money. So he risked his own personal fortune by buying the food first, hoping to raise enough money later from donations to recover all the millions of dollars it would take to pay for the food. It worked out in the end, but it didn't have to.

Had Hoover never become president, he would have gone down in history as simply one of the great humanitarians of the 20th century. As it was, he was demonized politically for decades as the calloused president who refused to take responsibility to help those ruined by the depression.

In reality, it was Hoover—not FDR—who became the first president to throw the power of the federal government into the effort to get the country out of a depression. In recent years, it has become more widely acknowledged that Roosevelt's New Deal was essentially Hoover's policies raised to the next exponent, spending on a more lavish scale and saddling the country with counterproductive programs that have lasted into the next century.

The fact that the first government efforts to get the country out of a depression—by both Hoover and FDR— were followed by the longest depression in our history has also not been lost on some economists. Quite aside from the specific harm done by specific programs, the general uncertainty generated by unpredictable government interventions made investors reluctant to make the long-term commitments needed to generate more jobs, more output, and more purchasing power.

Not only the Federal Reserve and two presidents managed to make the Great Depression worse, so did Congress. When Congress passed the Hawley-Smoot tariff of 1930, it contributed to a worldwide contraction in international trade, as country after country tried to "save jobs" by protectionism.

The notion that the stock market crash of 1929 caused the Great Depression that ravaged the 1930s has long been popular on the left, since this blames capitalism and casts government in the role of rescuer of the economy. However, Professor Peter Temin of MIT has pointed out that in 1987 the "stock market fell almost exactly the same amount on almost exactly the same days of the year"—and there was no depression.

The Reagan administration was not the New Deal. The economy recovered quickly on its own and kept on growing.

This year's scandals and stock market collapse could not have come at a worse time, with an election coming up and no other big issues around for politicians to use. It is also worth noting that there are only two economists in Congress and hundreds of lawyers, ready to say and do whatever will look good and feel good at the moment.

If Congress passes laws that put corporate crooks behind bars for a long time, that is fine. But if it passes laws that will enable politicians to micro-manage businesses, that is a proven formula for big economic problems for a long time to come.

Milton Friedman at 90

Milton Friedman's 90th birthday provides an occasion to think back on his role as the pre-eminent economist of the 20th century. To those of us who were privileged to be his students, he also stands out as a great teacher.

When I was a graduate student at the University of Chicago, back in 1959, one day I was waiting outside Professor Friedman's office when another graduate student passed by. He noticed my exam paper on my lap and exclaimed: "You got a B?"

"Yes," I said. "Is that bad?"

"There were only two B's in the whole class," he replied.

"How many A's?" I asked.

"There were no A's!"

Today, this kind of grading might be considered to represent a "tough love" philosophy of teaching. I don't know about love, but it was certainly tough.

Professor Friedman also did not let students arrive late at his lectures and distract the class by their entrance. Once I arrived a couple of minutes late for class and had to turn around and go back to the dormitory.

All the way back, I thought about the fact that I would be held responsible for what was said in that lecture, even though I never heard it. Thereafter, I was always in my seat when Milton Friedman walked in to give his lecture.

On a term paper, I wrote that either (a) this would happen or (b) that would happen. Professor Friedman wrote in the margin: "Or (c) your analysis is wrong."

"Where was my analysis wrong?" I asked him.

"I didn't say your analysis was wrong," he replied. "I just wanted you to keep that possibility in mind."

Perhaps the best way to summarize all this is to say that Milton Friedman is a wonderful human being—especially outside the classroom. It has been a much greater pleasure to listen to his lectures in later years, after I was no longer going to be quizzed on them, and a special pleasure to appear on a couple of television programs with him and to meet him on social occasions.

Milton Friedman's enduring legacy will long outlast the memories of his students and extends beyond the field of economics. John Maynard Keynes was the reigning demi-god among economists when Friedman's career began, and Friedman himself was at first a follower of Keynesian doctrines and liberal politics.

Yet no one did more to dismantle both Keynesian economics and liberal welfare-state thinking. As late as the 1950s, those with the prevailing Keynesian orthodoxy were still able to depict Milton Friedman as a fringe figure, clinging to an outmoded way of thinking. But the intellectual power of his ideas, the fortitude with which he persevered, and the ever more apparent failures of Keynesian analyses and policies, began to change all that, even before Professor Friedman was awarded the Nobel Prize in economics in 1976.

A towering intellect seldom goes together with practical wisdom, or perhaps even common sense. However, Milton Friedman not only excelled in the scholarly journals but also on the television screen, presenting the basics of economics in a way that the general public could understand.

His mini-series "Free to Choose" was a classic that made economic principles clear to all with living examples. His good nature and good humor also came through in a way that attracted and held an audience.

Although Friedrich Hayek launched the first major challenge to the prevailing thinking behind the welfare state and socialism with his 1944 book *The Road to Serfdom,* Milton Friedman became the dominant intellectual force among those who turned back the leftward tide that once seemed to be the wave of the future. Without Milton Friedman's role in changing the minds of so many Americans, it is hard to imagine how Ronald Reagan could have been elected president.

Nor was Friedman's influence confined to the United States. His ideas reached around the world, not only among economists, but also in political circles which began to understand why left-wing ideas that sounded so good produced results that were so bad.

Milton Friedman rates a 21-gun salute on his birthday. Or perhaps a 90-gun salute would be more appropriate.

"Price Gouging" in Florida

In the wake of the hurricanes in Florida, the state's attorney general has received thousands of complaints of "price gouging" by stores, hotels, and others charging far higher prices than usual during this emergency.

"Price gouging" is one of those emotionally powerful but economically meaningless expressions that most economists pay no attention to, because it seems too confused to bother with. But a distinguished economist named Joseph Schumpeter once pointed out that it is a mistake to dismiss some ideas as too silly to discuss, because that only allows fallacies to flourish—and their consequences can be very serious.

Charges of "price gouging" usually arise when prices are significantly higher than what people have been used to. Florida's laws in fact make it illegal to charge much more during an emergency than the average price over some previous 30-day period.

This raises questions that go to the heart of economics: What are prices for? What role do they play in the economy?

Prices are not just arbitrary numbers plucked out of the air. Nor are the price levels that you happen to be used to any more special or "fair" than other prices that are higher or lower.

What do prices do? They not only allow sellers to recover their costs, they force buyers to restrict how much they demand. More generally, prices cause goods and the resources that produce goods to flow in one direction through the economy rather than in a different direction.

How do "price gouging" and laws against it fit into this?

When either supply or demand changes, prices change. When the law prevents this, as with Florida's anti-price-gouging laws, that reduces the flow of resources to where they would be most in demand. At the same time, price control reduces the need for the consumer to limit his demands on existing goods and resources.

None of this is peculiar to Florida. For centuries, in countries around the world, laws limiting how high prices are allowed to go have led to consumers demanding more than was being supplied, while suppliers cut back on what they supplied. Thus rent control has consistently led to housing shortages and price controls on food have led to hunger and even starvation.

Among the complaints in Florida is that hotels have raised their prices. One hotel whose rooms normally cost $40 a night now charged $109 a night, and another hotel whose rooms likewise normally cost $40 a night now charged $160 a night.

Those who are long on indignation and short on economics may say that these hotels were now "charging all that the traffic will bear." But they were probably charging all that the traffic would bear when such hotels were charging $40 a night.

The real question is: Why will the traffic bear more now? Obviously because supply and demand have both changed. Since both homes and hotels have been damaged or destroyed by the hurricanes, there are now more people seeking more rooms from fewer hotels.

What if prices were frozen where they were before all this happened?

Those who got to the hotel first would fill up the rooms and those who got there later would be out of luck—and perhaps out of doors or out of the community. At higher prices, a family that might have rented one room for the parents and another for the children will now double up in just one room because of the "exorbitant" prices. That leaves another room for someone else.

Someone whose home was damaged, but not destroyed, may decide to stay home and make do in less than ideal conditions, rather than pay the higher prices at the local hotel. That too will leave another room for someone whose home was damaged worse or destroyed.

In short, the new prices make as much economic sense under the new conditions as the old prices made under the old conditions.

It is essentially the same story when stores in Florida are selling ice, plywood, gasoline, or other things for prices that reflect today's supply and demand, rather than yesterday's supply and demand. Price controls will not cause new supplies to be rushed in nearly as fast as higher prices will.

None of this is rocket science. But Justice Oliver Wendell Holmes said, "we need education in the obvious more than investigation of the obscure."

Economic "Power"

"Is Wal-Mart Good for America?"

That is the headline on a *New York Times* story about the country's largest retailer. The very idea that third parties should be deciding whether a particular business is good for the whole country shows incredible chutzpa.

The people who shop at Wal-Mart can decide whether that is good for them or not. But the intelligentsia are worried about something called Wal-Mart's "market power."

Apparently this giant chain sells 30 percent of all the disposable diapers in the country and the *Times* reporter refers to the prospect of "Wal-Mart amassing even more market power."

Just what "power" does a sales percentage represent? Not one of the people who bought their disposable diapers at Wal-Mart was forced to do so. I can't remember ever having bought anything from Wal-Mart and there is not the slightest thing that they can do to make me.

The misleading use of words constitutes a large part of what is called anti-trust law. "Market power" is just one of those misleading phrases. In anti-trust lingo, a company that sells 30 percent of the disposable diapers is said to "control" 30 percent of the market for that product. But they control nothing.

Let them jack up their prices and they will find themselves lucky to sell 3 percent of the disposable diapers. They will discover that they are just as disposable as their diapers.

Much is made of the fact that Wal-Mart has 3,000 stores in the United States and is planning to add 1,000 more. At one time, the A & P grocery chain had 15,000 stores but now they have shrunk so drastically that there are probably millions of people—especially in the younger generation— who don't even know that they exist.

An anti-trust lawsuit back in the 1940s claimed that A & P "controlled" a large share of the market for groceries. But they controlled nothing. As the society around them changed in the 1950s, A & P began losing millions of dollars a year, being forced to close thousands of stores and become a shadow of its former self.

Let the people who run Wal-Mart start believing the talk about how they "control" the market and, a few years down the road, people will be saying "Wal-Who?"

With Wal-Mart, as with A & P before them, the big bugaboo is that their low prices put competing stores out of business. Could anyone ever have doubted that low-cost stores win customers away from higher-cost stores?

It is one of the painful signs of the immaturity and lack of realism among the intelligentsia that many of them regard this as a "problem" to be "solved." Trade-offs have been with us ever since the late unpleasantness in the Garden of Eden.

How could industries have found all the millions of workers required to create the vast increase in output that raised American standards of living over the past hundred years, except by taking these workers away from the farms?

Historians have lamented the plight of the hand-loom weavers after power looms began replacing them in England. But how could the poor have been able to afford to buy adequate new clothing unless the price was brought down to their income level by mass production machinery?

Judge Robert Bork once said that somebody always gets hurt in a court room. Somebody always gets hurt in an economy that is growing. You can't keep on doing things the old way and still get the benefits of the new way.

This is not rocket science. But apparently some people just refuse to accept its logical implications. Unfortunately, some of those people are in Congress or in courtrooms practicing anti-trust law. And then there are the intelligentsia, perpetuating the mushy mindset that enables this counterproductive farce to go on.

This refusal to accept the fact that benefits have costs is especially prevalent in discussions of international trade. President Bush's ill-advised tariff on foreign steel was a classic example of trying to "save jobs" in one industry by policies which cost far more jobs in other industries making products with artificially expensive steel. Fortunately, he reversed himself.

Is it still news that there is no free lunch?

A Relic of the Recent Past

Only in California would a city that is less than 50 years old have a historical society. But, in California, anything more than a couple of decades old is considered historic and anything that is a century old is considered to be ancient history.

Nevertheless, the Foster City Historical Society has performed a useful service by publishing a little book titled simply "Foster City." It details the building of an attractive middle-class community with about 30,000 people on what was once swamp land.

What makes this story of more than local interest is that Foster City is the kind of community that would be difficult to build today and, in many places, virtually impossible. The very idea of draining a swamp—a sacrosanct "wetland"—would arouse the fury of environmental zealots.

Legalistic hassles over "environmental impact" reports alone might be enough to bankrupt the builders. Environmental impact reports often have little or nothing to do with the environment and everything to do with stopping development.

Nothing is easier than to claim that there will be horrible environmental consequences from building something. Moreover, there is no penalty whatsoever for making charges that can cost others millions of dollars to research and prove wrong.

The whole purpose of the charges may be precisely to cause builders to lose millions of dollars and perhaps have to give up the whole idea of building anything where the green zealots don't want anything built.

Foster City was built in the 1960s, just before the environmental protection racket went big time, with the aid of legislation and court decisions that gave green zealots the power to impose huge costs on others at little or no cost to themselves.

Nowhere is that power wielded more ruthlessly today than in San Mateo County, where Foster City is located. But, back when Foster City was built, the biggest challenges were physical.

In addition to draining the swamp, levees had to be built to hold back the tide waters of San Francisco Bay, and the land had to be filled in to make it strong enough to support the weight of homes and buildings.

Critics claimed that the first big earthquake would devastate a community built on land-fill—but their claims had no such legal clout as such claims would gain during the 1970s. In reality, Foster City came through the big 1989 earthquake with flying colors, while buildings collapsed and fires broke out from broken gas lines elsewhere in the San Francisco Bay area.

While Foster City is something of a triumph—a beautifully laid out community of attractive homes and condominiums, with parks and lovely lagoons on which boats sail, and miles of bicycle paths—it is also a reminder of the tragedy that no such community can be created today in many places, including the county in which it is located.

It is not that there is no vacant land left in San Mateo County. On the contrary, more than half the county consists of vacant land on which laws forbid the building of anything. Yet environmentalists there, as elsewhere, conjure up a vision in which the last few patches of greenery are threatened with being paved over.

Even when they are proved wrong by inescapable facts, green zealots often fall back on runaway extrapolations, claiming that they must stop development now or there will be ever increasing population densities, more pollution, more this, more that.

Runaway extrapolations are the last refuge of hysteria mongers when confronted with facts that demolish their lies. Think about it: The temperature has risen about 10 degrees since this morning. If you extrapolate that, we will all be burned to a crisp before the end of the month. Extrapolations prove nothing.

Ironically, many of the same people who have made "development" a dirty word that arouses outrage have nevertheless often looked favorably on "redevelopment."

What is the difference? Development means private initiative to build what people are willing to buy. Redevelopment means government tearing down "blighted" areas, so that whatever bureaucrats and politicians want can be built. Few redevelopments are anywhere near as well done as Foster City.

Who Can Afford It?

"Who can afford to buy a house in this place?" my wife asked, when I read her the average prices of homes in various northern California communities.

"We certainly can't," I said. Our home has more than doubled in value since we bought it 11 years ago. We couldn't live here if we had to pay today's prices. This is not unusual on the peninsula stretching from San Francisco to Silicon Valley.

Home prices can be very misleading in this area because many—if not most—of the people living here never paid those prices. These are the prices of current home sales. They are the prices that newcomers moving in have to pay.

That fact has a lot to do with skyrocketing home prices. The people who vote on the laws which severely restrict building, create costly bureaucratic delays, and impose arbitrary planning commission notions will not have to pay a dime toward the huge costs being imposed on anyone trying to build anything in the San Francisco Bay area. Newcomers get stuck with those costs.

The biggest of these costs is the cost of the land rather than the cost of the houses themselves. The average price of homes is a million dollars in some San Francisco Bay area communities where it would be hard to find a single house that anyone would call a mansion.

Nor are there many new homes being built in these communities. Old homes are simply being bid up in price, precisely because it is either impossible or ruinously expensive to build new homes.

Unlike other places, where people trying to sell their houses usually have an asking price that they bring down somewhat in the course of negotiations with a prospective buyer, in the San Francisco Bay area the asking price is usually bid up during the competition among people who want to buy.

Someone who bought a home for $100,000 back in the 1970s may put it on sale for $700,000 today—and watch the buyers bid it up to $900,000. The average home price in San Mateo County, where it is nearly impossible to build anything, is $921,000.

There are a lot of nice middle-class homes in San Mateo County, and some rather modest homes, but very few mansions.

One of the middle-class communities in the county is Foster City, a planned community built back in the 1960s. When the first homes went on sale there in 1963, you could buy a three-bedroom house for as little as $22,000. If you wanted something bigger or more fancy, or in a more scenic location, you could still get it for under $50,000.

Today, the average price of a home in Foster City is $1.2 million.

People who wring their hands about a need for "affordable housing" seldom consider that the way to have affordable housing is to stop making it unaffordable. Foster City housing was affordable before the restrictive land use laws in this area made all housing astronomically expensive.

Contrary to the vision of the left, it was the free market which produced affordable housing—before government intervention made housing unaffordable.

None of this is rocket science. Anyone who can

understand the concept of supply and demand can understand that putting most of the land in a whole county off-limits to building will cause the price of the remaining land to rise.

It is the land, rather than the houses that are built on it, which has become astronomically expensive in places with extreme "open space" laws and other severe restrictions on the use of land. In some places without such laws, a house can be bought for a fraction of what that same house would cost in parts of California.

The people who push restrictive laws and policies often try to blame everything else for high housing costs. "Overpopulation" is one such red herring. In reality, the population of San Mateo County has declined by 9,000 people in the past four years while housing prices have risen sharply.

Ironically, a consummately selfish policy of creating costs that force newcomers to pay high prices which existing homeowners will not have to pay is often wrapped in the mantle of idealism and washed down with pious expressions of hope for some way to try to create "affordable housing."

Free-Lunch Medicine

It is always fascinating to see elementary economics make front-page news. It was front-page news in the *Wall Street Journal* of November 12, 2003 that there are long waiting times for seeing medical specialists in Canada and in other countries with government-controlled medical care systems—but not in the United States, where some politicians are trying to get us to imitate those countries.

Shortages where the government sets prices have been common in countries around the world, for centuries on end, whether these shortages have taken the form of waiting lists, black markets, or other ways of coping with the fact that what people demand at an artificially low price exceeds what other people will supply at such prices.

This principle is not limited to medical care. There were waiting lines for food, undershirts, and all sorts of other things in the Communist bloc countries in Eastern Europe before the collapse of Communism in that region. You had to get on a waiting list to buy a poorly made car in India before they began to free up their economy from government controls.

You could go back literally thousands of years and find shortages under price controls in the Roman Empire or in ancient Babylon. But it is still front-page news today because elementary economics has not yet sunk in.

An OECD study shows that the percentage of patients waiting more than 4 months for elective surgery in English-speaking countries is in single digits only in the United

States, where we "lack" the "benefits" of a government-run medical system.

In Canada 27 percent of patients wait more than 4 months and in Britain 38 percent. Elective surgery includes some heart surgery.

Depending on what you are suffering from, and how much you are suffering, longer waits can be a cost that far outweighs monetary savings under price control or government subsidies. Sometimes the wait can be fatal.

There is another kind of waiting—waiting for new medicines to be developed for scourges like cancer, AIDS, and Alzheimer's. Countries with price controls on pharmaceutical drugs have far fewer of such drugs created than the United States does.

Yet Americans, who produce a wholly disproportionate share of the world's new life-saving drugs, are being asked to imitate price control policies in countries where such policies have dried up the costly research behind such discoveries.

These countries have left the development of new drugs to the United States. But if we follow their example by killing the goose that lays the golden egg, who can we turn to for developing new medicines? This could be the most costly free lunch of all.

None of the various schemes for lowering the prices of medicines seems willing to face up to the simple fact that each new medicine developed costs hundreds of millions of dollars. This huge inescapable fact just seems to evaporate from the discussion as politicians vie with one another for the best way to make these medicines "affordable" at "reasonable" prices.

Politicians who claim to be able to "bring down the cost of health care" are talking about bringing down the prices charged. But prices are not costs. Prices are what pay for costs.

No matter how much lower the government sets the prices paid to doctors, hospitals, or pharmaceutical drug manufacturers, none of this reduces the costs in the slightest.

It still takes just as much time, equipment, and training to turn a medical school student into a doctor. It still takes just as many hospitals to care for the sick. It still takes just as many years of scientific research and clinical trials to create a new medicine.

Those who are dying to control the prices of pharmaceutical drugs are oblivious to the fact that other people may be literally dying unnecessarily if they succeed. There is no free lunch, even though politicians get elected by promising free lunches.

Government price controls on medicines and medical care simply mean that these costs do not all get covered. This works in the short run—and the short run is what politicians are interested in, because elections are held in the short run. But the rest of us had better think ahead, if we value our health.

Free-Lunch Medicine: Part II

Any attempt at a rational discussion of the economic realities of government-controlled medical care is almost certain to run up against the trump card of the political left: The Poor.

The image that is often invoked is that of the elderly poor, forced to choose between food and medical treatment. Who could be so heartless as to abandon them to the vagaries of the free market?

This has proved to be a very effective political strategy for extending government power, not only over medical care but also over housing and other sectors of the economy.

The phoniness of this argument becomes apparent the moment you suggest that money be set aside specifically for dealing with the special problems of the poor, rather than bringing whole sectors of the economy under the dominance of politicians, bureaucrats and judges.

The amount of money needed to take care of the poor is often some minute fraction of what sweeping new government programs cost. But, while big government liberals are willing to use the poor as human shields in their political battles, their more basic strategy is to proclaim that everyone has a "right" to some "basic need" that they want the government to provide.

As a matter of practical politics, programs for the poor alone do not have as large a constituency as programs to give everybody some benefit, so that we can all have the illusion of getting something for nothing—or at some arbitrarily defined "reasonable" or "affordable" price.

It is completely unreasonable to talk about reasonable prices.

Such talk amounts to saying that economic realities have to adjust to what we are willing to pay, because we are not going to adjust to economic realities. The biggest economic reality that gets ignored in discussions of medical care is that developing a single new medicine or training a single new doctor takes huge amounts of resources.

What we think we can afford has nothing to do with what pharmaceutical drugs cost to develop. Nor does it have anything to do with the costs of training a new doctor or building a new hospital. We are either going to pay those costs or we are not going to get the quantity or the quality that we want.

Schemes for re-importing American drugs from Canada or buying in bulk from pharmaceutical companies are essentially ways of shifting costs around—without reducing these costs by one cent. Already government agencies, HMOs and others are engaged in shifting medical costs onto somebody else. But, for society as a whole, there is no somebody else.

No matter how much the costs are shifted around in clever shell games, those costs do not go away. That is the hard reality which no political rhetoric can change.

The only reason such rhetoric has even the appearance of plausibility is that price controls work in the short run—and that is good enough for politicians, since elections are held in the short run. After all, when the government drives down prices paid to doctors, hospitals or pharmaceutical companies, there is not much that doctors, hospitals or pharmaceutical companies can do about it immediately.

Doctors are not going to give up practicing medicine and become truck drivers. Medical schools are not going to be turned into bowling alleys or hospitals into skating rinks. Pharmaceutical companies cannot suddenly shift to manufacturing cars. So price controls seem to work in the short run—but only in the short run.

When you confront doctors with more hassles with bureaucrats and lower payments for their services, do not expect the medical profession to remain as attractive to bright young people deciding what careers to follow. In the long run, every single doctor is going to have to be replaced by someone from the younger generation, or else we are going to have a shortage of doctors.

Britain, for example, has had government-run medical care for decades and nearly half their doctors are imported, often from Third World countries with lower standards of medical training. Canadian hospitals have less modern equipment available than American hospitals do. They depend on American medicines after destroying incentives to develop their own with price controls.

Is this what we are supposed to imitate?

Free-Lunch Medicine: Part III

A successful political crusade is incomplete without a villain. To play St. George, you need a dragon. The crusade for government control of medical care has made the pharmaceutical industry its villain.

First, there are the "unconscionable" profits of the firms producing medications. Since there is no definition of unconscionable profits, this gives the politicians great flexibility. And, because there are a number of different ways of computing profit rates, that gives them even more flexibility.

A couple of years ago, during the Anthrax scare, there were loud denunciations of Bayer, the manufacturer of the leading drug for treating Anthrax, by liberal Senators like Ted Kennedy and Chuck Schumer. They claimed that Bayer was making too much profit on that drug and should lower the price during a national emergency.

Just for the record, it would have cost 50 dollars to use the drug in question for the time it was needed, after which you could switch to other and less expensive drugs. Also for the record, Bayer operated at a loss during that quarter. When even losses are considered to be unconscionable profits, you can see how flexible these terms are in the hands of political demagogues.

No doubt Bayer was making money on that particular drug but pharmaceutical drugs are a risky business, with many money-losing ventures that have to be covered by the profits on those drugs that do make money.

Ask yourself: If you had some money saved for your retirement and someone suggested that you invest it in the pharmaceutical industry, would all the denunciations of the industry by politicians, and threats to crack down with legislation, make you more willing or less willing to risk investing your money there?

Put differently, how high a rate of return would you require before putting your money into most industries, as compared to how high a rate of return you would require before being willing to invest in the pharmaceutical industry? With liberals breathing fire about "unconscionable profits" and threatening punitive legislation, the pharmaceutical industry would probably have to offer you a higher rate of return before you would risk investing in drug companies.

You might have to make an "unconscionable" rate of return to make the risk worth taking.

You can see the same process at work in some Third World countries, where local demagogues blame these countries' poverty on "exploitation" by foreign investors and threaten to put a stop to it. Whether or not these demagogues actually follow through and carry out their threats, such talk can cause foreign investors to stay away.

They say talk is cheap but political demagoguery can have very high costs. In the case of pharmaceutical drugs, these costs go beyond money to needless pain, disabilities and death, when the rate of new drug discovery suffers from threatening political rhetoric that discourages investment.

Now that we have talked about the dragon, what about St. George? Proponents of government-controlled medical care point out that, despite much longer waits for many medical treatments in Canada, Canadian life expectancy is slightly higher than that of Americans. Apparently St. George is a success.

That might be decisive evidence if medical care were the only determinant of life expectancy. But even the finest medical care in the world cannot help people who are killing themselves, whether suddenly with a gun or more slowly with drugs or obesity or other dangerous lifestyles.

Americans, for example, are obese more than twice as often as Canadians and our murder rates are higher. Those who resist the idea of personal responsibility are quick to blame objective circumstances, such as medical care.

Some years ago, there were media outcries because black pregnant women received less prenatal care than white pregnant women and their infant mortality rates were higher. But Americans of Chinese, Japanese, and Filipino ancestry also had less prenatal care than whites—and lower infant mortality rates than whites.

The effects of personal behavior cannot be ignored. Neither can the inescapable costs of medical care.

Manufacturing Confusion

"Manufacturing jobs" has become a battle cry of those who oppose free trade and are sounding an alarm about American jobs being exported to lower-wage countries overseas. However, manufacturing jobs are much less of a problem than manufacturing confusion.

Much of what is being said confuses what is true of one sector of the economy with what is true of the economy as a whole. Every modern economy is constantly changing in technology and organization. This means that resources—human resources as well as natural resources and other inputs—are constantly being sent off in new directions as things are being produced in new ways.

This happens whether there is or is not free international trade. At the beginning of the 20th century, 10 million American farmers and farm laborers produced the food to feed a population of 76 million people. By the end of the century, fewer than 2 million people on the farms were feeding a population of more than 250 million. In other words, more than 8 million agricultural jobs were "lost."

Between 1990 and 1995, more than 17 million American workers throughout the economy lost their jobs. But there were never 17 million workers unemployed during this period, any more than the 8 million agricultural workers were unemployed before.

People moved on to other jobs. Unemployment rates in fact hit new lows in the 1990s. None of this is rocket science.

But when the very same things happen in the international economy, it is much easier to spread alarm and manufacture confusion.

There is no question that many computer programming jobs have moved from the United States to India. But this is just a half-truth, which can be worse than a lie. As management consultant Peter Drucker points out in the current issue of *Fortune* magazine, there are also foreign jobs moving to the United States.

In Drucker's words, "Nobody seems to realize that we import twice or three times as many jobs as we export. I'm talking about the jobs created by foreign companies coming into the U.S.," such as Japanese automobile plants making Toyotas and Hondas on American soil.

"Siemens alone has 60,000 employees in the United States," Drucker points out. "We are exporting low-skill, low-paying jobs but are importing high-skill, high-paying jobs."

None of this is much consolation if you are one of the people being displaced from a job that you thought would last indefinitely. But few jobs last indefinitely. You cannot advance the standard of living by continuing to do the same things in the same ways.

Progress means change, whether those changes originate domestically or internationally. Even when a given job carries the same title, often you cannot hold that job while continuing to do things the way they were done 20 years ago—or, in the case of computers, 5 years ago.

The grand fallacy of those who oppose free trade is that low-wage countries take jobs away from high-wage countries. While that is true for some particular jobs in some particular cases, it is another half-truth that is more misleading than an outright lie.

While American companies can hire computer

programmers in India to replace higher paid American programmers, that is because of India's outstanding education in computer engineering. By and large, however, the average productivity of Indian workers is about 15 percent of that of American workers.

In other words, if you hired Indian workers and paid them one-fifth of what you paid American workers, it would cost you more to get a given job done in India. That is the rule and computer programming is the exception.

Facts are blithely ignored by those who simply assume that low-wage countries have an advantage in international trade. But high-wage countries have been exporting to low-wage countries for centuries. The vast majority of foreign investments by American companies are in high-wage countries, despite great outcries about how multinational corporations are "exploiting" Third World workers.

Apparently facts do not matter to those who are manufacturing confusion about manufacturing jobs.

A Cold Shower

Sometimes a phrase betrays a whole mindset. Someone quoted in the *New York Times* recently referred to the Bush tax cut as one in which "most of the benefits would be showered on the richest taxpayers."

Keeping money that you yourself earned is called having benefits "showered" on you! By this reasoning, anyone who has the power to take something from you and doesn't take it all is "showering" benefits on you. Anyone who has a gun and doesn't use it to kill you is showering life itself on you.

Big spenders and big taxers never want to face the fact that wealth is not created by government, but by the people that the government taxes. Moreover, these are seldom simply people who "happen to have money," as the phrase goes.

Most people who have money usually got it by providing other people with something that they wanted badly enough to pay for it. This is never called "public service" by the politically correct. Selling people what they want, in order to get what you want, is called "greed."

It's public service when you decide what other people "really" need and impose it at the taxpayers' expense. It's public service when you create hoops for other people to jump through—rules to follow, forms to fill out, lives to be lived as you prescribe—all for their own good.

Given this mindset, you can see why letting people keep more of the money they earn is considered to be indulging them with benefits that the government "showers" on them. It is like subsidizing sin.

Anyone who has read *The Federalist Papers*—or who has read between the lines in the Constitution—knows that the people who founded this country had a great fear of government's power over individuals. They knew that there are always busybodies who cannot be happy unless they are telling other people what to do and forcing them to do it.

Property rights were put into the Constitution to keep politicians on a short leash, instead of letting them roam at will over the land and treat the wealth created by others as something for them to dispense as largess and use to buy votes.

People had the right to bear arms, so that they could defend themselves, instead of letting their safety and the safety of their families be yet another playground for bright ideas about crime and criminals, such as unsubstantiated theories about "root causes" and pious hopes about "rehabilitation" of criminals and "prevention" of crime.

It is not just a question about the rightness or wrongness of particular notions in isolation, but the unending proliferation of these notions. Every little wonderful bright idea has its rationale. It will make us safer, or smarter, or more sensitive. Above all, it will make us more like the anointed who have thought up these grandiose notions.

To those with this self-flattering mindset, if they think it is more important to look out for caribou than to look out for people, then you must be a slob if you think people are more important than caribou.

When you add up all the requirements, restrictions, re-education, and re-diculous ideas dreamed by all the 57 varieties of busybodies, you end up hemmed in like a rat backed into a corner.

Literally from the moment you wake up in the morning and take a shower (with a government-prescribed rate of water flow) to the time you flush the toilet (also with a government-prescribed water flow rate) for the last time before going to bed, your life has been laid out for you.

An Old "New Vision"

Despite the fanfare of a televised speech at the National Press Club in Washington, a very old and hackneyed set of proposals was unveiled as a "new vision" for the creation of "affordable housing." The speech was by Richard Ravitch, co-chairman with former Congresswoman Susan Molinari of what is called the Millennial Housing Commission, a group making recommendations to Congress on housing policy.

These two members of the New York political establishment produced the kinds of proposals that such people have been turning out for years. "Affordable housing" for them means government-subsidized housing, and their report essentially spells out innumerable schemes by which the taxpayers can pick up part or all of the tab for tenants or home buyers.

Contrary to this political report, a recent economic and statistical analysis by Professors Edward L. Glaeser of Harvard and Joseph E. Gyourko of the Wharton School of Business concludes: "America is not facing a nationwide affordable housing crisis." There are astronomical housing prices in particular places for reasons peculiar to those places. The principal reason is the price of land.

"In large areas of the country," they find, "housing costs are quite close to the cost of new construction." These areas "represent the bulk of American housing" and they are areas where "land is quite cheap."

In high-price areas, "housing is expensive because of artificial limits on construction created by the regulation of

new housing." In other words, the government—which is
depicted by Molinari and Ravitch as the savior of those
seeking "affordable housing"—is in fact the very reason why
housing is so unaffordable in some places, according to
scholars who have actually analyzed the hard data.

What kinds of differences in housing prices are we
talking about? The average home price nationwide is about
$150,000 but it is $500,000 in the area extending from San
Francisco to Silicon Valley, about 30 miles south of the city.
Nor is this price difference due to grander homes in
California. Very ordinary homes just have grand prices.

You can in fact buy magnificent homes in some parts of
the country for less than rather nondescript houses in
pricier California communities. A recent issue of the *Wall
Street Journal* had an advertisement for a 4 bedroom, 6 bath
home, with 4,370 square feet of space and "a screen-
enclosed pool/spa," located adjacent to a golf course and
country club, for $550,000. It was in Leesburg, Florida.

Meanwhile, in Palo Alto, California, two houses were
advertised at nearly double that price—$1,095,000 each—
and neither house had as much as 1,500 square feet of
space. Nor were they located anywhere other than on an
ordinary city street, and no swimming pool was mentioned
in either ad.

Many things go into determining the price of housing,
both homes and apartments. But, after taking numerous
factors into consideration, the Harvard and Wharton
professors found that the key factor was the cost of the land
on which the housing was built.

Their statistical analysis indicates that a home on a
quarter-acre lot in Chicago is likely to sell for about
$140,000 more than its construction costs. In San Diego it
sells for $285,000 more than construction costs, in New York

City $350,000 more and in San Francisco nearly $700,000 more than construction costs.

"Only in particular areas, especially New York City and California, do housing prices diverge substantially from the costs of new construction," according to the study. Why the astronomical housing prices in some places? Strict zoning laws "are highly correlated with high prices," Glaeser and Gyourko find.

Long delays in getting permits to build are major factors in high housing prices. Millions of dollars can be tied up while bureaucrats dawdle and environmentalists carp. Indeed, delay is one of the chief weapons of environmental extremists who don't want anything built, and who know that delays cost developers a bundle. In the end, that ends up costing home buyers and apartment tenants a bundle.

More government is not the solution. Big, intrusive government is what creates the problem.

Third World Sweatshops

"Low-Wage Costa Ricans Make Baseballs for Millionaires."

That was the headline on one of those *New York Times* "news" stories that continued its recent tradition of editorials disguised as news. The headline said it all but the story ran on and on anyway, with details and quotes that added nothing to the familiar story that Third World workers don't earn nearly as much money as most Americans, even when they work for rich American companies.

Perhaps the best refutation of the implied message of this "news" story also appeared in the *New York Times*, in a frankly labeled op-ed piece by the paper's own Nicholas D. Kristof. Writing from Cambodia, Kristof reported: "Here in Cambodia factory jobs are in such demand that workers usually have to bribe a factory insider with a month's salary just to get hired."

The workers in Cambodia receive even lower wages than those in Costa Rica. But the difference is that the report from Cambodia spelled out what the local workers' alternatives were and how anxious they are to get the jobs denounced by intellectuals and politicians who live in affluent countries.

"Nhep Chanda averages 75 cents a day for her efforts. For her, the idea of being exploited in a garment factory— working only six days a week, inside instead of in the broiling sun, for up to $2 a day—is a dream."

By and large, multinational companies pay about double the local wages in Third World countries. As for "exploitation," the vast majority of American investment overseas goes to high-wage countries, not low-wage countries.

Why are these international capitalists passing up supposedly golden opportunities for exploitation? Because they understand economics better than most intellectuals and politicians, who are content to score cheap points, without worrying about the logic or the consequences.

If outsiders succeed in pressuring or forcing multinational companies to pay higher wages, that will make it more economical for those companies to relocate many of their operations to more affluent countries, where the higher productivity of the workers there will cover the higher wage rates.

Net result: Third World workers will be worse off for having lost better jobs than most of them can find locally. Meanwhile, Western intellectuals and politicians will be congratulating themselves for having ended exploitation.

At the heart of all this is a confusion between the vagaries of fate and the sins of man. All of us wish that workers in Costa Rica and Cambodia, not to mention other poor countries, were able to earn higher pay and live better lives. But wishing will not make it so and causing them to lose their jobs will not help.

It is tragic that people in some societies simply have not had the same opportunities to develop more valuable skills and that those societies have not had economic and political systems that promote material progress comparable to that in most Western countries.

Low pay is one symptom of that fact—and changing the symptom will not change the underlying problem, which is that the people in such countries got a raw deal from fate, history, geography or culture. These are the vagaries of fate but the left tries to turn this into the sins of man by blaming Western employers, who are in fact providing these workers with better options than they had before.

The left-wing spin is that the poor are poor because the rich are rich. That opens the door for a big power-grab by the left in the name of "fairness" or "social justice" or whatever other rhetoric resonates with the unwary and the ill-informed.

Unfortunately, the left's theory does not also resonate with the facts. Whether domestically or internationally, investors looking for the highest rates of return usually steer clear of poor areas and put their money where there are people with more advanced skills, living in more prosperous countries, even if businesses have to pay much higher salaries in such places.

The United States, for example, has long invested more in Canada than in all of poverty-stricken sub-Saharan Africa, where wage rates are a fraction of Canadian wage rates. If the facts mattered—and if the poor really mattered to their supposed saviors—the implications of that would have been understood long ago.

Third World Sweatshops: Part II

Those who vent their moral indignation over low pay for Third World workers employed by multinational companies ignore the plain fact that these workers' employers are usually supplying them with better opportunities than they had before, while those who are morally indignant on their behalf are providing them with nothing.

Some of the more rational among the indignant crusaders for "social justice" may concede that the employers are usually offering better pay than Third World workers would have had otherwise. But they see no reason why wealthy corporations should not pay wages more like the wages paid in affluent countries.

There are at least two reasons why not—one economic and one moral.

The economic reason is that output per man-hour in Third World countries is usually some fraction of what it is in Western industrial nations such as the United States. Pay rates raised without regard to productivity are a virtual guarantee of unemployment, whether it is done in the name of ending "exploitation" in the Third World or providing "a living wage" in the United States.

Most modern industrial nations have minimum wage laws but those with higher minimum wage rates or additional mandated workers' benefits tend to have higher unemployment rates.

Germany, for example, has perhaps the most employer-provided benefits mandated by government. These benefits include such huge severance pay that firing anyone is likely to be uneconomical. The costs of these benefits have been estimated as roughly double those of employer-provided benefits in the United States.

If you think that is great for the workers, remember that there is no free lunch, for workers or anybody else. The high cost of labor and the difficulties of firing anyone mean that employers are reluctant to hire, even when times are booming.

It is often cheaper to expand output by using more labor-saving machines, or to work the existing workforce overtime, rather than hire more employees. While Americans become alarmed when unemployment reaches 6 percent, double-digit unemployment has been common in Germany.

At one time, neither Switzerland nor Hong Kong had minimum wage laws. Last year, *The Economist* magazine reported: "Switzerland's unemployment rate neared a five-year high of 3.9% in February." For most countries that have minimum wage laws, a 3.9 % unemployment rate would be a five-year low, if not wholly unattainable.

Back when Hong Kong was a British colony and its wage rates were set by supply and demand, the *Wall Street Journal* reported that its unemployment rate was less than 2 percent. Then, after China took over Hong Kong and mandated various worker benefits—which add to labor costs, the same as higher wage rates—Hong Kong's unemployment rate went over 8%.

This was not high by European standards but it was unprecedented for Hong Kong. There is no free lunch in any part of the world.

Why cannot rich multinational corporations simply

absorb the losses of paying Third World workers more than their productivity is worth? Why shouldn't they?

First of all, multi-billion-dollar corporations are seldom owned by multi-billionaires. They are usually owned by thousands, if not millions, of stockholders, most of whom are nowhere close to being billionaires. Some may be teachers, nurses, mechanics, clerks and others who own stock indirectly by paying into pension funds that buy these stocks.

Indeed, the average incomes of all the stockholders—direct and indirect—may be no greater than the average incomes of those intellectuals, politicians, and others who want them to absorb the costs of higher pay in the Third World.

But if teachers, nurses, mechanics, and clerks are supposed to accept less money to live on in their retirement years, why shouldn't similar donations to the Third World come from reporters for the *New York Times* or Ivy League professors, movie stars or others who are morally indignant?

Or is this just one of many things that the morally indignant think is worth having others pay for, but not worth enough to pay for themselves?

Privatizing Social Security

Would you sign a contract that enabled the other party to change the terms of that contract at will, while you could neither stop him nor make any changes of your own? Probably not. Yet that is exactly what happens when you pay money into Social Security.

No matter what you were promised or at what age you were supposed to get it, the government can always pass a new law that changes all of that. But you still have to pay into the system.

A private annuity plan run by an insurance company is legally required to pay you what was promised, when it was promised, and to maintain assets sufficient to redeem its promises.

Why are liberals against letting people put part of their Social Security payments into private investments?

Risk is one of their arguments. Al Gore incessantly repeated the phrase "a risky scheme" during the 2000 election campaign and risk still seems to be the big objection to letting people put their own money where they want.

Some liberals may actually believe that politicians know what is best for you better than you know yourself. That is, after all, the philosophy behind many other government programs.

Another reason for liberal opposition to private investment of Social Security payments is that it deprives them of control of billions of dollars that they have been spending from the Social Security trust fund for years. They can buy a lot of votes with all sorts of giveaway programs, financed by money taken from Social Security.

As for the risk of making private investments, that might be a real concern if people were putting their money into commodity speculation or other volatile markets. Most people have better sense and privatization could limit where Social Security premiums could be invested.

Although the stock market bounces up and down from day to day, people are not investing today in order to retire next week. They begin paying Social Security premiums when they first get a job and they retire 40 or 50 years later.

Stocks are far less risky in the long run than they are in the short run because the ups and downs balance out over a long period of time. It is virtually impossible to find any 40-year or 50-year period in which the stock market has not paid a higher rate of return on your money than you get from Social Security.

You may get a slightly lower pension if you retire when the stock market is down than if you retire when the stock market is up—but even the lower pension is going to be more than you would get paying the same amount of money into Social Security.

Risks can be minimized in many ways. There are some mutual funds that simply buy a mixture of the stocks that make up the Dow Jones average (or Standard & Poor's), so that their clients will have the kind of return on their investments that the stock market as a whole has. They don't make a killing but they don't get killed either.

How did Social Security get into its present mess in the first place? Because politicians made it the "risky scheme" that they now claim privatization would be.

The same political expediency which caused Social Security to be called "insurance," in order to get public support, guaranteed that it would be nothing of the sort. Unlike an insurance company, Social Security has never had enough money to pay for all the pensions it promised.

Privatizing Social Security: Part II

Current Senate hearings on "mandatory retirement" may have more than a little relevance to the huge question of how to "save" Social Security. Unfortunately, there is far too little attention being paid to the question of why Social Security requires saving in the first place.

The key problem with Social Security is that it has never taken in enough to cover all the pensions it promised to pay. Promises win votes but collecting enough money to pay for those promises does not.

Should we be surprised that politicians take the easy way out by promising a lot and leaving it to future politicians to figure out how to pay for what was promised—or how to disguise their welshing on those promises?

We hear a lot about how changing demographics have created a problem for Social Security, since people now live longer, changing the ratio of people paying into the system compared to people getting money out of the system.

But you don't see insurance companies wringing their hands about how they can't pay out the pensions they promised when they sold annuities.

That is because each generation's premiums were invested to create additional future wealth to pay for that generation's pensions, regardless of whether the next generation is large or small. The big difference between private annuities and Social Security is that private investment creates future wealth for the country as a whole and Social Security does not.

More total wealth through privatization offers some hope of solving the problem of inadequate wealth to pay the pensions that Social Security promised to the baby boomers. Otherwise, the government will have to welsh on its promises, because the amount of tax increase needed exceeds what is politically feasible.

That is where so-called "mandatory retirement" comes in. That concept is as fraudulent as calling Social Security "insurance" when it has in fact always been a pyramid scheme, where each generation depends on the next generation to pay its pensions.

There has never been any such thing as mandatory retirement. By contract or custom, employers have had a general practice of no longer employing people after they reached a certain age. But there has been no requirement that those people retire. Many—if not most—have in fact continued working elsewhere, often while drawing a pension.

By passing laws forbidding "mandatory retirement," the government reduced the number of older people who would otherwise have retired and begun drawing Social Security pensions. This self-serving transfer of billions of dollars in financial liabilities from the government to private employers was thus presented as a virtuous rescue of older workers from unfair discrimination.

Never mind that the Constitution forbids the government from changing the terms of private contracts. Never mind that younger workers find their upward path blocked by older workers whom the employer cannot get rid of without legal hassles.

All of this is washed down with lofty rhetoric about how age need not mean a decline in efficiency, about how our senior citizens still have much to contribute, about how older Americans are "breaking the silver ceiling," in the words of Senator John Breaux at recent Senate hearings.

In other words, the assumption is that individual employers looking directly at individual workers, whose work they are already familiar with, are not smart enough to make as good a judgment as distant politicians talking in generalities.

Even in the past, when a particular employer's obligation to employ workers expired at a certain age, there was nothing to prevent a mutual agreement for particular workers to continue working past that age, when the employer saw that the particular worker's productivity made this advisable and the worker wanted to continue on.

In short, neither Senate hearings nor "expert" witnesses were necessary. Much of this is a charade to allow the government to raise or eliminate remaining retirement ages, in order to escape from the impossible situation that politicians created when they designed Social Security as a pyramid scheme.

"Living Wage" Kills Jobs

Give credit where credit is due. The political left is great with words. Conservatives have never been able to come up with such seductive phrases as the left mass produces.

While conservatives may talk about a need for "judicial restraint," liberals cry out for "social justice." If someone asks you why they should be in favor of judicial restraint, you have got to sit them down and go into a long explanation about Constitutional government and its implications and prerequisites.

But "social justice"? No explanation needed. No definition. No facts. Everybody is for it. Do you want social injustice?

The latest verbal coup of the left is the phrase "a living wage." Who is so hard-hearted or mean-spirited that they do not want people to be able to make enough money to live on?

Unfortunately, the effort and talent that the left puts into coining great phrases is seldom put into analysis or evidence. The living wage campaign shows that as well.

Just what is a living wage? It usually means enough income to support a family of four on one paycheck. This idea has swept through various communities, churches and academic institutions.

Facts have never yet caught up with this idea and analysis is lagging even farther behind.

First of all, do most low-wage workers actually have a family of four to support on one paycheck? According to a recent study by the Cato Institute, fewer than one out of five minimum wage workers has a family to support. Workers earning the minimum wage are usually young people just starting out.

So the premise is false from the beginning. But it is still a great phrase, and rhetoric is apparently what matters, considering all the politicians, academics and church groups who are stampeding all and sundry toward the living wage concept.

What the so-called living wage really amounts to is simply a local minimum wage policy requiring much higher pay rates than the federal minimum wage law. It's another name for a higher minimum wage.

Since there have been minimum wage laws for generations, not only in the United States, but in other countries around the world, you might think that we would want to look at what actually happens when such laws are enacted, as distinguished from what was hoped would happen.

Neither the advocates of this new minimum wage policy nor the media—much less politicians—show any interest whatsoever in facts about the consequences of minimum wage laws.

Most studies of minimum wage laws in countries around the world show that fewer people are employed at artificially higher wage rates. Moreover, unemployment falls disproportionately on lower skilled workers, younger and inexperienced workers, and workers from minority groups.

The new Cato Institute study cites data showing job losses in places where living wage laws have been imposed. This should not be the least bit surprising. Making anything more expensive almost invariably leads to fewer purchases. That includes labor.

While trying to solve a non-problem—supporting families that don't exist, in most cases—the living wage crusade creates a very real problem of low-skilled workers having trouble finding a job at all.

People in minimum wage jobs do not stay at the minimum wage permanently. Their pay increases as they accumulate experience and develop skills. It increases an average of 30 percent in just their first year of employment, according to the Cato Institute study. Other studies show that low-income people become average-income people in a few years and high-income people later in life.

All of this depends on their having a job in the first place, however. But the living wage kills jobs.

As imposed wage rates rise, so do job qualifications, so that less skilled or less experienced workers become "unemployable." Think about it. Every one of us would be "unemployable" if our pay rates were raised high enough.

I would love to believe that the Hoover Institution would continue to hire me if I demanded double my current salary. But you notice that I don't make any such demand. Third parties need to stop making such demands for other people. It is more important for people to have jobs than for busybodies to feel noble.

A Happy Birthday?

Only a few economic historians are likely to notice that June 17th marks the 75th anniversary of the signing of the Hawley-Smoot tariff bill, and even economic historians are unlikely to be nostalgic about that disastrous legislation.

Why not leave the bad news of the past in the past? After all, we have our own problems today.

Unfortunately, the same kind of thinking that led to the Hawley-Smoot tariffs is still alive and well—and in full youthful vigor—in the media and in politics today.

At the heart of past and present arguments for restricting imports that compete with American-made products is the notion that these imports will cost Americans their jobs. That fear was even more understandable back in 1930, when the Great Depression was getting under way and unemployment was at 9 percent.

The Hawley-Smoot bill raised American tariffs to record high levels, in an attempt to protect existing jobs and in hopes of helping the unemployed find work producing things that the United States had previously been importing from other countries. Many businesses were in favor of the new tariffs, hoping to retain or expand their markets, and farmers were especially big supporters of the Hawley-Smoot tariffs.

Who was opposed?

Most of the leading economists in the country were opposed. A front-page headline in the *New York Times* of May 5, 1930 read: "1,028 Economists Ask Hoover to Veto

Pending Tariff Bill." Those signing this public appeal against the new tariffs included many of the top economists of the day—25 professors of economics at Harvard, 26 at the University of Chicago, and 28 at Columbia.

But, to a politician, what do 1,028 votes matter in a country the size of the United States? Congressman Hawley and Senator Smoot both ignored them, as did President Herbert Hoover, who signed the legislation into law the next month.

The economic reasons for not restricting international trade then were the same as they are today. The only difference is that what happened then gives us a free home demonstration of what can be expected to happen if we go that route again.

The economists' appeal spelled it out: "The proponents of higher tariffs claim that the increase in rates will give work to the idle. This is not true. We cannot increase employment by restricting trade."

If 9 percent unemployment was troublesome in 1930, when the Hawley-Smoot tariff was passed, it was nothing compared to the 16 percent unemployment the next year and the 25 percent unemployment two years after that. The annual rate of unemployment in the United States never got back down to the 9 percent level again during the entire decade of the 1930s.

American industry as a whole operated at a loss for two consecutive years. Farmers, who had given strong support to the Hawley-Smoot tariffs, saw their own exports cut by two-thirds as countries around the world retaliated against American tariffs by restricting their imports of American industrial and agricultural products.

The economists' appeal had warned of "retaliatory tariffs" that would set off a wave of international trade restrictions which would hurt all countries economically. After everything that these economists had warned about happened, tariffs began to be reduced but throughout the 1930s they remained above where they were before the Hawley-Smoot tariffs—and so did unemployment.

Many factors, of course, affected the Great Depression of the 1930s. But later economists looking back have seen the Hawley-Smoot tariff as one of the factors needlessly prolonging the economic disaster.

How much wiser are we today? Not much, if at all.

Talk about import restrictions or complaints about "outsourcing" today proceed with the same mindless disregard of what other nations are doing and will do.

People who throw around statistics about how many American jobs have been outsourced don't even mention how many Americans have jobs that have been outsourced from other countries, much less how many Americans will lose those jobs if we start a new round of international trade restrictions.

PART III

LEGAL ISSUES

Calculated Confusion

Those who want to see judges who will apply the law instead of imposing their own policies face not only political obstruction to the appointment of such judges but also calculated confusion about the very words used in discussing what is at issue.

Judges who impose their own preferences, instead of following the law as it is written, have long been known as "judicial activists" while those who carry out the law, instead of rewriting it to suit themselves, have been said to be following the "original intent" of the law.

But now a massive effort to muddy the waters has been launched by those who want judges who will continue to impose the liberal agenda from the bench. Words like "activists" and "intent" are being twisted beyond recognition.

Senator Patrick Leahy has redefined "activist" judges to make the least activist Justices on the Supreme Court—Antonin Scalia and Clarence Thomas—suddenly activists by his new definition.

Senator Leahy has said: "The two most activist judges we have right now are Justice Thomas and Justice Scalia, who have struck down and thus written laws of their own in place of congressional laws more than anybody else on the current Supreme Court."

One of the major functions of the Supreme Court for more than two centuries has been to strike down acts of Congress, the President, or the lower courts when any of these exceed the authority granted to them by the

Constitution. Calling this "judicial activism" is playing games with words and befogging the real issues.

When Justices Scalia and Thomas enforce the limits set by the Constitution, that is not writing "their own new laws," no matter what Senator Leahy claims.

Those who are writing their own new laws are people like Justice John Paul Stevens, who arbitrarily expanded the Constitution's authorization of government taking of private property for "public use" to allow the taking of private property for a "public purpose"—which can be anything under the sun.

It is one thing to allow the government to take land needed to build a military base or a dam and something very different to allow the government to bulldoze people's homes to turn the land over to a private developer to build casinos or shopping malls.

Liberal law professors have joined in the redefining of words. One has given a numerical meaning to "judicial activism" by counting how many laws particular justices have declared unconstitutional. As Mark Twain said, there are three kinds of lies—lies, damned lies, and statistics.

Another law professor, Stanley Fish of Florida International University, likewise befogs the obvious with elegant nonsense.

Those who try to follow the "original intent" of the Constitution cannot do so, according to Professor Fish, because "the author's intent" cannot be discerned, "so the intention behind a text can always be challenged by someone else who marshals different evidence for an alternative intention."

Clever, but no cigar.

While the phrase "original intent" has been used as a loose label for the philosophy of judges who believe in sticking to the law as it is written, judges with this philosophy have been very explicit, for more than a century, that they did not—repeat, not—mean getting inside the heads of those who wrote the Constitution.

Justice Oliver Wendell Holmes said it in plain English, that interpreting what was meant by someone who wrote a law was not trying to "get into his mind" because the issue was "not what this man meant, but what those words would mean in the mouth of a normal speaker of English, using them in the circumstances in which they were used."

Such contemporary followers of Holmes as Judge Robert Bork have said the same thing in different words. More important, nobody ever voted on what was in the back of someone else's mind. They voted on the plain meaning of obvious words.

There is no confusion between the government's taking land for its own use and seizing land to turn it over to somebody else. The only confusion is the calculated confusion of the partisans of judicial activists.

Judges and Judgment

Many years ago, someone did a study of the IQs of municipal transit drivers and their accident rates. Those with below-average IQs had higher rates of accidents, as you might expect. What was unexpected was the discovery that drivers with IQs above a certain level also had higher rates of accidents.

Apparently driving a bus or trolley was not enough to keep the minds of very bright people occupied. So their minds wandered and they had more than their share of accidents as a result.

Something similar may have contributed to disasters in our legal system, especially in appellate courts, where the issue is not simply whether someone was innocent or guilty, or who caused what damage, but how all this fits into the framework of Constitutional law.

The Constitution of the United States is not some esoteric document, written to be understood only by people with high IQs and postgraduate education. It is written in rather plain language.

There is even a sort of instructors' guide on what the Constitution means in *The Federalist Papers*—a collection of popular 18th century essays by those who helped write the Constitution, explaining why they did what they did.

Despite all this, appellate court decisions interpreting Constitutional law today are often a huge maze of tangled reasoning, obscure concepts and complex confusion. The motto over the entrance to the Supreme Court of the

United States says, "Equal Justice Under Law" but sometimes you might wish that it said: "Brevity is the soul of wit."

It is not that the cases are so complicated in themselves but that high-IQ judges have turned simple realities into complex metaphysics. A few years ago, the Supreme Court voted 5 to 4 that carrying a gun near a school was not interstate commerce. To most people, the decision was obvious. So why 5 to 4?

You might think the decision should have been nine to nothing and it should not have taken more than one page to explain. Yet the good justices tied themselves into knots with lengthy explanations of their votes for and against.

The reason this decision was so complex and caused such consternation among some legal scholars was that previous generations of Supreme Court justices had turned the Constitution's simple concept of interstate commerce into a complicated rationalization of Congress' ever expanding exercises of power that it was never given when the Constitution was written.

Although the 10th Amendment says pretty plainly that the federal government can do only what it is specifically authorized to do, while the people can do whatever they are not specifically forbidden to do, this was not good enough for those who had visions of a more active government in Washington.

The terribly clever people who were put on the courts kept "interpreting" Congress' power to regulate interstate commerce so broadly that anything they wanted to regulate was called "interstate commerce." Thus the interstate commerce clause was used to virtually repeal the 10th Amendment.

Judges got so clever back in the 1940s that even a man who grew food for himself in his own backyard was said to be affecting interstate commerce—and was therefore subject to the power of Congress.

After generations of this kind of runaway "interpretation" of the Constitution, it was a shock to some legal scholars when the Supreme Court decided—5 to 4— that Congress could not pass a federal law forbidding people from carrying guns near local schools.

Most states had such laws anyway, and all states had the authority to pass such laws if they wanted to, so this decision did not leave school children unprotected. It just put a stop to one of the thousands of extensions of federal power beyond what the Constitution authorized.

These over-extensions of federal power were not due simply to the ideological biases of judges, though that was undoubtedly a big factor. It also grew out of judges with more brainpower than was necessary to deal with 90 percent of the cases that came before them. High IQs and low self-discipline led to more wrecks in the law, just as among municipal transit drivers.

Justice for Little Angelo

Little Angelo finally got justice, though he died too young to even know what justice meant. Angelo Marinda lived only eight months and it took more than twice that long to convict his father of his murder.

Tragically, the policies and the mindset among the authorities responsible for the well-being of children—the practices and notions that put this baby at risk—are still in place and more such tragedies are just waiting to happen. Little Angelo came to the authorities' attention only 12 days after he was born, when he turned up at a hospital with broken bones.

How would a baby less than two weeks old have broken bones? And what do you do about it?

Many of us would say that you get that baby away from whoever broke his bones and never let them near him again. But that is not what the "experts" say. Experts always have "solutions." How else are they going to be experts?

The fashionable solution is called "family reunification services." The severity of little Angelo's injuries would have made it legally possible to simply take him away and put him up for adoption by one of the many couples who are hoping to adopt a baby.

But no. Through the magic of "family reunification services" parents are supposed to be changed so that they will no longer be abusive.

A social worker told the court two years ago that the San Mateo County Children and Family Services Agency "will be recommending reunification services, as the parents are receptive to receiving services." The fact that little Angelo's sister had already had to be removed from that same home did not seem to dampen this optimism.

At the heart of all this is the pretense to knowledge that we simply do not have and may never have. There are all sorts of lofty phrases about teaching "parenting skills" or "anger management" or other pious hopes. And children's lives are being risked on such unsubstantiated notions.

Little Angelo himself apparently knew better. After months in a foster home, he was allowed back for a visit with his parents and "had a look of fear in his eyes" when he saw them.

But "expertise" brushes aside what non-experts believe— and little Angelo was not an expert, at least not in the eyes of the social workers who were in charge of his fate. The fact that he had returned from a previous visit with bruises did not make a dent on the experts.

Social workers thought it would be nice if little Angelo could have a two-day unsupervised visit with his parents at Christmas. It was a visit from which he would not return alive.

Now, more than 16 months after the baby's death, Angelo's father has been convicted of having literally shaken him to death.

Incidentally, there were experts who testified on the father's behalf at the trial, one of whom gave testimony that contradicted what he himself had written in a book. This expert had never seen little Angelo, dead or alive.

The time is long overdue for us to stop pretending to know things that nobody knows—not even people with impressive letters in front of their names or behind their names. Whether these experts are simply cynical guns for hire or really believe their own theories and rhetoric is beside the point. Unsubstantiated theories are no foundation for risking the lives of the helpless.

How anyone could break the bones of a newborn baby is something that people may speculate about. But to claim to know how to turn such parents into decent human beings is reckless. And to risk a baby's life on such speculation is criminal.

It is too bad that only one man will go to jail for this crime. There ought to be room in a cell somewhere for the social workers and their bosses who made this murder possible in the face of blatant evidence about the dangers that an infant could see, even if the responsible adults refused to see.

The pretense of knowledge allows judges, social workers, and others to "do something" by sending people to "training" in "parenting skills" and other psychobabble with no track record of success. And it allows children like little Angelo to be killed.

Property Rites

Two centuries ago, British Prime Minister William Pitt said that the poorest man in the country is so secure in his little cottage that the King of England and his men "dare not cross the threshold" without his permission. That is what property rights are all about—keeping the government off the backs of the people.

Beginning last September 19th, however, laws went into effect giving the British public the right to walk on certain privately owned land. These are large estates that critics on the left have called "private kingdoms," which are to be private no more.

Envy and resentment of the rich have always been potent political weapons for those seeking the expansion of government power.

Often the power first applied to the rich gradually comes down the income scale to apply to people who are far from rich, just as the income tax has done. But it may be a while before ordinary Britons find that their own little cottage gardens can be trampled on by strangers.

In Norway and Sweden, people are not only allowed to walk on other people's privately owned land but also to go riding and skiing there and to pick fruit. Europe has long been politically further to the left than the United States, so it provides a sneak preview of where our own liberals are headed.

In the more left-leaning parts of California, for example, public access to privately owned land is being pushed under a variety of labels. A builder in San Mateo, California, wanted to wall off a small development for the elderly, in the interest of security, but was told by the Planning Commission that he must allow "street presence" rather than block out the public, if he expects to get their approval to build.

Some private homeowners on the Monterey peninsula have discovered that they are not quite as private as they would like to be because local authorities there have created an easement which allows the public to have access to a road across their property.

Officials who violate homeowners' property rights may have some pretty words that are in vogue in their circles but they pay no price if strangers burglarize or vandalize homes to which they have been given free access, or even murder the homeowners.

Paying a price is what decision-making through a market is all about. But getting something for nothing is increasingly what politics is all about. Why anyone would expect better decisions to be made by third parties who pay no price for being wrong is one of the mysteries of our time.

All across this country, planning commissions, zoning boards, and environmental agencies take more and more decisions out of the hands of the people, who are told in increasing detail what they can and cannot do on their own property.

People who live where there are strong winds and tall trees with shallow roots on their property know that this a formula for falling trees to create costly damage or even death. But these homeowners have in some places found that they cannot cut down those trees because that would go against environmental fetishes.

Rivers and streams may need to be dredged, in order to

prevent flooding, but the danger of a flooded home or a drowned child is not a price that has to be paid by bureaucrats at an environmental agency that is preoccupied with keeping everything "natural."

The Constitution of the United States protected property rights for the same reason that it protected other rights—a fear, based on the history of the human race, that those with power would abuse it if you let them. But liberal judges have increasingly "interpreted" the Constitution's property rights out of existence when those rights have gotten in the way of government officials promoting liberal agendas.

Although much of this arbitrary power is wielded by unelected officials on zoning boards, planning commissions, and the like, the laws that create these boards and commissions are passed by elected officials whom we can vote out of office. But that requires that we stop letting ourselves be duped by pretty phrases like "open space" or "smart growth." There will never be a lack of pretty phrases, if that is all it takes to get us to give up our rights and submit to those who can feel fulfilled in their own lives only when they are controlling our lives.

Property Rites: Part II

When I was house-hunting, one of the things that struck me about the house that I eventually settled on was the fact that there were no curtains or shades on the bathroom window in the back. The reason was that there was no one living on the steep hillside in back, which was covered with trees.

Since I don't own that hillside, someday someone may decide to build houses there, which means that the bathroom would then require curtains or shades and our back porch would no longer be as private. Fortunately for me, local restrictive laws currently prevent houses from being built on that hillside.

Also fortunately for me, my continued criticisms of such laws in this column have not made a dent in the local authorities. But suppose that someday either the courts will strike down land use restrictions or local officials will respect property rights.

Maybe I will be long gone by then and the new owner of this house will be angry at the diminished privacy—and consequently the diminished value of the house, caused by the building of houses on the hillside. Would that anger be justified?

The fundamental question is: What did the homeowner buy? And would the change in laws deprive him of what he paid for? Since the house and the wooded hillside are separate properties, the homeowner never paid for a hillside wooded in perpetuity.

If whoever owns the hillside finds that his property is worth more with houses on it, what right does the adjacent homeowner have to deprive the other owner of the benefits of building on that hillside or selling it to a builder?

True, my house was worth more because of the privacy provided by the wooded hillside. But there was no guarantee that the hill would remain wooded forever. Whoever buys the house buys its current privacy and the chance—not a certainty—that the hill will remain wooded.

If a homeowner wanted a guarantee that the hill would remain as is, he could have bought the hill. That way he would be paying for what he wanted, rather than expecting the government to deprive someone else for his benefit.

Many restrictive land use laws in effect turn a chance that someone paid for into a guarantee that they did not pay for, such as a guarantee that a given community would retain its existing character.

Existing homeowners get huge windfall gains, in the form of rising appreciation of their homes, when laws prevent farmers from selling their land for the purpose of building houses. It's supply and demand.

Without laws restricting land use, supply and demand would make much farm land more valuable for building homes that people want, rather than creating agricultural surpluses that people don't want, but are forced to pay for as taxpayers under our agricultural subsidy laws.

The rationale is the "preservation" of agricultural land. But nothing is easier than to dream up a rationale to put a fig leaf on naked self-interest. Far from being in danger of losing our food supply, for more than half a century we have had chronic agricultural surpluses.

Another rationale for laws restricting land use is that "open space" is a good thing, that it prevents "overcrowding" for example. But preventing people from building homes in one place only makes the crowding greater in other places. This is just another fig leaf for the self-interest of those who want other people to be forced to live somewhere else.

Esthetics or other benefits of "open space," can be a good thing. But how good? When you have to buy up the land in competition with others who want to use it for their purposes, that is when you have to put your money where your mouth is.

When the power of government is used to take the land off the market, instead of buying it, then the Constitutional right of "equal protection of the laws" is denied to others.

None of this is rocket science. But it does require taking a moment to think. Unfortunately, our schools are increasingly turning out people who can only "feel" and who are therefore easy prey for those who know how to use rhetoric to manipulate emotions.

Property Rites: Part III

You may own your own home and expect to live there the rest of your life. But keep your bags packed, because the Supreme Court of the United States has decreed that local politicians can take your property away and turn it over to someone else, just by using the magic words "public purpose."

We're not talking about the government taking your home in order to build a reservoir or a highway for the benefit of the public. The Constitution always allowed the government to take private property for "public use," provided the property owner was paid "just compensation."

What the latest Supreme Court decision does with verbal sleight-of-hand is change the Constitution's requirement of "public use" to a more expansive power to confiscate private property for whatever is called "public purpose"—including turning that property over to some other private party.

In this case—*Kelo v. New London*—the private parties to whom the government would turn over confiscated properties include a hotel, restaurants, shops, and a pharmaceutical company.

These are not public uses, as the Constitution requires, but are said to serve "public purposes," as courts have expanded the concept beyond the language of the 5th Amendment—reflecting those "evolving" circumstances so dear to judges who rewrite the Constitution to suit their own tastes.

No sane person has ever denied that circumstances

change or that laws need to change to meet new circumstances. But that is wholly different from saying that judges are the ones to decide which laws need changing and in what way at what time.

What are legislatures for except to legislate? What is the separation of powers for except to keep legislative, executive, and judicial powers separate?

When the 5 to 4 Supreme Court majority "rejected any literal requirement that condemned property be put into use for the general public" because of the "evolving needs of society," it violated the Constitutional separation of powers on which the American system of government is based.

When the Supreme Court majority referred to its "deference to legislative judgments" about the taking of property, it was as disingenuous as it was inconsistent. If Constitutional rights of individuals are to be waved aside because of "deference" to another branch of government, then the citizens may as well not have Constitutional rights.

What are these rights supposed to protect the citizens from, if not the government?

This very Court showed no such deference to a state's law permitting the execution of murderers who were not yet 18. Such selective "deference" amounts to judicial policy-making rather than the carrying out of the law.

Surely the justices must know that politicians whose whole careers have been built on their ability to spin words can always come up with some words that will claim that there is what they can call a "public purpose" in what they are doing.

How many private homeowners can afford to litigate such claims all the way up and down the judicial food chain? Apartment dwellers who are thrown out on the street by the bulldozers are even less able to defend themselves with litigation.

The best that can be said for the Supreme Court majority's opinion is that it follows—and extends—certain judicial precedents. But, as Justice Clarence Thomas said in dissent, these "misguided lines of precedent" need to be reconsidered, so as to "return to the original meaning of the Public Use Clause" in the Constitution.

Justice Sandra Day O'Connor's dissent points out that the five Justices in the majority—Ginsburg, Breyer, Souter, Stevens, and Kennedy—"wash out any distinction between private and public use of property." As a result, she adds: "The specter of condemnation hangs over all property. Nothing is to prevent the State from replacing any Motel 6 with a Ritz-Carlton, any home with a shopping mall, or any farm with a factory."

In other words, politicians can replace your home with whatever they expect will pay more taxes than you do—and call their money grab a "public purpose."

Foreign Law Is Not Law

One of the ironies of our time is that economists have been discovering the importance of law, as such—as distinguished from the specific merits of particular laws— while judges seem increasingly to be losing sight of the rule of law.

"I can hardly imagine any laws so bad, to which I would not rather be subject than to the caprice of a man," John Stuart Mill said more than a century and a half ago.

Modern economists usually have in mind the economic advantages to a society of having a framework of known, enduring, and dependable rules—the rule of law—within which economic activities can be planned and long-term commitments and investments can be made. But Mill saw the benefits of living under known rules to extend far beyond economic benefits.

Mill spoke of the danger of having to lead "a life of anxiety lest by some of my acts I should unwittingly infringe against a will which had never been made known to me." Some of today's vague and ambiguous anti-trust, anti-discrimination, and environmental laws strike like lightning out of the blue to hit people who had no idea that they were doing something wrong.

The Constitution of the United States expressly forbad retroactive laws—"ex post facto" laws, it called them—but judicial decisions creating new rights, duties, and nuances out of thin air are for all practical purposes ex post facto law.

"Evolving standards" are also ex post facto law, for who can know in advance how someone else's standards are going to evolve, much less which evolving standards will get a majority of the votes in the Supreme Court?

The recent practice of using foreign laws as bases for judicial decisions about American laws likewise turns law into the caprices that John Stuart Mill feared more than he feared bad laws.

There is no such thing as generic foreign law. There are the specific laws of France and the very different specific laws of Saudi Arabia and of hundreds of other countries around the world. It is a matter of individual prejudice or caprice which of these laws any given judge chooses to cite.

Justice Anthony Kennedy, for example, referred to foreign laws as a reason for declaring an American state's law unconstitutional because it permitted the execution of murderers who were not yet 18 years old, which some foreign governments do not. In other words, laws enacted by the elected representatives of an American state can be wiped out if people in Spain or New Zealand think otherwise.

Not only does this prevent the millions of people who want to be law-abiding citizens from knowing which laws to abide by, it deprives American voters of the right of self-government through elected representatives that is at the heart of American society.

If our votes decide only which candidates get which offices, but not what laws and policies those elected representatives can enact for us to live under, our elections will become more and more like placebos, with the real power being exercised from the judicial bench by people we never voted for.

Liberal judicial activists have been citing laws from

countries more to the political left than the United States is, but there is no reason why other judges at other times could not cite very different laws to justify or rationalize decisions that could not be justified or rationalized on the basis of the Constitution of the United States that all judges have sworn to uphold.

In one of Justice Clarence Thomas' opinions, he noted in passing that the distinguished British 18th century legal scholar William Blackstone had said that people condemned to death should be executed within 48 hours. Surely this is not an idea that liberal judicial activists would want to import and Justice Thomas did not rely on it.

But there is no reason in principle why this or any other ideas from abroad should be any less eligible to be imported than the ideas from foreign countries which have been cherry-picked from an almost endless assortment of possibilities.

The question is not even whether particular foreign laws should become American law. It is not possible for them to become American law, in the sense of rules known in advance, unless they are openly enacted into law by elected officials, rather than imposed by judicial fiat after the fact.

Medical Lawsuits

When a friend told me recently that he was going to undergo a painful medical procedure to see if he has cancer, it reminded me of a time years ago when I faced a similar prospect. The testing procedure in my case would have been both painful and with some risk of infection.

Fortunately, it was a two-part procedure. The first part was uncomfortable but not painful or with any great risk of infection. After a young doctor had put me through that part, an older specialist took over and examined the results—and he decided not to proceed with the second part of the test.

When my wife asked me if that meant that I did not have cancer, my answer was, "No."

"What it means," I said, "was that the doctor weighed the alternatives and decided that, since the chance that I had cancer was sufficiently small, and the danger of infection from the test itself was sufficiently large, the best choice was not to go any further."

My wife seemed not completely put at ease by that, so I added: "Like anybody else, this doctor can be wrong. But, if it turns out that I do have cancer and die, I don't want anybody to sue that man. Nobody is infallible and no patient has a right to infallibility."

Since this was many years ago, apparently the doctor's choice was the right one. But how many doctors feel free to make such choices in today's legal climate, where frivolous lawsuits and junk science can lead to multimillion-dollar awards or settlements?

After so many megabucks awards grew out of claims that babies born with cerebral palsy could have been spared if only the doctor had delivered them by Caesarean section, C-section births rose sharply. But it did not reduce cerebral palsy.

While the C-section births may not protect babies from cerebral palsy, they protect doctors from being ruined financially by glib lawyers and gullible juries. Those lawyers who claim that their big-bucks awards don't add much to the cost of medical care are counting only the sums of money they collect.

But needless operations and needless tests are not free, either financially or otherwise.

Today, I cannot help wondering whether my friend is going to be put through a painful procedure for his sake or because the doctor dares not fail to do this test, for fear of a lawsuit somewhere down the road. This is one of the hidden costs of frivolous lawsuits and runaway damage awards, quite aside from the sums of money pocketed by lawyers.

When I was growing up, it would never have occurred to me that Dr. Chaney, our family physician, was doing anything other than giving it his best shot for the sake of our health.

It probably never occurred to Dr. Chaney that we might sue him. For one thing, he knew we didn't have enough money to hire a lawyer, so that was out of the question in the first place.

Trust between doctor and patient is not a small thing. Sometimes it can be the difference between life and death. Our laws recognize the enormous importance of that relationship by exempting doctors from having to testify to what a patient has told them, even if it is a murder case.

To go to these lengths to protect the doctor-patient relationship—and then blithely throw it away with easy access to frivolous lawsuits makes no sense. Neither does creating a massive medical bureaucracy to pay for treatments and medication, where that means that patients can go only to those doctors preselected for them by some insurance company or the government.

One of my favorite doctors retired early and spent some time explaining to me why he was doing so. The growing red tape was bad enough but the deterioration of the doctor-patient relationship soured him even more.

Earlier in his career, patients came to him because someone had recommended him and they came with a wholly different attitude from that of someone who had been assigned to him by an insurance company. He now found much more of a distrustful, if not adversarial, attitude that didn't do him any good or the patient any good.

That may be the biggest cost of our current bureaucratic and legal environment.

Fixing the Jury System

Now that the case against Tyco executives has ended in a mistrial, there is much outcry against the juror whose holdout will cause a $12 million trial to have to be done all over again from scratch. Whether that juror was principled or just pig-headed, this trial reveals something more fundamentally wrong with our jury system—and with the media.

It was not some trashy supermarket scandal sheet, but the *Wall Street Journal* and the *New York Post,* that published the juror's name. The Associated Press published her photograph. It was not this juror's holdout itself which ultimately led to a mistrial but a report of her receiving a phone call and a letter that were seen as putting pressure on her.

The jury was described as being minutes away from reaching a verdict when the judge called a mistrial. But the judge was right. There was no way of knowing whether the holdout juror was now agreeing with the other 11 because of an outside threat.

The media who are condemning this woman ought to be condemning themselves for their own irresponsibility, which is not only costing taxpayers millions of dollars but can corrupt the whole system of justice. The *New York Times* pioneered such irresponsibility years ago, when it published the name of the foreman of the jury that acquitted the policemen who beat Rodney King.

Newspapers have every right to complain about any jury

verdict they don't like. But that is wholly different from putting jurors in personal jeopardy when they don't vote the way the media wants them to vote. Do we want future jurors to decide cases on the basis of facts or on the basis of fear?

In the Diallo police shooting case four years ago, a witness whose testimony tended to support the defense was forced by the prosecutor to reveal in open court not only his name and address, but also the very apartment in which he and his family lived.

In an atmosphere where mobs were being whipped up outside the courthouse by demagogues, this was a shot across the bow of any other potential witness who might testify in ways that the prosecutor did not like.

Do you wonder why witnesses do not come forward? When they do come forward, are they supposed to testify to what they actually saw or to what they think will keep them out of trouble?

If we are serious about wanting justice in our courts, then we need to start getting serious about preventing witnesses and jurors from being intimidated. We might start by getting all cameras out of the courtroom.

There is no reason why the identity of the jurors has to be known by the media. The whole jury could be put behind one-way glass, so that they can see the proceedings but cannot be seen. It can be made a felony to publish their names.

The requirement for unanimous jury verdicts is long overdue for reconsideration. One pig-headed juror can cause not only a costly mistrial but also verdicts that do not reflect the seriousness of the crime.

People who commit murder should be convicted of murder, not manslaughter because one juror is too squeamish to risk the death penalty. There are too many people around who think they have "a right to my own opinion," as they put it, which translates as: "My mind is made up, so don't confuse me with the facts."

The time is also long overdue to reconsider the current practice of having jurors selected with vetoes by the lawyers in the case. When prospective jurors are given 30-page questionnaires made up by lawyers, asking intrusive questions about their personal lives and beliefs, the situation has gotten completely out of hand.

Courts do not exist for the sake of lawyers but for the sake of the public. Allowing lawyers to fish around in hopes of finding one mush head who can save their client makes no sense.

Anonymous jurors, selected by lottery, and not restricted to unanimous verdicts, should be good enough for anyone in an inherently imperfect world. In such a system, cranks and ideologues would not have nearly the leverage that they do now.

There could also be professional jurors, trained in the law, for cases involving complex legal issues. That would cost more—or rather, the cost would be visible in money, rather than hidden in the corruption of the legal system, the way it is now.

Half a Century after *Brown*

May 17, 1954 saw one of the most momentous decisions in the history of the Supreme Court of the United States. Some observers who were there said that one of the black-robed justices sat on the great bench with tears in his eyes.

The case was of course *Brown v. Board of Education*, and the decision declared that racially segregated schools were unconstitutional. In rapid succession, all kinds of other racial segregation, which were common across most of the South and even in some border states, were likewise declared unconstitutional.

This was a reversal of the old 1896 Supreme Court decision in *Plessy v. Ferguson* that racially "separate but equal" facilities were constitutional—and an end to the pretense that the segregated facilities for blacks were in fact equal.

As a young government clerk going to a black college at night—Howard University in Washington—I first heard of the decision when our professor entered the classroom in an obvious state of agitation and announced that something momentous had happened that day, and that we would discuss that, instead of the planned lesson.

As various people around the room expressed themselves, it was clear that we were all in favor of the decision. In fact, many of my classmates seemed to have the most Utopian expectations that this was going to lead to some magic solution to problems of race and poverty. When my turn came, I said:

"It's been more than fifty years since *Plessy v. Ferguson*—

and we still don't have 'separate but equal.' What makes you think this is going to go any faster?"

This discordant note was brushed aside in the general celebration. My classmates seemed to think that racial integration was going to do it all. They were not alone.

Looking back after half a century, what has *Brown v. Board of Education* accomplished and what has it failed to accomplish? What has it made worse?

After a very long struggle, the courts finally put an end to official racial segregation in states where it had been a barrier and a degradation to blacks. This included the District of Columbia, whose schools were racially segregated.

The anticipated economic benefits, however, lagged far behind. Blacks were already rising out of poverty at a rapid rate that was not accelerated by the civil rights laws and court decisions of the 1950s and 1960s, though of course the progress continued. Yet half a century of political spin has convinced much of the media and the public that black progress began with the civil rights revolution.

It did not. The first two decades after 1940 saw a more rapid rise of blacks out of poverty and into higher paying jobs than the decades following the Civil Rights Act of 1964 or the affirmative action policies that began in the 1970s. Check out the facts.

The key fallacy underlying the civil rights vision was that all black economic lags were due to racial discrimination. That assumption has survived to this day, in the courts, in the media, in academia, and above all in politics.

No amount of factual evidence can make a dent in that assumption. This means that a now largely futile crusade against discrimination distracts attention from the urgent need to upgrade educational standards and job skills among blacks.

Where has *Brown v. Board of Education* been positively harmful?

The flimsy and cavalier reasoning used by the Supreme Court, which based its decision on grounds that would hardly sustain a conviction for jay-walking, set a pattern of judicial activism that has put American law in disarray on all sorts of issues that extend far beyond racial cases. The pretense that the Court was interpreting the Constitution of the United States added insult to injury.

The Court got away with this, despite some calls for impeachment, because it was outlawing a set of racial practices that the country as a whole found abhorrent. If the justices took a few liberties with the law and the facts, who cared?

After half a century of unbridled judicial activism on many fronts, we now know that victims of frivolous lawsuits and violent crime cared, among others. And restoring law to our courts may take another 50 years—if it can be done at all.

Half a Century after *Brown*: Part II

The landmark case of *Brown v. Board of Education* was immediately about schools, even though it quickly became a precedent for outlawing racial segregation in other government-controlled institutions and programs.

What was the basis for that landmark decision and what have been the actual effects of *Brown v. Board of Education* on the education of black students?

The key sentence in the *Brown* decision was: "Separate educational facilities are inherently unequal." It was not just that the previous "separate but equal" doctrine was not being followed in practice. Rather, the Supreme Court argued that there was no way to make separate schools equal. All-black schools were inherently inferior.

It so happened that, within walking distance of the Supreme Court where this sweeping pronouncement was made, there was an all-black high school that had produced quality education for more than 80 years. Back in 1899 this school outscored two out of three white academic high schools in Washington on standardized tests.

Today, in the 21st century, it would be considered Utopian even to hope for such a result. Moreover, this was not an isolated fluke. This same school had an average IQ of 111 in 1939—fifteen years before the Supreme Court declared such things impossible.

Most schools for blacks were in fact inferior, mainly because most were in the South, where the educational standards for blacks and whites alike tended to be lower.

Racial discrimination, as distinguished from segregation alone, tended to make black schools the worst of all.

This was not due to their being all black, however. Back in the early 1940s, the black schools in Harlem had test scores very similar to those in white working class neighborhoods on New York's lower east side. Sometimes the Harlem schools' scores were a little higher than those of schools on the lower east side, and sometimes they were a little lower, but these scores were always comparable.

In short, it was not segregation, as such, that made schools inferior. If this seems like hair-splitting, consider the consequences of the Supreme Court's reasoning.

Once you say that racial separation makes the education itself inferior, you are launched on a course that leads straight to court-ordered busing of school children hither and yon to mix and match them racially, in hopes of educational improvement.

The polarization and bitterness of this crusade has lasted for decades—and has left black children still far behind educationally. Many are now much further below national norms than black students were in Harlem more than half a century ago.

Medical authorities have long recognized that a quack remedy that is harmless in itself can nevertheless be fatal in its effects, if it keeps sick people from getting the treatment that can cure them. Racial mixing and matching has been the great quack remedy for the educational lags of black school children that has substituted for higher standards and harder work.

Brown v. Board of Education did not prescribe compulsory busing for racial balance. But the logic of its argument led inexorably to that conclusion, whether that was the original intent or not.

More broadly, both the explicit language and the implicit assumptions of the Supreme Court in *Brown* depicted the answer to problems of blacks in general as being essentially the changing of white people. This was yet another line of reasoning that led straight into a blind alley.

Today, there are all-black schools that succeed, all-black schools that fail, and racially mixed schools that do either. Neither race nor racial segregation can explain such things. But both can serve as distractions from the task of creating higher standards and harder work.

The judicial mythology of racial mixing has led to an absurd situation where a white student can get into a selective public high school in San Francisco with lower qualifications than a Chinese American student. This farcical consequence of judicial mythology about a need for racial mixing does nothing to improve education for blacks or anyone else.

Half a Century after *Brown*: Part III

Although *Brown v. Board of Education* dealt with race and with schools, its judicial philosophy spread rapidly to issues having nothing to do with race or schools. In the half century since *Brown*, judges at all levels have become unelected legislators imposing the vision of the political left across a wide spectrum.

For example, the anti-business vision of the left was apparent in another Supreme Court case with *Brown* in its title—*Brown Shoe Co. v. United States*. In this 1962 case, the same Chief Justice Earl Warren who delivered the landmark racial decision now ruled that a merger between the Brown Shoe Company and the Kinney retail shoe store chain had to be broken up.

Why? Because the Kinney chain, which sold about one percent of the shoes in the United States, could be "foreclosed" to other shoe manufacturers if it merged with Brown Shoe. According to Chief Justice Warren, such mergers, "if left unchecked, will be likely 'substantially to lessen competition.'"

If ever there was a runaway extrapolation, this was it. If Brown and Kinney had been allowed to remain merged, together they would still have sold less than 6 percent of the shoes in the United States. But the Warren Court wanted to nip monopoly in the bud.

The same anti-business bias has over the years allowed frivolous lawsuits, based on junk science, to ruin or destroy companies and whole industries, costing vast numbers of workers their jobs. All of this happened, not because the written laws compelled it, but because activist judges stretched and twisted the laws to fit their own biases and preconceptions.

Nowhere did this free-wheeling judicial activism do more damage to more people than in the Warren Court's remaking of the criminal law.

Under the much disdained "traditional" approach of criminal law, murders had been declining dramatically over the years. The murder rate in 1960 was just under half of what it had been in 1934.

All of that changed quickly and dramatically for the worse after the Warren Court began imposing its own notions about crime in the 1960s. The most famous of these changes was the "Miranda warning" that police have to give suspects, stating that they have a right to remain silent and to have an attorney supplied free.

For more than a century and a half, not one of the great Supreme Court Justices—not Holmes, not Brandeis, nor anybody else—had ever discovered any such requirement in the Constitution of the United States. Nor had Congress passed any law requiring any such thing.

It was just another part of the liberal vision imposed from the bench by an unelected judiciary. Moreover, *Miranda* was just one in a string of Supreme Court decisions that made it easier for criminals to escape punishment.

The theory was that a more "enlightened" understanding of crime would reduce the crime rate. Whatever the plausibility of this belief, the facts to the contrary were devastating.

The murder rate, which had been going down for decades, suddenly shot up. By 1974, the murder rate was twice as high as in 1961. The average person's chances of becoming a victim of a violent crime tripled between 1960 and 1976.

Anyone can make a mistake but judicial mistakes are set in concrete. Moreover, the very possibility that they might be mistaken never seemed to occur to headstrong justices.

When a former police commissioner addressed a gathering of judges in 1965, warning of the consequences to expect from their rulings in criminal cases, Justices Warren and Brennan "roared with laughter," according to the *New York Times*, when a law professor poured scorn and derision on the commissioner's statements.

How many crime victims or their widows or orphans would have laughed is another question.

Brown v. Board of Education was not just about race or schools but was about a whole judicial mindset with ramifications across a whole spectrum of issues—and reverberations that are still with us in the 21st century. Its pluses and minuses have to be added up with that in mind.

Umpires, Judges, and Others

Major league umpires are complaining about an electronic device that is being used to check how accurately they are calling balls and strikes. They say that the device itself is too variable to be relied on.

Whatever the merits of each side in this issue, it all sounds much like judges complaining about restrictive sentencing guidelines and the "three strikes and you are out" laws which lock up repeat felons for life. From neither the umpires nor the judges is there the slightest acknowledgement that their own willful and arbitrary behavior is what brought on this reaction.

For years now, there have been complaints that every umpire seems to have his own personal strike zone, despite the rules of baseball which specify what is a strike and what is a ball. Some umpires have even complained when television cameras took overhead pictures showing that some pitches that were called strikes had in fact never passed over any part of the plate.

Some umpires called "high strikes," some called "low strikes" and some were said to retaliate against pitchers or batters who complain by adjusting the size of the strike zone to their disadvantage.

All of history says that arbitrary power goes to people's heads, whether they are umpires, judges, or Howell Raines of the *New York Times*. When judges get headstrong and disregard the rules, the consequences can be far more disastrous than they are in a baseball game or a newspaper.

Only after years—indeed, decades—of judges bending over backwards to let criminals off the hook have legislators begun passing laws to keep felons behind bars where they belong, instead of out on the street victimizing more people. These laws are not perfect, but those who whine about their imperfections pass over in utter silence the reckless judicial behavior that made such laws necessary.

It is much the same story in our public schools. Teachers' unions complain bitterly about outside testing of students, claiming that the tests are flawed, that "teaching to the test" distorts education and miscellaneous other whines and smoke screens.

The cold fact is that these tests came about only after decades of dumbing down of academic standards—which the education establishment ignored, denied or blamed on every conceivable thing other than themselves. Anything wrong with parents, students or society was taken as proof that there was nothing wrong with the schools.

All the complaints about the imperfections of the tests fail to acknowledge the irresponsible self-indulgences— including iron-clad tenure for incompetent teachers—that made tests necessary.

I don't know whether the new electronic camera for calling balls and strikes is better or worse than the umpires, or how much it will improve over time. But I do know that it was not just a bolt from the blue.

Neither were the restrictions put on judges who seemed hell-bent to let murderers roam the streets again. Nor were tests for schools where students are treated as a captive audience to be propagandized with political correctness or as guinea pigs to be experimented with to try out the latest fads.

We the public have been far too trusting and gullible

when it comes to putting arbitrary powers in the hands of people who are not accountable to anyone.

One group that has not yet been reined in are social workers, who have wreaked havoc in the lives of children, whether by ripping them out of their homes because of unsubstantiated accusations by anonymous informants or by putting them back into homes where they have already been abused—and where some have subsequently been killed.

Like teachers, social workers indulge themselves in all sorts of unsubstantiated notions which turn into dogmas when their establishment refuses to test those notions against evidence. Dogmas about teaching "parenting skills" or "anger management" can cost children their lives.

Accountability may be old-fashioned but it is still not obsolete. It is our only hope when there are headstrong people with power.

Big Business and Quotas

Anyone who thinks that business is gung ho for the free market has just not been paying attention to business. Adam Smith knew better, back in the 18th century.

Although he was the patron saint of capitalism, Smith was no fan of capitalists. Any policy advocated by businessmen, he said, "ought never to be adopted till after having been long and carefully examined, not only with the most scrupulous, but with the most suspicious attention."

In our own time, as in Adam Smith's time, businesses have not hesitated to advocate government interference with free markets. Tariffs on steel and other import restrictions are obvious examples. Many, if not most, anti-trust cases begin with some business complaining because a competitor is gaining market share by charging lower prices or offering an improved product.

While businesses will use the rhetoric of the free market when it suits their purpose, they will dump it in a minute when it does not. Against this background, it is not surprising that big business is filing briefs in favor of affirmative action in the University of Michigan case before the Supreme Court.

Big business has long been in favor of racial quotas. When an effort was begun back in the 1980s, within the Reagan administration, to get rid of affirmative action, the influence of corporate America helped squelch this effort.

Why does big business want racial quotas? Because it is in their own self-interest.

If a corporation does not have enough minority employees to satisfy government agencies, that can lead to racial discrimination lawsuits. But if they hire by quotas and quotas are outlawed, they can be sued by whites for reverse discrimination. Keeping affirmative action legal solves their problem.

But that is not how it was presented in the January 27, 2003 issue of *BusinessWeek*, where columnist Roger O. Crockett portrayed corporations as courageously "sticking out their necks" for the sake of that mystic thing called "diversity."

Sticking their necks out? Just who is going to do what to them for supporting quotas? It is safer than playing checkers with your maiden aunt.

If there is anything more ridiculous than endlessly repeating the magic word "diversity," it is trying to come up with plausible arguments in favor of the racial quotas that this euphemism really means.

According to *BusinessWeek*, corporate CEOs "believe that as minorities' share of the U.S. population has mounted, diversity has become a critical workforce requirement." They get this diversity by hiring graduates of "a campus where diversity thrives" because that is where "students develop an understanding of different cultures." And that, in turn means that these graduates know how to "appeal to a variety of consumers" as well as how to get along with "colleagues and clientele from many ethnic backgrounds."

How do companies in Japan manage to sell everything from cars to cameras, in countries around the world, without having that mystic "diversity"? How does a country with such a racially homogeneous population even manage to educate its young people if "diversity" is such an essential factor in education?

Yet big business CEOs "rightly worry," according to *BusinessWeek*, that without racial quotas the result would be "a smaller supply of minority college grads, which would damage the economy and the society alike."

Actually, the result of getting rid of racial quotas in college admissions is likely to be a *larger* supply of minority college graduates, because minority students will be attending colleges where they meet the same standards as others and are more likely to be able to do the work and graduate, instead of punching out as often as they do when they are admitted under lower standards.

The end of affirmative action in state colleges and universities in California and Texas has not led to declining enrollments of minorities, but to their redistribution among academic institutions. But facts carry no such weight as the "diversity" mantra.

The Grand Fraud

No issue has been more saturated with dishonesty than the issue of racial quotas and preferences. Many defenders of affirmative action are not even honest enough to admit that they are talking about quotas and preferences, even though everyone knows that that is what affirmative action amounts to in practice.

Despite all the gushing about the mystical benefits of "diversity" in higher education, a recent study by respected academic scholars found that "college diversity programs fail to raise standards" and that "a majority of faculty members and administrators recognize this when speaking anonymously."

This study by Stanley Rothman, Seymour Martin Lipset, and Neil Nevitte found that "of those who think that preferences have some impact on academic standards those believing it negative exceed those believing it positive by 15 to 1."

Poll after poll over the years has shown that most faculty members and most students are opposed to double standards in college admissions. Yet professors who will come out publicly and say what they say privately in these polls are as rare as hen's teeth.

Such two-faced talk is pervasive in academia and elsewhere. A few years ago, in Berkeley, there was a big fight over whether a faculty vote on affirmative action would be by secret ballot or open vote. Both sides knew that the result of a secret ballot would be the direct opposite of the result in a public vote at a faculty meeting.

When any policy can only be defended by lies and duplicity, there is something fundamentally wrong with that policy. Virtually every argument in favor of affirmative action is demonstrably false. It is the grand fraud of our time.

The need for "role models" of the same race or sex is a key dogma behind affirmative action in hiring black or female professors. But a recent study titled *Increasing Faculty Diversity* found "no empirical evidence to support the belief that same-sex, same-ethnicity role models are any more effective than white male role models."

The related notion that a certain "critical mass" of black students is needed on a given campus, in order that these students can feel comfortable enough to do their best, has become dogma without a speck of evidence being offered or asked for. Such evidence as there is points in the opposite direction.

Without affirmative action, its advocates claim, few black students would be able to get into college. In reality, there are today more black students in the University of California system and in the University of Texas system than there were before these systems ended affirmative action.

These black students are simply distributed differently within both systems—no longer being mismatched with institutions whose standards they don't meet. They now have a better chance of graduating.

What of the idea that affirmative action has helped blacks rise out of poverty and is needed to continue that rise? A far higher proportion of blacks in poverty rose out of poverty in the twenty years between 1940 and 1960—that is, before any major federal civil rights legislation—than in the more than 40 years since then. This trend continued in the 1960s, at a slower pace. The decade of the 1970s—the first affirmative action decade—saw virtually no change in the poverty rate among blacks.

In other words, most blacks lifted themselves out of poverty but liberal politicians and black "leaders" have claimed credit. One side effect is that many whites wonder why blacks cannot lift themselves out of poverty like other groups, when that is in fact what most blacks have done.

Affirmative action is great for black millionaires but it has done little or nothing for most people in the ghetto. Most minority business owners who get preferences in government contracts have net worths of more than one million dollars.

One of the big barriers to any rational discussion of affirmative action is that many of those who are for or against it are for or against the theory or the rationales behind group preferences and quotas. As for facts, the defenders simply lie.

The Grand Fraud: Part II

Fraud is as pervasive in arguments for affirmative action for women as in arguments for affirmative action for blacks. In fact, a whole fraudulent history has been concocted to explain the changing economic position of women over the years.

In the feminist movement's version of history, women's changing economic position is explained by women's being repressed by men until they began to be rescued in the 1960s by the women's movement, anti-discrimination policies, and affirmative action.

Hard facts tell a very different story. Women had achieved a higher representation in higher education and in many professions in earlier decades of the twentieth century than they had when the feminist movement became prominent in the 1960s.

This earlier success can hardly be attributed to Gloria Steinem, Betty Friedan and the like. Nor should they be allowed to claim credit for the later resumption of that earlier trend, which had more to do with demographics than politics.

The percentage of master's degrees and doctoral degrees that went to women was never as great during any year of the 1950s or 1960s as that percentage was back in 1930. The percentage of women who were listed in "Who's Who in America" was twice as high in 1902 as in 1958.

Women were also better represented in higher education and in a number of professions in the 1920s or

1930s than they were in the 1950s or 1960s, though none of this fits the fashionable fairy tales of the feminists.

Women received 34 percent of the bachelor's degrees in 1920 but only 24 percent in 1950. In mathematics, women's share of doctorates declined from 15 percent to 5 percent over a span of decades, and in economics from 10 percent to 2 percent.

What was going on? After all, there was no feminist movement and no affirmative action in those earlier years when women were doing better.

What really happened was that, as the birth rate fell from the late nineteenth century into the 1930s, women rose in the professions and in the postgraduate education necessary for these professions. Then, as women began marrying younger and having more children during the years of the baby boom, their representation in both the professions and in the education that led to those professions fell.

There is nothing mysterious about the fact that motherhood is a time-consuming activity, leaving less time to pursue professional careers. It is just plain common sense— which is to say, it does not provide the moral melodrama needed by movements such as radical feminism.

In later years, as women again began to have fewer children, they rose again in higher education and in the professions, though it was often some years before they regained the position they had achieved decades earlier. But now their rise was accompanied by a drumbeat of feminist propaganda, loudly claiming credit.

Yet the role of motherhood in explaining male-female differences is far more readily demonstrated. Data from more than 30 years ago show that women who remained unmarried and worked continuously from high school into their thirties earned higher incomes than men of the same description.

What about the rise of women's income relative to that of men after the 1960s? Surely that must have been due to the feminist movement or to affirmative action, no? No!

What the hard data show is that more women began working full time, both absolutely and relative to men. Obviously, full-time workers get paid more than part-time workers.

Among those women who worked full-time and year around, their income as a percentage of the income of men of the same description showed no real trend throughout the 1960s and 1970s, despite all the hoopla about the feminist movement and affirmative action.

The income of women who worked full-time and year around began an upward trend relative to the income of men in the 1980s—during the Reagan administration, which is not when most feminists would claim to have had their biggest impact.

How do the feminists explain away all this earlier history of women's progress? They don't. They ignore it. By the simple expedient of tracing women's progress only since the 1960s, the fraud is protected from contact with inconvenient facts.

The Grand Fraud: Part III

If you would like to be taller than you are, do you think that joining a basketball team would help? After all, statistics prove that members of basketball teams are taller than other people.

If this seems like a strange way to reason, it is the same kind of reasoning used by those who argue that minority students need affirmative action to get into top-rated colleges and universities, because graduates of those institutions have more upscale careers.

I am sure that my graduating class at Harvard has had a high income. After all, it contained a Rockefeller and the Aga Khan, so even if the rest of us became unemployed bums, the class would still have a high average income. Of course, that wouldn't do the rest of us any good.

As hand-wringing begins in many quarters over the prospect that affirmative action might end, and fewer black students get admitted to Ivy League schools and flagship state universities, it is well to keep in mind that statistics about how well the graduates of such institutions do in later life may have little or no relevance to those black students who are admitted under lower standards.

Most black students who enter college do not graduate—and that is especially so for those admitted with qualifications well below those of the other students at the same institution. So how well the graduates of this or that college or university do in later life has no relevance to those who do not survive to make it up to the graduation platform.

These casualties of the double-standards admissions process do not even get the dignity of being recognized as the "collateral damage" of affirmative action. They would have been far better off succeeding on some campus where the admissions standards matched their academic background and capabilities.

For example, a study some years ago showed that the average black student at MIT scored in the top 10 percent in mathematics among students nationwide—but in the bottom 10 percent at MIT. One-fourth of those black students failed to graduate.

There is neither glory nor money to be had from flunking out of MIT. But you can have a fulfilling professional career after graduating from Texas Tech or Cal State Pomona.

The end of affirmative action in the state-supported universities of California and Texas was decried and denounced by those who said that it would mean the end of black students' "access" to college, the "resegregation of higher education" and other irresponsible rhetorical flourishes.

In reality, the end of affirmative action in California and Texas state institutions meant that fewer black students would go to Berkeley or Austin, and more would go to other state colleges and universities in the same systems. There are now more black students in these systems than there were under affirmative action.

A liberal think tank in New York has joined the hand-wringing over the current University of Michigan affirmative action case, currently under consideration by the U. S. Supreme Court, by publishing statistics supposedly showing how the percentage of minority students will decline in selective colleges. But being admitted to a selective college does not make anyone become a better student, any more than joining a basketball team makes anyone taller.

In reality, affirmative action increases the chance that a minority student will fail where the standards are higher, instead of succeeding where the standards are at a level that matches the student's academic capabilities.

Incidentally, when a minority student is admitted to a highly-rated college without meeting the standards, do you think that the white student who is displaced to make room is likely to be a Rockefeller or the Aga Khan? Or is the white student who is turned down more likely to be the son or daughter of some working-class family who is kept out so that the son or daughter of a black doctor can get in and make the statistics look good?

Both those who are kept out, despite meeting the qualifications standards, and those who are let in without meeting those standards, are likely to lose from affirmative action.

The Grand Fraud: Part IV

Someone once said of Lillian Hellman that every word she uttered was a lie, including "and" and "the." Many defenders of affirmative action deserve a Lillian Hellman award.

Not only is much of what they say contradicted by readily available facts, much of what they say publicly contradicts what they themselves say privately. Often their very reasons for favoring affirmative action are false.

Supposedly, affirmative action in college admissions is to help black students. But why are so many big businesses filing briefs with the Supreme Court in support of affirmative action in academia? Is it because they are so gung ho for black students? Or does this have something to do with their own bottom line?

Big business has a lot to lose if the courts stop buying the "diversity" mantra that has now become the stock defense of group preferences and quotas. Take away the legal protection of affirmative action and businesses can be sued by blacks if they are "under-represented" and by whites if blacks get hired with lower qualifications to make the numbers look good.

It would be a lawyer's heaven and a corporate CEO's hell. Money that might otherwise go to the stockholders or into reinvestment in the business would instead end up in the pockets of trial lawyers. Trying to steer a course between statistical "under-representation" and "reverse discrimination" would be a task that would be as interminable as it is impossible.

At the heart of the problem is that the courts have allowed both private plaintiffs and government agencies to equate statistical disparity with discrimination. At the very least, the burden of proof shifts to the employer—and usually nobody can prove anything, so the employer loses.

Since it is virtually impossible to find two groups with the same qualifications in any industry or in any country, applying the same standards to all applicants for employment or promotion virtually guarantees a "disparate impact" on different groups—which in turn virtually guarantees charges of discrimination.

Even when the same employer hires people for different jobs—say, third basemen and centerfielders—there can be very different racial representation in those two jobs. Check out the races of third basemen and centerfielders in the major leagues. Is the employer a racist when he hires third basemen but not a racist when he hires centerfielders?

You may have seen hundreds of black football players score touchdowns but when did you last see a black player kick the point after? Do you believe that white clubowners are willing to hire black running backs and wide receivers, and to pay them millions of dollars each, but that those very same clubowners cannot abide the thought of a black man kicking a football through the uprights?

These are just some of the absurd conclusions you would have to reach if you took "disparate impact" statistics seriously. But disparate impact theory is like the emperor who has no clothes. Everybody knows he has no clothes. But they have to pretend that he does. Otherwise, the whole system is in jeopardy.

Take away disparate impact theory and you would have widespread unemployment in government agencies that enforce anti-discrimination laws. Trial lawyers might have so much time on their hands that they would have to sue more doctors, in order to make ends meet.

Back during the Reagan administration, when there was some talk about a new presidential executive order, rescinding the executive orders of Presidents Lyndon Johnson and Richard Nixon, on which affirmative action is based, big business made their opposition known and the idea was quietly dropped.

This was not the Reagan administration's finest hour. Nor was it the Supreme Court's finest hour when the justices made their first big ruling on affirmative action, 25 years ago, and ended up with a cacophony of opinions, as they tried to square the circle and split the baby, so that quotas could continue—provided that you didn't call them quotas.

There has been a quarter of a century of national discord based on their indecision.

Saving Quotas

There was some talk recently about upcoming vacancies on the Supreme Court because some retirements were expected. However, the High Court's decision on affirmative action suggests that there are already vacancies, even though no one has resigned. We can only hope that, when President Bush gets a chance to nominate replacements, he does not fill an existing vacancy with another vacancy.

Justice Sandra Day O'Connor's majority decision upholding affirmative action in admissions to the University of Michigan Law School was her classic split-the-baby formula, washed down with rambling rhetoric, and making a mockery of the law. This decision provoked not only dissent from four other justices, but sarcasm and disgust—as it should have.

Justice O'Connor's argument is hard to summarize because it consists largely of repeating unsubstantiated claims about the "educational benefits that flow from a diverse student body" and the need for a "critical mass" of minority students for their own educational needs and those of other students. She uses the phrase "compelling interest" to get around the 14th Amendment's requirement of equal treatment, much as earlier generations of justices used the phrase "interstate commerce" to evade Constitutional limits on the powers of Congress.

This exercise in verbal dexterity included the pronouncement that "race-conscious admissions policies must be limited in time," that "all government use of race must have a logical end point." But, having uttered these pieties, Justice O'Connor imposed no time limit nor defined any criterion for an end point. In other words, she talked the talk but she didn't walk the walk.

Justice Antonin Scalia's response was that the "mystical 'critical mass' justification" for racial preferences "challenges even the most gullible mind." He pointed out how academics who talk about multiculturalism and diversity in the courts have "tribalism and racial segregation" on their own campuses, including "minority-only student organizations, separate minority housing opportunities, separate minority student centers, even separate minority-only graduation ceremonies."

Verbal pieties and cynical realities have thoroughly corrupted affirmative action from the beginning. A quarter of a century ago, the Bakke case brought a great outpouring of noble rhetoric from the Supreme Court but the bottom line was that you could continue to have racial quotas, so long as you didn't call them racial quotas.

Today's Supreme Court has not only reaffirmed that principle—or lack of principle—but also, by striking down a companion case involving undergraduate admissions, added that you can't blatantly award points for race. That would be giving the game away so obviously that even the great unwashed masses would see what you are doing.

Racial preferences and quotas are favored by what Justice Clarence Thomas' dissent called "the know-it-all elites." It has become a badge of their identity and what its actual consequences are for others in the real world is of no real interest to them. Justice Thomas is unimpressed by the endlessly repeated mantra of "diversity," which to him is just "a fashionable catch-phrase."

Far from buying Justice O'Connor's many reiterations of

claims for its educational benefits, Justice Thomas cited empirical studies indicating that the much vaunted diversity "actually impairs learning among black students."

No one epitomizes the know-it-all elites more than the *New York Times*, whose front-page story by Linda Greenhouse refers to "the broad societal consensus in favor of affirmative action in higher education," despite polls which have repeatedly shown the public's grave misgivings about racial quotas and preferences.

Justice Thomas' devastating dissent is deftly evaded by Ms. Greenhouse, who says that he "took as his text not the briefs but his own life story."

If you want to find out whether you can rely on what the *New York Times* says, now that Jayson Blair is gone, read Justice Thomas' dissent for yourself and see if you can find anything there that would lead you to believe that it was about his own life story.

The High Cost of Nuances

The Supreme Court's recent decision saying that the federal government can prosecute those using marijuana for medical purposes, even when state laws permit such use, has been seen by many as an issue of being for or against marijuana. But the real significance of this decision has little to do with marijuana and everything to do with the kind of government that we, our children, and our children's children are going to live under.

The 10th Amendment to the Constitution says that all powers not granted to the federal government belong to the states or to the people.

Those who wrote the Constitution clearly understood that power is dangerous and needs to be limited by being separated—separated not only into the three branches of the national government but also separated as between the whole national government, on the one hand, and the states and the people on the other.

Too many people today judge court decisions by whether the court is "for" or "against" this or that policy. It is not the court's job to be for or against any policy but to apply the law.

The question before the Supreme Court was not whether allowing the medicinal use of marijuana was a good policy or a bad policy. The legal question was whether Congress had the authority under the Constitution to regulate something that happened entirely within the boundaries of a given state.

For decades, judges have allowed the federal government to expand its powers by saying that it was authorized by the Constitution to regulate "interstate commerce." But how can something that happens entirely within the borders of one state be called "interstate commerce"?

Back in 1942, the Supreme Court authorized the vastly expanded powers of the federal government under Franklin D. Roosevelt's administration by declaring that a man who grew food for himself on his own land was somehow "affecting" prices of goods in interstate commerce and so the federal government had a right to regulate him.

Stretching and straining the law this way means that anything the federal government wants to do can be given the magic label "interstate commerce"—and the limits on federal power under the 10th Amendment vanish into thin air.

Judicial activists love to believe that they can apply the law in a "nuanced" way, allowing the federal government to regulate some activities that do not cross state lines but not others. The problem is that Justice Sandra Day O'Connor's nuances are different from Justice Antonin Scalia's nuances—not only in the medical marijuana case but in numerous other cases.

Courts that go in for nuanced applications of the law can produce a lot of 5 to 4 decisions, with different coalitions of justices voting for and against different parts of the same decision.

A much bigger and more fundamental problem is that millions of ordinary citizens, without legal training, have a hard time figuring out when they are or are not breaking the law. Nuanced courts, instead of drawing a line in the sand, spread a lot of fog across the landscape.

Justice Clarence Thomas cut through that fog in his

dissent when he said that the people involved in this case "use marijuana that has never been bought or sold, that has never crossed state lines, and that has had no demonstrable effect on the national market for marijuana."

Instead of going in for fashionable "nuance" talk, Justice Thomas drew a line in the sand: "If Congress can regulate this under the Commerce Clause, then it can regulate virtually anything—and the Federal Government is no longer one of limited and enumerated powers."

In short, the kinds of limitations on the power of the national government created by the Constitution are being nuanced out of existence by the courts.

Ironically, this decision was announced during the same week when Janice Rogers Brown was confirmed to the Circuit Court of Appeals. One of the complaints against her was that she had criticized the 1942 decision expanding the meaning of "interstate commerce." In other words, her position on this was the same as that of Clarence Thomas—and both are anathema to liberals.

The Polio Fallacy

The disappearance of an American teenager in Aruba has been more than a tragedy for her and for her family. It is the latest of many tragedies to strike trusting people who have long been sheltered from dangers and who have acted as if there were no dangers.

Not only individuals but whole nations have lost their sense of danger after having been protected from those dangers.

After the devastating disease of polio was finally conquered by vaccines, back in the 1960s, the number of people afflicted declined almost to the vanishing point. Some people then began to see no need to take the vaccine, since apparently no one was getting polio any more, so who was there to catch it from?

The result was a needless resurgence of crippling and death from this terrible disease.

The kind of thinking involved in the polio fallacy has appeared in many other contexts. When some public disorder gets underway and a massive arrival of police on the scene brings everything under control immediately, many in the media and in politics deplore such "over-reaction" on the part of the police to a minor disturbance.

It never occurs to such people that it was precisely the arrival of huge numbers of cops on the scene that brought the disturbance to a screeching halt without having to use force.

During the Cold War, Communist expansionism around

the world somehow never struck Western Europe, which was protected by the American nuclear umbrella. Western Europeans often accused the United States of unnecessary militarism. American military power was like the polio vaccine that was considered unnecessary.

The latest version of the polio fallacy is the demonizing of the Patriot Act. Some people are yelling louder than ever that they have been silenced, that we have had our freedom destroyed, all as a result of the Patriot Act.

Let us go back to square one, to the terrorist attacks of 9/11, which were the reason for passage of the Patriot Act.

Do you remember how long every major public event— the World Series, Christmas celebrations, the Super Bowl— was a time of fear of a new terrorist attack? Do you remember all the advice to stock up on medicines or food, so that we could ride out any new terrorist onslaught?

Do you remember all the places that terrorists were expected to strike? The different colors of national alerts being announced regularly?

Now, after years have passed without any of these feared disasters actually happening, the eroding of a sense of danger has led many to repeat the polio fallacy and act as if the dangers from which we have been protected did not exist—and that the enhanced protection is therefore unnecessary.

The many crackdowns on domestic terrorists under the Patriot Act, as well as the ability to intercept and disrupt their communications under the powers of that Act, receive little or no credit for the fact that there has been no repetition of anything like 9/11.

The man principally responsible for law enforcement crackdowns on terrorists in the United States during this dangerous period—Attorney General John Ashcroft—not only received no gratitude for our safety, the complacency to which that safety led allowed many to indulge themselves in the luxury of vilifying Ashcroft at every turn.

Like the police who arrive in large numbers to quell disturbances and are then accused of "over-reacting," the Patriot Act has been depicted as an over-reaction to terrorist activity. Indeed, the very word "terrorist" has been banned in much of the politically correct media.

The Patriot Act is no closer to perfection than anything else human. It has costs, as every benefit has had costs, hard as it is for many among the intelligentsia to accept anything less than "win-win" situations.

"I have a real problem with fascism," as one lady in a trendy California bookstore said fiercely, when discussing the Patriot Act.

She was aghast when I replied, "I hadn't noticed any fascism."

Have you?

PART IV

POLITICAL ISSUES

Spoiled Brat Politics

An editorial in a recent issue of the *National Geographic*'s *Traveler* magazine complained that kayakers in Maine found "residential development" near national parks and urged its readers to use their "influence" to prevent such things.

"You are the stakeholders in our national parks," it said.

Really? What stake do kayakers and others of like mind have that is not also a stake held by people who build the vacation homes whose presence offends the kayak set? Homeowners are just as much citizens and taxpayers as kayakers are, and they are even entitled to equal treatment under the 14th Amendment.

The essence of bigotry is denying others the same rights you claim for yourself. Green bigots are a classic example.

The idea that government is supposed to make your desires override the desires of other citizens has spread from the green bigots to other groups who claim privileges in the name of rights.

In California, a group of golfers in wheelchairs are suing a hotel chain for not providing them with special carts that will enable them to navigate the local hotel's golf course more comfortably and play the game better.

According to a newspaper account, the kinds of carts the golfers in wheelchairs want "have rotating seats so a golfer can swing and strike a ball from the tee, the fairway and on the green without getting out of the vehicle." If golfers want this kind of cart, there is nothing to stop them from buying one—except that they would rather have other people be forced to pay for it.

One of the golfers in this lawsuit has been confined to a wheelchair as a result of a diving accident and another as a result of a gunshot wound. Apparently the hotel had nothing to do with either event.

There was a time when people would have said that the hotel is not responsible for these golfers being in wheelchairs and therefore it has no obligation to spend additional money for special carts in order to help their scores on the links. But that was before the Americans with Disabilities Act, under which the hotel is being sued.

If the government wanted to do something for the disabled or the handicapped, it could have spent its own tax money to do so. Instead, it passed the Americans with Disabilities Act, which created a right to sue private institutions, in order to force them to spend their money to solve the problems of individuals with special problems or special desires, whether serious or frivolous.

It was a lawyer's full-employment act, creating another legally recognized victim group, empowered to claim special privileges, at other people's expense, in the name of equal rights.

Nor could such legislation make the usual claim that it was coming to the defense of the poor and the downtrodden. Golf courses are not the natural habitat of the poor and the downtrodden.

One of the plaintiffs in the golf-course lawsuit has been the managing partner in a large law firm. He says, "I just want the same opportunity as everyone else" to "get out and play 18 holes with my friends and colleagues."

Equal opportunity does not mean equal results, despite

how many laws and policies proceed as if it does, or how much fashionable rhetoric equates the two.

An example of that rhetoric was the title of a recent *New York Times* column: "A Ticket to Bias." That column recalled bitterly the experience of a woman in a wheelchair who bought a $300 ticket to a rock concert but was unable to see when other people around her stood up. This was equated with "bias" on the part of those who ran the arena.

The woman in the wheelchair declared, "true equality remains a dream out of reach." Apparently only equality of results is "true" equality.

A recent publication of the American Historical Association shows this same confusion when it says that doors "are largely closed" to people who want to become historians if they didn't graduate from a top-tier college. In other words, unequal results proves bias that closed doors, according to this rhetoric.

Confusion between equal opportunity and equal results is a dangerous confusion behind many kinds of spoiled brat politics.

Spoiled Brat Politics: Part II

The idea that what I want overrides what you want has increasingly become part of our thinking, our policies and even our laws. There is literally a federal case before the Supreme Court over the fact that many colleges and universities refuse to allow military recruiters on campus.

Why? Because, as the academics will tell you, they are opposed to the military, either in general or because they think the military are discriminating against homosexuals or for whatever other reasons they have.

These academics have every right to be against the military, for any reason or for no reason.

If they don't like the military, they can stay away from the military, since there is no draft. But what they want is to keep other people away from the military, by preventing students from hearing what the military recruiters have to say, as students hear what recruiters from all sorts of other institutions and movements have to say on campus.

The reason there is a legal issue is that a federal law has been passed, saying that colleges and universities that forbid military recruiters from coming on campus are no longer eligible to receive federal money.

Academics are outraged. They see this law as a violation of their freedom—including their right to violate their students' freedom. It is classic spoiled brat politics, based on the idea that what I want overrides what you want.

The same principle underlies growing legal restrictions

on building anything that existing residents in a community don't want built.

A young "planning consultant" to a local politician in New York says: "These neighborhoods substantially have not changed in 40 years. What we are trying to do is make sure they are recognizable 40 years from now. I don't think there is anything wrong with that. In fact, in many other places in the country, that is celebrated. So why shouldn't we celebrate it here?"

That young man probably has a bright future in politics, where the ability to confuse the issues is a highly rewarded talent.

"Everybody is doing it" is a very effective political argument, requiring neither facts nor logic, and widely accepted in this era of dumbed-down education. Focusing on the benefits to some and ignoring the costs to others is another tried-and-true political tactic.

Since people who are already in a community are the ones who vote, making what they want override what other people want is a winner in spoiled brat politics.

At one time, courts took seriously the 14th Amendment's guarantee of equal rights for all, regardless of where they lived and voted. Courts even enforced the 5th Amendment's guarantee of property rights.

In other words, local voters and local politicians could not arbitrarily deprive other people of the right to come in and buy and use property as they saw fit, simply because some planning consultants or planning commissions preferred that they do otherwise. But Constitutional protection of property rights is no longer "in the mainstream" of fashionable legal thinking.

Let's go back to square one. The people who bought homes in a neighborhood 40 years ago did not buy the neighborhood, nor did they pay for a guarantee that the neighborhood would stay the same for 40 years, much less in perpetuity.

The only way the government can give current residents such a guarantee is to take away other people's property rights, which exist precisely in order to keep politicians at bay.

Buying a chance and asking the government to turn that chance into a guarantee has become a common occurrence under spoiled brat politics.

When you buy a home with a great view of the ocean, you do not pay for a guarantee that nothing will ever be built between you and the ocean. You ask politicians to give that to you, at someone else's expense.

Some people even call that idealism because you are "preserving" something good. But preserving it from whom? And why is what you want more important than what they want?

The "Compassion" Racket

Our hearts automatically go out to the people of Florida, who are being battered by a series of hurricanes in rapid succession. But we have brains as well as hearts—and the time is long overdue to start using them.

Hurricanes come through Florida every year about this time. And, every year, politicians get to parade their compassion by showering the taxpayers' money on the places that have been struck.

What would happen if they didn't?

First of all, not as many people would build homes in the path of a well-known disaster that comes around like clockwork virtually every year. Those who did would buy insurance that covers the costs of the risks they choose to take.

That insurance would not be cheap—which would provide yet another reason for people to locate out of harm's way. The net result would be fewer lives lost and less property damage. Is it not more compassionate to seek this result, even if it would deprive politicians of television time?

In ABC reporter John Stossel's witty and insightful book *Give Me A Break*, he discusses how he built a beach house with only "a hundred feet of sand" between him and the ocean. It gave him a great view—and a great chance of disaster.

His father warned him of the danger but an architect pointed out that the government would pick up the tab if anything happened to his house. A few years later, storm-driven ocean waves came in and flooded the ground floor of Stossel's home. The government paid to have it restored.

Still later, the waves came in again, and this time took out the whole house. The government paid again. Fortunately for the taxpayers, Stossel then decided that enough was enough.

In politics, throwing the taxpayers' money at disasters is supposed to show your compassion. But robbing Peter to pay Paul is not compassion. It is politics.

The crucial fact is that a society does not have one dime more money to devote to the resources available to help victims of natural disasters by sending that money through government agencies. All that it does is change the incentives in such a way as to subsidize risky behavior.

The same money can just as well come through insurance companies. Even if most insurance companies are unwilling to insure people living in particularly vulnerable areas, or living in homes that are inadequate to withstand hurricane-force winds, there are always insurers who specialize in high risks—and who charge correspondingly higher premiums.

Lloyds of London, for example, has already been moving into the market for insurance for homes costing half a million dollars or more and located along coastal waters, whether in Florida or the Hamptons or elsewhere. If rich people want to put their mansions at risk, there is no reason why they shouldn't pay the costs, instead of forcing the taxpayers to pay those costs.

What about "the poor"? As in so many other cases, the poor are the human shields behind which big-government advocates advance. If you are seriously concerned about the poor themselves, you can always subsidize them and avoid subsidizing others by having means tests.

Means tests are anathema to the political left because it puts an end to their game of hiding behind the poor. Compassion is a laudable feeling but it can also be a political racket.

As with so many government programs that people have come to rely on, phasing out state and federal disaster relief programs would not be easy. In an election year, it is impossible.

Fortunately, there are years in between elections, in which it is at least theoretically possible to talk sense. Whether the risks are hurricanes, earthquakes, floods or forest fires, people who have gotten themselves out on a limb by taking risks in the expectation that the government will bail them out can be gradually weaned away from that expectation by phasing out disaster relief.

The alternative is to keep on forcing taxpayers to be patsies forever, while politicians bask in the glow of the compassion racket by throwing the taxpayers' money hither and yon, while the media applaud the courage of those who rebuild in the path of known disasters.

Ronald Reagan (1911–2004)

There are many ways to judge a President or anyone else. One old-fashioned way is by results. A more popular way in recent years has been by how well someone fits the preconceptions of the intelligentsia or the media.

By the first test, Ronald Reagan was the most successful President of the United States in the 20th century. By the second test, he was a complete failure.

Time and time again President Reagan went against what the smug smarties inside the beltway and on the TV tube said. And time and again he got results.

It started even before Ronald Reagan was elected. When the Republicans nominated Governor Reagan in 1980, according to the late *Washington Post* editor Meg Greenfield, "people I knew in the Carter White House were ecstatic." They considered Reagan "not nearly smart enough"—as liberals measure smart.

The fact that Ronald Reagan beat President Jimmy Carter by a landslide did not cause any re-evaluation of his intelligence. It was luck or malaise or something else, liberals thought.

Now the media line was that this cowboy from California would be taught a lesson when he got to Washington and had to play in the big leagues against the savvy guys on Capitol Hill.

The new President succeeded in putting through Congress big changes that were called "the Reagan revolution." And he did it without ever having his party in control of both houses of Congress. But these results caused no re-evaluation of Ronald Reagan.

One of his first acts as President was to end price controls on petroleum. The *New York Times* condescendingly dismissed Reagan's reliance on the free market and repeated widespread predictions of "declining domestic oil production" and skyrocketing gasoline prices.

The price of gasoline fell by more than 60 cents a gallon. More luck, apparently.

Where the new President would really get his comeuppance, the smart money said, was in foreign affairs, where a former governor had no experience. Not only were President Reagan's ideas about foreign policy considered naive and dangerously reckless, he would be going up against the wily Soviet rulers who were old hands at this stuff.

When Ronald Reagan referred to the Soviet Union as an "evil empire," there were howls of disapproval in the media. When he proposed meeting a Soviet nuclear buildup in Eastern Europe with an American nuclear buildup in Western Europe, there were alarms that he was going to get us into a war.

The result? President Reagan's policies not only did not get us into a war, they put an end to the Cold War that had been going on for decades.

Meanwhile, Soviet Premier Mikhail Gorbachev, who was the media's idea of a brilliant and sophisticated man, had a whole Communist empire collapse under him when his policies were put into effect. Eastern Europe broke free and Gorbachev woke up one morning to find that the Soviet Union that he was head of no longer existed—and that he was now a nobody in the new Russian state.

But that was just bad luck, apparently.

For decades it had been considered the height of political wisdom to accept as given that the Soviet bloc was here to stay—and its expansion was so inevitable that it would be foolhardy to try to stop it.

The Soviet bloc had in fact expanded through seven consecutive administrations of both Republicans and Democrats. The first territory the Communists ever lost was Grenada, when Ronald Reagan sent in American troops.

But, once again, results carried no weight with the intelligentsia and the media.

Reagan was considered to be completely out of touch when he said that Communism was "another sad, bizarre chapter in human history whose last pages even now are being written." But how many "smart" people saw the end of the Soviet Union coming?

Ronald Reagan left this country—and the world—a far better place than he found it. And he smiled while he did it. That's greatness—if you judge by results.

Gun Control Myths

Professor Joyce Lee Malcolm of Bentley College deserves some sort of special prize for taking on the thankless task of talking sense on a subject where nonsense is deeply entrenched and fiercely dogmatic. In her recently published book, *Guns and Violence*, Professor Malcolm examines the history of firearms, gun control laws and violent crime in England. What makes this more than an exercise in history is its relevance to current controversies over gun control in America.

Gun control zealots love to make highly selective international comparisons of gun ownership and murder rates. But Joyce Lee Malcolm points out some of the pitfalls in that approach. For example, the murder rate in New York City has been more than five times that of London for two centuries—and during most of that time neither city had any gun control laws.

In 1911, New York state instituted one of the most severe gun control laws in the United States, while serious gun control laws did not begin in England until nearly a decade later. But New York City still continued to have far higher murder rates than London.

If we are serious about the role of guns and gun control as factors in differing rates of violence between countries, then we need to do what history professor Joyce Lee Malcolm does—examine the history of guns and violence. In England, as she points out, over the centuries "violent crime continued to decline markedly at the very time that guns were becoming increasingly available."

England's Bill of Rights in 1688 was quite unambiguous that the right of a private individual to be armed was an individual right, independently of any collective right of militias. Guns were as freely available to Englishmen as to Americans, on into the early 20th century.

Nor was gun control in England a response to any firearms murder crisis. Over a period of three years near the end of the 19th century, "there were only 59 fatalities from handguns in a population of nearly 30 million people," according to Professor Malcolm. "Of these, 19 were accidents, 35 were suicides and only 3 were homicides—an average of one a year."

The rise of the interventionist state in early 20th century England included efforts to restrict ownership of guns. After the First World War, gun control laws began restricting the possession of firearms. Then, after the Second World War, these restrictions grew more severe, eventually disarming the civilian population of England—or at least the law-abiding part of it.

It was during this period of severe restrictions on owning firearms that crime rates in general, and the murder rate in particular, began to rise in England. "As the number of legal firearms have dwindled, the numbers of armed crimes have risen," Professor Malcolm points out.

In 1954, there were only a dozen armed robberies in London but, by the 1990s, there were more than a hundred times as many. In England, as in the United States, drastic crackdowns on gun ownership by law-abiding citizens were accompanied by ever greater leniency to criminals. In both countries, this turned out to be a formula for disaster.

While England has not yet reached the American level

of murders, it has already surpassed the United States in rates of robbery and burglary. Moreover, in recent years the murder rate in England has been going up under still more severe gun control laws, while the murder rate in the United States has been going down as more and more states have allowed private citizens to carry concealed weapons—and have begun locking up more criminals.

In both countries, facts have no effect whatever on the dogmas of gun control zealots. The fact that most guns used to murder people in England were not legally purchased has no effect on their faith in gun control laws there, any more than faith in such laws here is affected by the fact that the gun used by the recent Beltway snipers was not purchased legally either.

In England as in America, sensational gun crimes have been seized upon and used politically to promote crackdowns on gun ownership by law-abiding citizens, while doing nothing about criminals. American zealots for the Brady Bill say nothing about the fact that the man who shot James Brady and tried to assassinate President Reagan has been out walking the streets on furlough.

Gun Control Myths: Part II

Talking facts to gun control zealots is only likely to make them angry. But the rest of us need to know what the facts are. More than that, we need to know that much of what the gun controllers claim as facts will not stand up under scrutiny.

The grand dogma of the gun controllers is that places with severe restrictions on the ownership of firearms have lower rates of murder and other gun crimes. How do they prove this? Simple. They make comparisons of places where this is true and ignore all comparisons of places where the opposite is true.

Gun control zealots compare the United States and England to show that murder rates are lower where restrictions on ownership of firearms are more severe. But you could just as easily compare Switzerland and Germany, the Swiss having lower murder rates than the Germans, even though gun ownership is three times higher in Switzerland. Other countries with high rates of gun ownership and low murder rates include Israel, New Zealand, and Finland.

Within the United States, rural areas have higher rates of gun ownership and lower rates of murder, whites have higher rates of gun ownership than blacks and much lower murder rates. For the country as a whole, hand gun ownership doubled in the late 20th century, while the murder rate went down. But such facts are not mentioned by gun control zealots or by the liberal media.

Another dogma among gun control supporters is that

having a gun in the home for self-defense is futile and is only likely to increase the chances of your getting hurt or killed. Your best bet is to offer no resistance to an intruder, according to this dogma.

Actual research tells just the opposite story. People who have not resisted have gotten hurt twice as often as people who resisted with a firearm. Those who resisted without a firearm of course got hurt the most often.

Such facts are simply ignored by gun control zealots. They prefer to cite a study published some years ago in the *New England Journal of Medicine* and demolished by a number of scholars since then. According to this discredited study, people with guns in their homes were more likely to be murdered.

How did they arrive at this conclusion? By taking people who were murdered in their homes, finding out how many had guns in the house, and then comparing them with people who were not murdered in their homes.

Using similar reasoning, you might be able to show that people who hire bodyguards are more likely to get killed than people who don't. Obviously, people who hire bodyguards already feel at risk, but does that mean that the bodyguards are the reason for the risk? Similarly illogical reasoning has been used by counting how many intruders were killed by homeowners with guns and comparing that with the number of family members killed with those guns. But this is a nonsense comparison because most people who keep guns in their homes do not do so in hopes of killing intruders.

Most uses of guns in self-defense—whether in the home or elsewhere—do not involve actually pulling the trigger. When the intended victim turns out to have a gun in his hand, the attacker usually has enough brains to back off. But the lives saved this way do not get counted.

People killed at home by family members are highly atypical. The great majority of these victims have had to call the police to their homes before, because of domestic violence, and just over half have had the cops out several times. These are not just ordinary people who happened to lose their temper when a gun was at hand.

Neither are most "children" who are killed by guns just toddlers who happened to find a loaded weapon lying around. More of those "children" are members of teenage criminal gangs who kill each other deliberately.

Some small children do in fact get accidentally killed by guns in the home—but fewer than drown in bathtubs. Is anyone for banning bathtubs? Moreover, the number of fatal gun accidents fell, over the years, while the number of guns was increasing by tens of millions. None of this supports the assumption that more guns mean more fatal accidents.

Most of the gun controllers' arguments are a house of cards. No wonder they don't want any hard facts coming near them.

A Painful Anniversary

August 20, 2004 marked the 40th anniversary of one of the major turning points in American social history. That was the date on which President Lyndon Johnson signed legislation creating his "War on Poverty" program in 1964.

Never had there been such a comprehensive program to tackle poverty at its roots, to offer more opportunities to those starting out in life, to rehabilitate those who had fallen by the wayside, and to make dependent people self-supporting. Its intentions were the best. But we know what road is paved with good intentions.

The War on Poverty represented the crowning triumph of the liberal vision of society—and of government programs as the solution to social problems. The disastrous consequences that followed have made the word "liberal" so much of a political liability that today even candidates with long left-wing track records have evaded or denied that designation.

In the liberal vision, slums bred crime. But brand new government housing projects almost immediately became new centers of crime and quickly degenerated into new slums. Many of these projects later had to be demolished. Unfortunately, the assumptions behind those projects were not demolished, but live on in other disastrous programs, such as Section 8 housing.

Rates of teenage pregnancy and venereal disease had been going down for years before the new 1960s attitudes toward sex spread rapidly through the schools, helped by

War on Poverty money. These downward trends suddenly reversed and skyrocketed.

The murder rate had also been going down, for decades, and in 1960 was just under half of what it had been in 1934. Then the new 1960s policies toward curing the "root causes" of crime and creating new "rights" for criminals began. Rates of violent crime, including murder, skyrocketed.

The black family, which had survived centuries of slavery and discrimination, began rapidly disintegrating in the liberal welfare state that subsidized unwed pregnancy and changed welfare from an emergency rescue to a way of life.

Government social programs such as the War on Poverty were considered a way to reduce urban riots. Such programs increased sharply during the 1960s. So did urban riots. Later, during the Reagan administration, which was denounced for not promoting social programs, there were far fewer urban riots.

Neither the media nor most of our educational institutions question the assumptions behind the War on Poverty. Even conservatives often attribute much of the progress that has been made by lower-income people to these programs.

For example, the usually insightful quarterly magazine *City Journal* says in its current issue: "Beginning in the mid-sixties, the condition of most black Americans improved markedly."

That is completely false and misleading.

The economic rise of blacks began decades earlier, before any of the legislation and policies that are credited with producing that rise. The continuation of the rise of blacks out of poverty did not—repeat, did not—accelerate during the 1960s.

The poverty rate among black families fell from 87

percent in 1940 to 47 percent in 1960, during an era of virtually no major civil rights legislation or anti-poverty programs. It dropped another 17 percentage points during the decade of the 1960s and one percentage point during the 1970s, but this continuation of the previous trend was neither unprecedented nor something to be arbitrarily attributed to the programs like the War on Poverty.

In various skilled trades, the incomes of blacks relative to whites more than doubled between 1936 and 1959—that is, before the magic 1960s decade when supposedly all progress began. The rise of blacks in professional and other high-level occupations was greater in the years immediately preceding the Civil Rights Act of 1964 than in the years afterwards.

While some good things did come out of the 1960s, as out of many other decades, so did major social disasters that continue to plague us today. Many of those disasters began quite clearly during the 1960s.

But what are mere facts compared to a heady vision? Liberal assumptions—"two Americas," for example—are being recycled this election year, even by candidates who evade the "liberal" label.

The High Cost of Shibboleths

A recent e-mail from a reader said that he could not find the word "shibboleth" in his desk dictionary, even though he had seen this word in my column. That was an unfortunate omission in his dictionary because shibboleths explain a lot about what is said and done in politics today.

Back in Biblical times, the word "shibboleth" was used as a password, because people from one side could say it easily and their enemies couldn't. It identified who you were and which side you were on.

Today, many things that are said and done in our political life serve that same purpose—and often make no sense otherwise. When people say that they are for "diversity" or gun control or campaign finance reform, they are declaring themselves to be on one side in the political wars as a whole. In their own eyes, their positions on such issues identify them as one of the good, caring and compassionate people.

What political shibboleths do is transform questions about facts, causation and evidence into questions about personal identity and moral worth. Shibboleths are also a great labor-saving device. You don't need to find out what the actual consequences of affirmative action have been if being for "diversity" serves the purpose of identifying you as one of those good people who care about racial justice and the advancement of the disadvantaged.

You don't have to find out what actually happens when there are more relaxed or more stringent gun control laws, if you only need to show that you are on the side of the angels. How many lives have actually been lost under one policy versus the other is a factual question whose answer you need not bother learning.

Mere facts cannot compete with shibboleths when it comes to making people feel good. Moreover, shibboleths keep off the agenda the painful question of how dangerous it is to have policies which impact millions of human beings without a thorough knowledge of the hard facts needed to understand just what that impact has actually been.

Shibboleths are the life blood of the media. Stories which seem to support the side of the angels are trumpeted from coast to coast, while stories which support the other side are either downplayed or ignored altogether.

For example, vicious crimes committed by white people against black people are big news because these stories fit the shibboleths which establish the moral identity of the journalists who tell these stories. Vicious crimes committed by blacks against whites are not big news because these stories undermine the shibboleths—or, as it is phrased, "feed stereotypes." Ditto with stories about crimes committed by the homeless, homosexuals and others favored by current shibboleths.

Shibboleths are dangerous, not only because they mobilize political support for policies that most of the supporters have not thought through, but also because these badges of identity make it harder to reverse those policies when they turn out to be counterproductive or even disastrous. When admitting a mistake means renouncing one's identity as one of "us" and being identified with a demonized "them," do not expect as many people to do it as if all that was involved was the question whether policy *A* produces better results than policy *B*.

Those who strain for moral equivalence—itself one of the shibboleths of our time—may assume that shibboleths are part of all political or ideological positions. But, for at least two centuries, shibboleths have been at the heart of the ideology of the left, whether moderate left or radical left.

Assumptions of being more concerned, caring and compassionate than their opponents can be found on the left from Godwin and Condorcet in the 18th century to a whole galaxy of liberal-left journalists, academics, organizations and movements today. But there were no such assumptions in the writings of Adam Smith in the 18th century or in those of Milton Friedman today. It was enough for them to say that their opponents were mistaken and their policies harmful—and why.

What we need are more factual arguments and counter-arguments. With shibboleths, we are flying blind into the future, through mountains of hard facts that are being ignored when they contradict the vision that gives many people their sense of self-worth.

"Why Do They Hate Us?"

The idea that what goes around comes around applies not only to individuals but to nations and whole civilizations. It was just a few centuries ago—not long, as history is measured—that China had the highest standard of living in the world and the Dutch were the world's largest exporters, while North Africans were enslaving a million Europeans.

Nowhere have whole peoples seen their situation reversed more visibly or more painfully than the peoples of the Islamic world. In medieval times, Europe lagged far behind the Islamic world in science, mathematics, scholarship, and military power.

Even such ancient European thinkers as Plato and Aristotle became known to Europeans of the Middle Ages only after their writings, which had been translated into Arabic, were translated back into European languages.

Today that is all reversed. The number of books per person in Europe is more than ten times that in Africa and the Middle East. The number of books translated into Arabic over the past thousand years is about the same as the number translated into Spanish in one year.

There are only 18 computers per thousand persons in the Arab world, compared to 78 per thousand persons worldwide. Fewer than 400 industrial patents were issued to people in the Arab countries during the last two decades of the 20th century, while 15,000 industrial patents were issued to South Koreans alone.

Human beings do not always take reversals of fortune

gracefully. Still less can those who were once on top quietly accept seeing others leaving them far behind economically, intellectually, and militarily.

Those in the Islamic world have for centuries been taught to regard themselves as far superior to the "infidels" of the West, while everything they see with their own eyes now tells them otherwise. Worse yet, what the whole world sees with their own eyes tells them that the Middle East has made few contributions to human advancement in our times.

Even Middle Eastern oil was largely discovered and processed by people from the West. After oil, the Middle East's most prominent export has been terrorism.

Those who look at the world in rationalistic terms may say that the Middle East can use some of its vast oil wealth to expand its own educated classes and move back to the forefront of human achievement. They did it once, why not do it again?

All sorts of things can be done in the long run, but you have to live through the short run to get there. Moreover, even the short run, as history is measured, can be pretty long in terms of the human lifespan.

Even if the Islamic world set such goals and committed the material resources and individual efforts required, they could not expect to pull abreast of the West for generations, even if the West stood still. More realistically, it would take centuries, as it took the West centuries to catch up to them.

What will happen in the meantime? Are millions of proud human beings supposed to quietly accept inferiority for themselves and their children, and perhaps their children's children?

Or are they more likely to listen to demagogues, whether political or religious, who tell them that their lowly place in the world is due to the evils of others—the West, the Americans, the Jews?

If the peoples of the Islamic world disregarded such demagogues, they would be the exceptions, rather than the rule, among people who lag painfully far behind others. Even in the West, there have been powerful political movements based on the notion that the rich have gotten rich by keeping others poor—and that things need to be set right "by all means necessary."

These means seldom include concentration on self-improvement, with 19th-century Japan being one of the rare exceptions. Lashing out at others is far more immediately satisfying—and modern communications, transportation, and weaponry make it far easier to lash out destructively across great distances.

Against this background, we may want to consider the question asked by hand-wringers in the West: Why do they hate us? Maybe it is because the alternative to hating us is to hate themselves.

Foreign "Allies"

To those who do not want to face up to hard and brutal choices in a nuclear age, the magic formula is to turn to something called "the international community"—or, more concretely, the United Nations or "our European allies." As with so many rhetorical solutions to hard problems, the specific realities behind the rhetoric get very little attention.

What is the actual track record of the UN or Europe? Is it something to rely on, in life and death decisions?

The UN stood idly by in Rwanda while mass slaughters went on. The UN passed resolution after resolution on Iraq for years, without taking any action to enforce them. Indeed, the UN was part of the massive corruption in the oil-for-food program, which enabled Saddam Hussein to divert money intended to feed the Iraqi people into buying weapons and palaces for himself.

When the UN seated Libya on its human rights committee, that was a sign of its moral bankruptcy. So was its conference on racism, which featured anti-Semitic propaganda by Arab countries.

What of our European allies, who are automatically assumed to be so much wiser and more sophisticated than American "cowboy" presidents, whether Reagan or Bush?

Europe's track record throughout the 20th century was one unbelievable disaster after another. European countries blundered their way into two world wars—from which every country involved emerged worse off than before, with a continent devastated and its people hungry amid the rubble. Both times American food fed them.

The two biggest ideological disasters of the 20th century—Communism and Fascism—were both created in Europe. Both of these blind fanaticisms led to innocent civilians being killed by the millions, during peacetime as well as in wars.

For more than half a century, Western Europe has not had to defend itself because it has been protected by the American nuclear umbrella. Without that, there was nothing to stop the Soviet army from marching right across the continent to the Atlantic Ocean.

American protection enabled Western Europe to neglect its own military defenses, and in some cases use their armed forces as another government featherbedding program. NATO's forces include unionized soldiers who absorb a much higher share of Europe's military spending than do American soldiers in the U.S. That leaves less money for NATO to buy up-to-date equipment.

NATO's troops get generous vacations and light enough schedules that many of them have part-time civilian jobs. The average age of soldiers in Belgium is 40, compared to 28 for American soldiers.

No country could afford to have to fight a war with over-age soldiers and obsolete equipment, unless its military defense was left to someone else. That someone else is the United States.

Like so many people who have been sheltered from the harsh realities of life and not forced to stand on their own two feet, Western Europeans have been able to indulge themselves in illusions. The most unrealistic of these illusions has been that we can just talk our way out of international threats with "negotiations," treaties and UN resolutions.

That approach was tried for two decades after the First World War. That is what led to the Second World War.

France was the worst. In the 1920s, its foreign minister Aristide Briand negotiated much-ballyhooed agreements renouncing war—agreements that won him the Nobel Prize but did nothing to deter war. In fact, such things lulled peaceful countries into a dangerous complacency that emboldened aggressor nations.

France's record of cowardice and betrayal of its allies during the 1930s, was climaxed by its own surrender to Hitler after just six weeks of fighting in 1940. At the 11th hour, France appealed to the United States, which was not in the war at that point, for military equipment—that is, for the kind of "unilateral" American intervention at which the French would sneer so often in later years.

Are these the people to whom we should defer on life-and-death questions? Are our actions to be limited to what is acceptable to the lowest common denominator at the UN or in Europe? Are the lofty rhetoric and condescending airs of foreigners to impress us more than their dismal track records?

My Platform

From time to time some kind readers suggest that I run for public office, including President of the United States. No need for those on the left to panic. It is not going to happen.

Such suggestions, however, cause me to imagine what my platform would be if I were in politics. Once you see what that platform would be, you can understand why it will never happen.

Since politicians like to have campaign slogans, instead of "Bring it On!" my slogan might be "Get rid of it!" to describe all the laws, policies, and government agencies that I would abolish.

A more positive slogan would be "Conservative Radicalism." That is, my policies would be based on traditional values but would make radical changes in order to restore or enhance those values.

Cabinet-level departments, for example, would be reduced to just two—the Defense Department and the State Department, with the latter purged of the weak-kneed internationalist crowd who have dominated it for so long. Departments of Agriculture, Commerce, Labor, etc., would all be abolished as just money-wasting bureaucracies serving outside special interests, instead of the people whose taxes support them.

Government subsidies would be drastically reduced, starting at the top. That is, there would be a prohibition against giving a dime of government money to anyone whose annual income or total assets exceed one billion dollars. Why should agricultural subsidies be going to Ted Turner and David Rockefeller, or "universal health care" pay for their medicine?

Who could object to cutting off subsidies to billionaires? Once that was done, however, the next step would be to cut off millionaires. Then we could proceed on down the income scale until people making a hundred grand a year could no longer expect to be subsidized with the taxpayer's money.

The great advantage of this way of proceeding is that it would rob the media of opportunities to run sob stories about how some poor person was hurt by cutbacks in some government program—even when the vast majority of those who were hurt were the bureaucrats who run these programs and slick special interests who hide behind the poor.

By the time we got down to cutting off all government subsidies to people making $100,000 a year or more, the federal budget would probably not only be balanced but have a surplus. Of course, there would be hordes of unemployed bureaucrats being interviewed on TV, complaining that the world was going to end without their vital contributions. But that could be brushed aside.

With all the money saved by ending vast numbers of subsidies, the government could afford to pay the kinds of salaries that would attract highly qualified people from the private sector. For example, if every member of Congress were paid a million dollars a year, that would cost less than one percent of what it costs to run the Department of Agriculture.

As things stand today, a successful doctor, lawyer, executive, engineer or economist would lose money by becoming a member of Congress. This means that Congress is largely filled with people who either already have great wealth or people who don't have what it takes to earn a high income in the private sector—or people hungry for power, who are the worst of all.

These are not the kinds of people who should dominate the making of laws in Congress or enforcing them in the courts. Short-sighted critics might object that the kinds of people we have in politics and the courts don't deserve to get a million dollars a year. But that is the very reason for trying to get better people.

If a million dollars a year won't do it, you could raise the pay to ten million and it would still be chump change compared to what is wasted by cheap politicians, who turn out to be very expensive politicians when wasting the taxpayers' money.

Then there should be term limits. In fact, elected officials should be limited to just one term. Otherwise, they and their staffs would be spending most of their time doing things to get re-elected in all but the last term.

These are just some of the things I would do in the name of "conservative radicalism." But it may be enough to show why there is no clear and present danger of my being nominated, much less elected.

The Oldest Fraud

Election frauds are nothing new and neither are political frauds in general. The oldest fraud is the belief that the political left is the party of the poor and the downtrodden.

The 2004 election results in California were only the latest evidence to give the lie to that belief. While the state as a whole went for Kerry, 55 percent versus 44 percent for Bush, the various counties ranged from 71 percent Bush to 83 percent Kerry. The most affluent counties were where Kerry had his strongest support.

In Marin County, where the average home price is $750,000, 73 percent of the votes went for Kerry. In Alameda County, where Berkeley is located, it was 74 percent Kerry. San Francisco, with the highest rents of any major city in the country, gave 83 percent of its votes to Kerry.

Out where ordinary people live, it was a different story. Thirty-six counties went for Bush versus 22 counties for Kerry, and usually by more balanced vote totals, though Bush went over 70 percent in less fashionable places like Lassen County and Modoc County. If you have never heard of them, there's a reason.

It was much the same story on the votes for Proposition 66, which would have limited the "three strikes" law that puts career criminals away for life. Affluent voters living insulated lives in places well removed from high-crime neighborhoods have the luxury of worrying about whether we are not being nice enough to hoodlums, criminals and terrorists.

They don't like the "three strikes" law and want it weakened. While most California voters opposed any weakening of that law, a majority of the voters in the affluent and heavily pro-Kerry counties mentioned wanted us to stop being so mean to criminals.

This pattern is not confined to California and it is not new. There were limousine liberals before there were limousines. The same pattern applies when you go even further left on the political spectrum, to socialists and communists.

The British Labor Party's leader in the heyday of its socialist zealotry was Clement Attlee, who grew up in a large home with servants—and this was not the only home his family owned. Meanwhile, Margaret Thatcher's family ran a grocery store and lived upstairs over it.

While the British Labor Party was affiliated with labor unions, it was the affluent and the intellectuals in the party who had the most left-wing ideologies and the most unrealistic policies. In the years leading up to World War II, the Labor Party was for disarmament while Hitler was arming Germany to the teeth across the Channel.

Eventually, it was the labor union component of the party that insisted on some sanity, so that Britain could begin preparing to defend itself militarily—not a moment too soon.

When Karl Marx and Friedrich Engels wrote the *Communist Manifesto,* they were a couple of spoiled young men from rich families. All their talk about the working class was just talk, but it appealed to other such young men who liked heady talk.

As Engels himself put it, when the Communist group for

whom the *Manifesto* was written was choosing delegates, "a working man was proposed for appearances sake, but those who proposed him voted for me." This may have been the first rigged election of the Communist movement but it was certainly not the last.

All sorts of modern extremist movements, such as the Weathermen in the United States or the Baader-Meinhof gang in Germany, have attracted a disproportionate number of the affluent in general and the intellectuals in particular.

Such people may speak in the name of the downtrodden but they themselves are often people who have time on their hands to nurse their pet notions about the world and their fancies about themselves as leaders of the poor, saviors of the environment or whatever happens to be the Big Deal du jour.

Osama bin Laden is not someone embittered by poverty. He is from a very rich family and has had both the time to nurse his resentments of the West and the money to organize terrorists to lash out in the only way that can give them any significance.

The belief that liberal, left-wing or extremist movements are for the poor may or may not be the biggest fraud but it is certainly the oldest.

The Left's Vision

Santa Monica, California, has decreed a fine of $2,500 a day—for not cutting your hedges!

Has someone discovered some terrible health hazard or other danger from hedges that are too high? Not at all. The politicians who run Santa Monica have simply decided that people should not be able to build a high wall of hedges around themselves.

Santa Monica has long been called "the People's Republic of Santa Monica" for all the far left laws and rhetoric it generates. Like other governments called "people's republic," the last thing they care about is people. The ideology, or even whims, of those in power routinely take away other people's right to live their own lives as they see fit.

Santa Monica is not unique. Wherever you get enough far left people in power, you can find a similar willingness to force everyone into collectivist conformity at all costs.

Too often these selfish ego trips of the left are called idealism, and issues are discussed in terms of the wonderful goals they proclaim—"social justice," "open space" or "saving" this or that—rather than in terms of what is actually being done and the costs entailed on others, even when that cost is $2,500 a day.

None of this is peculiar to the United States. In fact, the same mindset is more prevalent in a number of Western European countries and has been carried even further in practice.

In Britain, for example, the right to defend yourself is being taken away in many ways. Gun control laws there have not only tightened restrictions on gun ownership—with the murder rate rising as they do—these laws ban anything that looks like a gun, especially if it is used in self-defense.

Britons who have held burglars in their homes until the police arrived, by using toy pistols, have been arrested along with the burglars. To the collectivist mindset, independent self-help of any sort is a threat to their vision of the government as the sole source of protection and direction.

If someone attacks you in Britain and you knock him down, you are not allowed to hit him again or you will be charged with assault. Apparently they think that someone who has been knocked down is now harmless. People who have led sufficiently sheltered lives may believe such things—and impose such notions on others through the power of government.

The British Broadcasting Corporation (BBC) has even advised that you are not to yell "help" when you are attacked in a public place. You are to yell "Call the police."

Both self-defense and coming to the aid of others are lumped together as "vigilante" actions. That mindset has made inroads into the American media as well.

Years ago, Bernard Goetz was called "the subway vigilante" in the media because he shot some young hoodlums who attacked him directly. He had sat quietly minding his own business while the thugs harassed other people in the same subway car. But even to defend himself was "vigilante" action, as far as those in the liberal media were concerned.

The left takes its vision seriously—more seriously than it takes the rights of other people. They want to be our shepherds. But that requires us to be sheep.

Even in the raising of our own children, the left wants to take charge—without taking responsibility. Schools have long ago taken over the role of introducing children to sex when, how, and with whatever beliefs are in vogue. But, if your child ends up pregnant or stricken with AIDS, that is your problem, not theirs.

In some European countries, it is illegal to spank your own children. They apparently believe, like Hillary Clinton, that "it takes a village" to raise a child. But, if the child ends up rotten, it is not the village that lies awake at night. It is the parents.

Making other people's decisions for them without being held accountable for the consequences is the left's vision in many different contexts—including outsourcing our foreign policy to the United Nations or to the International Court of Justice, whom nobody elected and whom nobody can hold accountable.

Hedges in Santa Monica are just one of the signs of our times. The left wants to cut our freedom down, not just hedges.

The Left's Vocabulary

A recent angry e-mail from a reader said that certain issues should not be determined by "the dictates of the market." With a mere turn of a phrase, he had turned reality upside down.

Decisions by people free to make their mutual accommodations with other free people were called "dictates" while having third parties tell all of them what they could and couldn't do was not.

Verbal coups have long been a specialty of the left. Totalitarian countries on the left have called themselves "people's democracies" and used the egalitarian greeting "comrade"—even though some comrades had the arbitrary power of life and death over other comrades.

In democratic countries, where public opinion matters, the left has used its verbal talents to change the whole meaning of words and to substitute new words, so that issues would be debated in terms of their redefined vocabulary, instead of the real substance of the issues.

Words which have acquired connotations from the actual experiences of millions of human beings over generations, or even centuries, have been replaced by new words that wipe out those connotations and substitute more fashionable notions of the left.

The word "swamp," for example, has been all but erased from the language. Swamps were messy, sometimes smelly, places where mosquitoes bred and sometimes snakes lurked. The left has replaced the word "swamp" with "wetlands," a word spoken in pious tones usually reserved for sacred things.

The point of this verbal sleight-of-hand is to impose the left's notions of how other people can use their own land. Restrictive laws about "wetlands" have imposed huge costs on farmers and other owners of land that happened to have a certain amount of water on it.

Another word that the left has virtually banished from the language is "bum." Centuries of experience with idlers who refused to work and who hung around on the streets making a nuisance—and sometimes a menace—of themselves were erased from our memories as the left verbally transformed those same people into a sacred icon, "the homeless."

As with swamps, what was once messy and smelly was now turned into something we had a duty to protect. It was now our duty to support people who refused to support themselves.

Crimes committed by bums are covered up by the media, by verbally transforming "the homeless" into "transients" or "drifters" whenever they commit crimes. Thus "the homeless" are the only group you never hear of committing any crimes.

More to the point, third parties' notions are imposed by the power of the government to raise our taxes to support people who are raising hell on our streets and in parks where it has often become too dangerous for our children to play.

The left has a whole vocabulary devoted to depicting people who do not meet standards as people who have been denied "access."

Whether it is academic standards, job qualifications or credit requirements, those who do not measure up are said to have been deprived of "opportunity," "rights" or "social justice."

The word games of the left—from the mantra of "diversity" to the pieties of "compassion"—are not just games. They are ways of imposing power by evading issues of substance through the use of seductive rhetoric.

"Rights," for example, have become an all-purpose term used for evading both facts and logic by saying that people have a "right" to whatever the left wants to give them by taking from others.

For centuries, rights were exemptions from government power, as in the Bill of Rights. Now the left has redefined rights as things that can be demanded from the taxpayers, or from private employers or others, on behalf of people who accept no mutual obligations, even for common decency.

At one time, educators tried to teach students to carefully define words and systematically analyze arguments. They said, "We are here to teach you how to think, not what to think."

Today, they are teaching students what to think— political correctness. Instead of knowledge, students are given "self-esteem," so that they can vent their ignorance with confidence.

Abstract People

Most people have to deal with the reality that confronts them. They start with that reality and try to do the best they can within its limitations and within their own limitations.

But there are large and growing numbers of people—especially among the intelligentsia—whose starting point is some abstraction that they wish to apply to reality. For example, even in the face of a worldwide terrorist organization that has declared open warfare on every American man, woman and child, those whose starting point is abstraction focus on the "civil rights" of terrorists.

No one in World War II worried about Hitler's or Goering's civil rights. The very concept would have been considered absurd. Hitler and Goering were not part of our civil world. In fact, they were trying to destroy that world and replace it with their own tyranny. That is exactly what the world terrorist networks are trying to do today.

How can anyone have rights within a framework that he rejects and is trying to destroy? Rights are not just abstractions plucked out of thin air. Rights are part of a whole set of mutual obligations binding people together. If enemy soldiers have any rights, it is as a result of international agreements such as the Geneva Convention on prisoners of war. And they have those rights only after they have surrendered and become prisoners of war.

So long as they are still fighting, enemy soldiers do not even have the right to live, without which all other rights are meaningless. If these enemy soldiers have infiltrated wearing

civilian clothes or disguised in the uniform of some other
country, then they can be killed legally, even after
surrendering. Spies have been shot or hanged for centuries.

At one time, all this would have been considered too
obvious to require saying. But today, when some people talk
blithely about "animal rights," as if animals were part of
some system of mutual obligations, even the obvious has to
be explained to some of the products of our dumbed-down
education.

A sense of decency limits what we do to enemies or to
animals, but this is not a matter of rights, civil or otherwise.
Nor is it a threat to the rights of American citizens when we
fail to treat foreign terrorists as if they were American
citizens. Citizens are people who have a legal obligation to
play by certain rules, and who are therefore protected by
that same national system of rules. But people who are
trying to destroy both the citizens and the rules they live by
have no such claim.

The hand-wringers among us seem to be worried that
foreign terrorists are not being treated as nicely as they
would like or that illegal aliens from the Middle East will be
"singled out" to be sent back where they came from. In the
abstract, there is no more reason to focus on Middle Eastern
males than on Scandinavian females, when it comes to
deporting illegal aliens. It is just that we do not live in the
abstract. We live in the world that exists. And we want to
keep on living.

Some of these hand-wringers even seem to think that we
have to "set an example" that will vindicate us in the eyes of
"world opinion." In short, they put these abstractions first—
ahead of the deadly realities facing us now and in the years
ahead.

Why the United States of America needs to vindicate

itself in the eyes of the despotic and failing governments that make up much of the rest of the world is a mystery. Whether foreigners will in fact respect us for bending over backward or despise us for our apologetic weakness is another question.

Worse yet, other nations considering whether to cooperate or ally themselves with us—at some risk to themselves—will have to consider whether we are dependable and realistic enough to make the gamble worthwhile or whether we are terminally addicted to shibboleths that can jeopardize ourselves and them.

The great political affliction of the 20th century was putting abstractions ahead of flesh-and-blood human beings, especially in ideological totalitarian states under Nazism and Communism. Do we need to repeat that staggering tragedy in the 21st century?

Looking Back

We may look back on some eras as heroic—that of the founding fathers or "the greatest generation" that fought World War II—but some eras we look back on in disbelief at the utter stupidity with which people ruined their economies or blundered into wars in which every country involved ended up worse off than before.

How will people a century from now look back on our era? Fortunately, most of us will be long gone by then, so we will be spared the embarrassment of seeing ourselves judged.

What will future generations say about how we behaved when confronted by international terrorist organizations that have repeatedly demonstrated their cutthroat ruthlessness and now had the prospect of getting nuclear weapons from rogue nations like Iran and North Korea?

What will future generations think when they see the front pages of our leading newspapers repeatedly preoccupied with whether we are treating captured cutthroats nicely enough? What will they think when they see the Geneva Convention invoked to protect people who are excluded from protection by the Geneva Convention?

During World War II, German soldiers who were captured not wearing the uniform of their own army were simply lined up against a wall and shot dead by American troops.

This was not a scandal. Far from being covered up by the military, movies were taken of the executions and have since been shown on the History Channel. We understood then that the Geneva Convention protected people who obeyed the Geneva Convention, not those who didn't—as terrorists today certainly do not.

What will those who look back on these times think when they see that the American Civil Liberties Union, and others who have made excuses for all sorts of criminals, were pushing for the prosecution of our own troops for life-and-death decisions they had a split second to make in the heat of combat?

The frivolous demands made on our military—that they protect museums while fighting for their lives, that they tiptoe around mosques from which people are shooting at them—betray an irresponsibility made worse by ingratitude toward men who have put their lives on the line to protect us.

It is impossible to fight a war without heroism. Yet can you name a single American military hero acclaimed by the media for an act of courage in combat? Such courage is systematically ignored by most of the media.

If American troops kill a hundred terrorists in battle and lose ten of their own men doing it, the only headline will be: "Ten More Americans Killed in Iraq Today."

Those in the media who have carped at the military for years, and have repeatedly opposed military spending, are now claiming to be "honoring" our military by making a big production out of publishing the names of all those killed in Iraq. Will future generations see through this hypocrisy—and wonder why we did not?

What will the generations of the future say if we allow Iran and North Korea to develop nuclear weapons, which are then turned over to terrorists who can begin to annihilate American cities?

Our descendants will wonder how we could have let this happen, when we had the power to destroy any nation posing such a threat. Knowing that we had the power, they would have to wonder why we did not have the will—and why it was so obvious that we did not.

Nothing will more painfully reveal the irresponsible frivolity of our times than the many demands in the media and in politics that we act only with the approval of the United Nations and after winning over "world opinion."

How long this will take and what our enemies will be doing in the meantime while we are going through these futile exercises is something that gets very little attention.

Do you remember Osama bin Laden warning us, on the eve of the 2004 elections, that he would retaliate against those parts of the United States that voted for Bush? The United States is not Spain, so we disregarded his threats.

But what of future generations, after international terrorists get nuclear weapons? And what will our descendants think of us—will they ever forgive us—for leaving them in such a desperate situation because we were paralyzed by a desire to placate "world opinion"?

PART V

SOCIAL ISSUES

Mealy Mouth Media

The British Broadcasting Corporation has made itself look ridiculous by issuing orders that its reporters are not to refer to Saddam Hussein as an ex-dictator. Apparently using the word "dictator" would compromise the BBC's neutrality and call its objectivity into question.

Unfortunately, the BBC is not alone. In much of the American mainstream media, terrorists are referred to as "militants" or "insurgents." Rioters are called "demonstrators."

As American flags went up around the country in the wake of the September 11, 2001 attacks, even the wearing of little American flag lapel pins by TV journalists was banned by some broadcasters, with the notable exception of Fox News.

What makes all this straining for neutrality more than just another passing silliness is that it reveals a serious confusion between neutrality and objectivity. Such verbal posturing has been at its worst in some of the most biased media, such as the BBC.

During World War II, legendary journalist Edward R. Murrow never pretended to be neutral as between the Nazis and the Allies. Yet you would have trouble today finding anyone in the media with anything resembling the stature and integrity of Ed Murrow.

Honesty does not require posturing. In fact, the two things are incompatible. Nor does objectivity require neutrality.

Medical science is no less scientifically objective because it is completely biased in favor of people and against bacteria. Medical researchers are studying cancer cells with scientific objectivity in order to discover what the hard facts are about those cells, regardless of anyone's preconceived beliefs. But they are doing so precisely in order to destroy cancer cells and, if possible, prevent their existence in the first place.

Objectivity refers to an honest seeking of the truth, whatever that truth may turn out to be and regardless of what its implications might be. Neutrality refers to a preconceived "balance," which subordinates the truth to a preconception.

Journalists who reported the horrors of the Nazi concentration camps were not violating canons of objectivity by failing to use such neutral language as calling these places "residential facilities" or those who ran them "hosts."

Nor did the use of the term "dictator" to describe Hitler mean that World War II journalists did not come up to the supposedly high standards of today's media. What does the much-vaunted "public's right to know" mean when mealy mouth words filter out essential facts?

During the Cold War, the confusion between objectivity and neutrality led many journalists to balance negative things said about the Soviet Union with negative things said about the United States. In the circles of the media anointed, a phrase like "the free world" was disdained because it violated this verbal neutrality.

Journalistic sophisticates referred to "the so-called free world." Meanwhile, for decades on end, in countries around the globe, millions of ordinary human beings broke the personal ties of a lifetime, left behind their worldly belongings, and took desperate chances with their lives, and with the lives of their children—all in order to try to escape to "the so-called free world."

One of the pious phrases of the mealy mouth media is that "the truth lies somewhere in between." It may or it may not. Only after you have found the truth do you know where it is.

For years, there were people who denied that there was a famine in the Soviet Union during the 1930s and others who said that millions died during that famine. Did the truth lie somewhere in between?

The leading scholar who argued that millions starved during Stalin's man-made famine was Robert Conquest of the Hoover Institution, often described in the media as a right-wing think tank. When Mikhail Gorbachev finally opened the official records in the last days of the Soviet Union, it turned out that even more people had died during the famine than Dr. Conquest had estimated.

The truth is where you find it—and you don't find it with a preconceived "balance" expressed in mealy mouth words.

Achievements and Their Causes

In this age of specialization, experts are said to know more and more about less and less. There are undoubtedly specialists who can tell you more than you ever wanted to know about toenails or toads. However, the grand study of sweeping events has not died out entirely.

What could be more sweeping than a book titled *Human Accomplishment?* It is Charles Murray's latest book and it is dynamite.

The subtitle spells out how sweeping this book is: *The Pursuit of Excellence in the Arts and Sciences, 800 B.C. to 1950.* It is more than a historical survey of the landmark figures in many fields from various cultures around the world. It is an analysis of where, why, and how historic advances have been made in some places and not in others.

Just to pose this as a question goes against the grain of today's multiculturalism, in which all cultures are seen as equally valuable, and the non-judgmentalism that is too squeamish to declare some achievements more important than others.

Charles Murray, however, clearly believes that being able to cure fatal diseases is more important than some other things and that Rembrandt was a greater artist than your local sidewalk cartoon sketcher. Most people might regard this as obvious common sense but some of the intelligentsia may be seething with resentment at seeing their pet fetishes ignored.

Once you begin looking at the history of great human

achievements—whether in science or art, mathematics or literature—you discover that they are not random over time or random from one place to another. They cluster in time and in space.

Landmark figures in Western art clustered in the northern half of the Italian peninsula in the 15th to the 17th centuries and on the Channel coast of France and the Netherlands in the 19th through the mid-20th centuries. Landmark figures in literature, science and music have all had their own special concentrations at different times and places.

What never seems to have happened, either in Western or non-Western civilizations, was a random distribution of achievements. Even at the individual level, achievements are skewed.

Among professional golfers, for example, just over half have never won any tournament, anywhere. Even among the relatively small number who have ever won a major golf tournament, more than half have won just one. But Jack Nicklaus won 18.

Cities have been the scene of more than their share of great achievements in many fields. This is not just because many people have been concentrated in cities. Even in proportion to population, cities have turned out far more than their share of leading figures.

Particular groups have also had more than their share of spectacular achievements. In the first half of the 20th century, Jews won 14 percent of all Nobel Prizes in literature and the sciences combined, and in the second half of the century they won 29 percent. In both periods, Jews were less than one percent of the world's population.

Once we understand that achievements are not random and never have been, the question that arises is: What causes so much more achievement in some places than in others, at some times rather than others, and among some individuals and groups more than others?

Charles Murray's answers to these big question are too long for a newspaper column and can be found in the book. But just to have established a basis for such questions is a major contribution.

Let us not forget that we live in a time when a failure to have a random distribution of individuals and groups in the workplace or on an academic campus is regarded as a sign of bias or discrimination. The very thought that groups might differ among themselves in the required skills, attitudes and performances is anathema to many in academia, the media and even the courts.

This study of landmark achievements is itself a landmark achievement. If it does no more than get people to think about things that have been accepted as social dogmas, that will be a major contribution.

Talkers versus Doers

The big divide in this country is not between Democrats and Republicans, or women and men, but between talkers and doers.

Think about the things that have improved our lives the most over the past century—medical advances, the transportation revolution, huge increases in consumer goods, dramatic improvements in housing, the computer revolution. The people who created these things—the doers—are not popular heroes. Our heroes are the talkers who complain about the doers.

Those who have created nothing have maintained a constant barrage of criticism against those who created something, because that something was considered to be not good enough or the benefits turned out to have costs.

Every time I get on my bicycle and go pedalling down the road, I remember from my childhood that old geezers in their 70s didn't go biking in those days. They sat around on the porch in their rocking chairs.

Partly that was the style of the times but partly it was because old people did not have the energy and vigor that they have today. Much of that has been due to medical advances that not only added years to our lives but life to our years.

Doctors and hospitals have helped but much of the improvement in our health has been due to pharmaceutical drugs that keep us from having to go to hospitals, and have enabled doctors to head off many serious medical problems with prescriptions.

Yet the people who produce pharmaceutical drugs have been under heated political attack for years—attacks which often do not let the facts get in their way.

During the anthrax scare of 2001, for example, the maker of the leading antidote for anthrax was accused of making "obscene profits" even though (1) the total cost of treatment with their drug was just $50 and (2) the company actually operated at a loss while they were being denounced for obscene profits.

People who know nothing about advertising, nothing about pharmaceuticals, and nothing about economics have been loudly proclaiming that the drug companies spend too much on advertising—and demanding that the government pass laws based on their ignorance.

Today, we take the automobile so much for granted that it is hard to realize what an expansion of the life of ordinary people it represented. There was a time when most people lived and died within a 50-mile radius of where they were born.

The automobile opened a whole new world to these people. It also enabled those living in overcrowded cities to spread out into suburbs and get some elbow room. Trucks got goods to people more cheaply and ambulances got people to hospitals faster to save their lives.

Yet who among the people who did this are today regarded as being as big a hero as Ralph Nader, who put himself on the map with complaints about cars in general and the Corvair in particular?

Hard data on automobile safety and tests conducted on the Corvair both undermined Nader's claims. But he will always be a hero to the talkers. So will those who complain about commerce and industry that have raised our standard of living to levels that our grandparents would not have dreamed of.

Home-ownership is far more widespread among ordinary people today than in the past because of entrepreneurs who have figured out how to produce more, bigger and better houses at prices that more and more people could afford. But can you name any of those entrepreneurs who have been celebrated for their contributions to their fellow human beings?

Probably not. In California, anyone in the business of producing housing is more likely to be demonized as a "developer," a word that causes hostile reactions among Californians conditioned to respond negatively—and automatically, like Pavlov's dog.

As for computers, no one made them more usable by more people around the world than Microsoft. And no one has been hit with more or bigger lawsuits as a result.

Why can't the talkers leave the doers alone? Perhaps it is because that would leave the talkers on the sidelines, with their uselessness being painfully obvious to all, instead of being in the limelight and "making a difference"—even if that difference is usually negative.

Talkers versus Doers: Part II

The fact that benefits have costs means that those who create these benefits are tempting targets for accusations from those who know how to dramatize the costs. This means that the doers are constantly on the defensive when attacked by the talkers.

These attacks are especially effective in a society where most people have not been taught to weigh costs against benefits or to subject hot rhetoric to cold logic.

"Safety" issues are ideal for talkers because nothing is absolutely safe. A vaccine may save the lives of 10,000 children but, if five children die from the vaccine itself, that can set off loud denunciations of "corporate irresponsibility" and "greed" on the part of the companies that produced the vaccine.

Some people die from reactions to peanut butter. If the government banned every food from which some people can die, we would all die of starvation. If they banned every vaccine or drug from which people die, more people would die from diseases.

More than sloppy thinking and runaway rhetoric enables the talkers to harass the doers. The ever-growing jungle of laws and regulations provides a virtually unlimited number of grounds for lawsuits.

The talkers are in their natural habitat in courts where judges allow junk science to be used as evidence and juries are gullible enough to be impressed by glib and clever lawyers. The low cost of attacks and the high cost of defense tilts the system in favor of the talkers, especially since the talkers need pay no price for having made totally unfounded accusations.

Both the talkers and the doers know this. That is why the doers so often settle out of court, rather than be tied up in endless litigation. This is then taken as proof of guilt.

Anyone who wants to build anything can be hit with costly delays by environmental activists demanding environmental impact reports. It doesn't matter what the facts are, the talkers can always demand more information and object to the analysis.

All this takes time—and more time adds to the costs of borrowed money, on which interest must be paid, no matter whether the building for which it was borrowed is being built or the machines and workers are idled while speculative complaints are being investigated by bureaucrats who are in no hurry.

Not only the legal system and the regulatory bureaucrats enable talkers to impose high costs on the doers at low costs to themselves. So does the talkers' ready access to the media.

Talkers are usually more articulate than doers, since talk is their specialty. Moreover, they can stage demonstrations that the media will not only broadcast but give free air time for the talkers to make their accusations.

Jesse Jackson has made a science—and a lucrative occupation—out of accusations of "racism" against businesses. There is no way to prove that you are not a racist, so the doer's choice is to pay off the talker or face losses of customers from either the bad publicity or an organized boycott.

These kinds of incentives and constraints help explain a strange anomaly that many have noticed—big corporations contributing much more to left-wing causes than to conservative or libertarian causes.

"For every $1.00 major corporations gave to conservative and free-market groups, they gave $4.61 to organizations seeking more government," according to a study by the Capital Research Center, a Washington think tank.

Why? According to the Capital Research Center: "Many advocacy groups win corporate funding by threatening lawsuits and boycotts and by petitioning government regulatory bodies. Regulatory policies, in particular, give corporations a built-in incentive to pay-off left-wing activists."

Talkers cultivate an aura of morally lofty goals, while depicting doers as mere selfish money-grubbers. But professional talkers are pretty good at collecting big bucks, some through legalized extortion and others by creating huge windfall gains as their building restrictions cause housing prices to skyrocket.

The talkers' admirers include people struggling to pay inflated apartment rents and make huge monthly mortgage payments. Even their victims often admire the talkers more than the doers.

Liberals and Class

The new trinity among liberal intellectuals is race, class and gender. Defining any of these terms is not easy, but it is also not difficult for liberals, because they seldom bother to define them at all.

The oldest, and perhaps still the most compelling, of these concerns is class. In the vision of the left, we are born, live, and die in a particular class—unless, of course, we give power to the left to change all that.

The latest statistics seized upon to support this class-ridden view of America and other Western societies show that most people in a given part of the income distribution are the children of other people born into that same part of the income distribution.

Among men born in families in the bottom 25 percent of income earners only 32 percent end up in the top half of the income distribution. And among men born to families in the top 25 percent in income earners, only 34 percent end up down in the bottom half.

How startling is that?

More to the point, does this show that people are trapped in poverty or can coast through life on their parents' wealth? Does it show that "society" denies "access" to the poor?

Could it just possibly show that the kind of values and behavior which lead a family to succeed or fail are also likely to be passed on to their children and lead them to succeed or fail as well? If so, how much can government policy—

liberal or conservative—change that in any fundamental way?

One recent story attempting to show that upward mobility is a "myth" in America today nevertheless noted in passing that many recent immigrants and their children have had "extraordinary upward mobility."

If this is a class-ridden society denying "access" to upward mobility to those at the bottom, why is it that immigrants can come here at the bottom and then rise to the top?

One obvious reason is that many poor immigrants come here with very different ambitions and values from that of poor Americans born into our welfare state and imbued with notions growing out of attitudes of dependency and resentments of other people's success.

The fundamental reason that many people do not rise is not that class barriers prevent it but that they do not develop the skills, values and attitudes which cause people to rise.

The liberal welfare state means they don't have to and liberal multiculturalism says they don't need to change their values because one culture is just as good as another. In other words, liberalism is not part of the solution, but part of the problem.

Racism is supposed to put insuperable barriers in the path of non-whites anyway, so why knock yourself out trying? This is another deadly message, especially for the young.

But if immigrants from Korea or India, Vietnamese refugees, and others can come here and move right on up the ladder, despite not being white, why are black and white Americans at the bottom more likely to stay at the bottom?

The same counterproductive and self-destructive attitudes toward education, work and ordinary civility found in many of America's ghettos can also be found in lower-class British communities. Anyone who doubts it should read British doctor Theodore Dalrymple's book *Life at the Bottom* about the white lower class communities in which he has worked.

These chaotic and violence-prone communities in Britain do not have the excuse of racism or a legacy of slavery. What they do have in common with similar communities in the United States is a similar reliance on the welfare state and a similar set of intellectuals making excuses for their behavior and denouncing anyone who wants them to change their ways.

The latest round of statistics emboldens more intellectuals to blame "society" for the failure of many people at the bottom to rise to the top. Realistically, if nearly a third of people born to families in the bottom quarter of income earners rise into the top half, that is not a bad record.

If more were doing so in the past, that does not necessarily mean that "society" is holding them down more today. It may easily mean that the welfare state and liberal ideology both make it less necessary today for them to change their own behavior.

Liberals and Class: Part II

Someone once defined a social problem as a situation in which the real world differs from the theories of intellectuals. To the intelligentsia, it follows, as the night follows the day, that it is the real world that is wrong and which needs to change.

Having imagined a world in which each individual has the same probability of success as anyone else, intellectuals have been shocked and outraged that the real world is nowhere close to that ideal. Vast amounts of time and resources have been devoted to trying to figure out what is stopping this ideal from being realized—as if there was ever any reason to expect it to be realized.

Despite all the words and numbers thrown around when discussing this situation, the terms used are so sloppy that it is hard even to know what the issues are, much less how to resolve them.

Back in mid-May, both the *New York Times* and the *Wall Street Journal* had front-page stories about class differences and class mobility. The *Times'* article was the first in a long series that is still going on a month later. Both papers reached similar conclusions, based on a similar sloppy use of the word "mobility."

The *Times* referred to "the chance of moving up from one class to another" and the *Wall Street Journal* referred to "the odds that a child born in poverty will climb to wealth." But the odds or probabilities against something happening are no measure of whether opportunity exists.

Anyone who saw me play basketball and saw Michael Jordan play basketball when we were both youngsters would have given odds of a zillion to one that he was more likely to make the NBA than I was. Does that mean I was denied opportunity or access, that there were barriers put up against me, that the playing field was not level?

Or did it mean that Michael Jordan—and virtually everyone else—played basketball a lot better than I did?

A huge literature on social mobility often pays little or no attention to the fact that different individuals and groups have different skills, desires, attitudes and numerous other factors, including luck. If mobility is defined as being free to move, then we can all have the same mobility, even if some end up moving faster than others and some of the others do not move at all.

A car capable of going 100 miles an hour can sit in a garage all year long without moving. But that does not mean that it has no mobility.

When each individual and each group trails the long shadow of their cultural history, they are unlikely even to want to do the same things, much less be willing to put out the same efforts and make the same sacrifices to achieve the same goals. Many are like the car that is sitting still in the garage, even though it is capable of going 100 mph.

So long as each generation raises its own children, people from different backgrounds are going to be raised with different values and habits. Even in a world with zero barriers to upward mobility, they would move at different speeds and in different directions.

If there is less upward movement today than in the past, that is by no means proof that external barriers are responsible. The welfare state and multiculturalism both reduce the incentives of the poor to adopt new ways of life that would help them rise up the economic ladder. The last thing the poor need is another dose of such counterproductive liberal medicine.

Many comparisons of "classes" are in fact comparisons of people in different income brackets—but three-quarters of Americans in the lowest 20 percent move up to the highest 40 percent over time. Yet those who are obsessed with classes treat people in different brackets as if they were classes permanently stuck in those brackets.

The *New York Times* series even makes a big deal about disparities in income and lifestyle between the rich and the super-rich. But it is hard to get worked up over the fact that some poor devil has to make do flying his old propeller-driven plane, while someone further up the income scale flies around a mile or two higher in his twin-engine luxury jet.

Only if you have overdosed on disparities are you likely to wax indignant over things like that.

Liberals and Class: Part III

Sometimes it seems as if liberals have a genius for producing an unending stream of ideas that are counterproductive for the poor, whom they claim to be helping. Few of these notions are more counterproductive than the idea of "menial work" or "dead-end jobs."

Think about it: Why do employers pay people to do "menial" work? Because the work has to be done. What useful purpose is served by stigmatizing work that someone is going to have to do anyway?

Is emptying bed pans in a hospital menial work? What would happen if bed pans didn't get emptied? Let people stop emptying bed pans for a month and there would be bigger problems than if sociologists stopped working for a year.

Having someone who can come into a home to clean and cook and do minor chores around the house can be a godsend to someone who is an invalid or who is suffering the infirmities of age—and who does not want to be put into an institution. Someone who can be trusted to take care of small children is likewise a treasure.

Many people who do these kinds of jobs do not have the education, skills or experience to do more complex kinds of work. Yet they can make a real contribution to society while earning money that keeps them off welfare.

Many low-level jobs are called "dead-end jobs" by liberal intellectuals because these jobs have no promotions ladder.

But it is superficial beyond words to say that this means that people in such jobs have no prospect of rising economically.

Many people at all levels of society, including the richest, have at some point or other worked at jobs that had no promotions ladder, so-called "dead-end jobs." The founder of the NBC network began work as a teenager hawking newspapers on the streets. Billionaire Ross Perot began with a paper route.

You don't get promoted from such jobs. You use the experience, initiative, and discipline that you develop in such work to move on to something else that may be wholly different. People who start out flipping hamburgers at McDonald's seldom stay there for a full year, much less for life.

Dead-end jobs are the kinds of jobs I have had all my life. But, even though I started out delivering groceries in Harlem, I don't deliver groceries there any more. I moved on to other jobs—most of which have not had any promotions ladders.

My only official promotion in more than half a century of working was from associate professor to full professor at UCLA. But that was really just a pay increase, rather than a real promotion, because associate professors and full professors do the same work.

Notions of menial jobs and dead-end jobs may be just shallow misconceptions among the intelligentsia but they are a deadly counterproductive message to the poor. Refusing to get on the bottom rung of the ladder usually means losing your chance to move up the ladder.

Welfare can give you money but it cannot give you job experience that will move you ahead economically. Selling drugs on the streets can get you more money than welfare but it cannot give you experience that you can put on a job application. And if you decide to sell drugs all your life, that life can be very short.

Back around the time of the First World War, a young black man named Paul Williams studied architecture and then accepted a job as an office boy at an architectural firm. He agreed to work for no pay, though after he showed up the company decided to pay him something, after all.

What they paid him would probably be dismissed today as "chump change." But what Paul Williams wanted from that company was knowledge and experience, more so than money.

He went on to create his own architectural company, designing everything from churches and banks to mansions for movie stars—and contributing to the design of the theme building at Los Angeles International Airport.

The real chumps are those who refuse to start at the bottom for "chump change." Liberals who encourage such attitudes may think of themselves as friends of the poor but they do more harm than enemies.

The Autism "Spectrum"

When Billy's mother sees her twelve-year-old son's popularity with teammates on his baseball team, she thinks back to predictions made when he was a pre-schooler that he would have so much trouble making friends that, among other things, he would probably never be able to get married and have children.

It is a little early for Billy to be getting married, but the predictions have been off by miles so far. Why were such dire predictions made in the first place?

Billy was late in beginning to talk and was supposed to have been autistic. Once that label had been put on him, nothing could change the minds of those who saw him that way.

Contrary evidence from his emotional attachment to a little girl in his pre-school was dismissed, even though the two of them were inseparable on the playground—and even though an inability to form emotional attachments is at the heart of autism.

There is another kind of dogmatism from people who are not going to give up on the "autism" label. That is redefining the word to include a wide range of children who are said to be on the autism "spectrum." Billy's mother raised a fundamental question that seems to have eluded many professionals: Would you say that someone who is near-sighted is on the "blindness spectrum"?

What would we gain by such manipulations of words? And what would we lose?

Blindness, like autism, is a major tragedy. When some little toddler doesn't see quite as well as other kids, and may need glasses, what would be the point of alarming his parents by saying that he is on the blindness spectrum?

In the decade that has passed since I organized a support group of parents of late-talking children in September 1993, I have heard from literally hundreds of parents of such children, many of them re-living the anguish they went through when their children were diagnosed as autistic.

With the passage of time, it has become obvious that many of these children are not autistic, any more than Billy is autistic. Parents who are grateful that the hasty diagnoses their children received were wrong are also bitter that such labels were applied so irresponsibly—often by people who never set foot in a medical school or received any comparable training that would qualify them to diagnose autism. But professionals have been wrong as well.

Instead of trying to reduce mistaken diagnoses that inflict needless trauma on parents and often direct children into programs for autistic children that are counterproductive for children who are not autistic, the expansive new concept of an "autism spectrum" provides wiggle room for those who were wrong, so that they can avoid having to admit that they were wrong—and avoid having to stop being wrong.

It is as if people who told you that your little toddler would need a seeing-eye dog are able to get off the hook when the passage of time proved them wrong by saying that, because he now wears glasses, he is still on the blindness spectrum.

There is another aspect of this that affects the public in general and the taxpayers in particular. Time and again over the past decade, parents have told me that they have been urged to allow their late-talking children to be labeled "autistic" so that they would be eligible to get government money that can be used for speech therapy or whatever else the child might need.

Against that background, consider the widely publicized statistics showing an unbelievable rate of increase in autism in recent years. Is this a real change in the same thing or a redefinition of words? Worse yet, is this the corrupting effect of government money intended for children who are genuinely autistic?

Apparently no one knows the answer. But what is very disturbing is that such questions are not even on the agenda.

Studies of highly intelligent children show them to have many of the characteristics that can get them labeled autistic if they happen to be late in beginning to speak. For example, the book *Gifted Children* by Ellen Winner shows that such children "often play alone and enjoy solitude," have "almost obsessive interests" and "prodigious memories."

Such characteristics are an open invitation to false diagnoses of autism by those who are on the irresponsibility spectrum.

The High Cost of Busybodies

It was gratifying news when fans around the country volunteered to donate their kidneys to basketball star Alonzo Mourning, who would otherwise have to cut short his career because of life-threatening medical problems with his own kidneys. However, the head of the New York Organ Donor Network said that it was a shame "that it takes a personal tragedy of someone famous like Alonzo to raise awareness" of a need for organ donations when 17 people on the waiting list die daily.

What is an even bigger shame is that laws block the supply of organs to people who may be dying needlessly as a result.

Take the case of Alonzo Mourning and suppose that not a living soul was willing to give him a kidney. He was going to have to either give up a $23 million a year career or risk death by subjecting his kidneys to the stresses of playing. Suppose the law allowed him to offer half of that amount to anyone who would sell him a kidney.

Do you doubt that there would be someone willing to part with a kidney for that kind of money? There might well have been even more people willing to part with a kidney than there were.

I happen to know a lady who was born with three kidneys—and in poverty. Do you think she would have minded parting with a spare kidney, in order to have a better life for herself and her children?

With more than 80,000 people on waiting lists for various

organs, and many dying while waiting, why prevent such transactions? One reason is that third parties would be offended.

You know the words and the music: How terrible that the rich can buy other people's body parts—and that the poor are so desperate as to sell.

If you think that you have a right to forbid other people from making such voluntary transactions, then you are saying that your delicate sensibilities are more important than the poverty or even the deaths of other people.

Banning organ sales does nothing to make the poor less poor. Nor do those 80,000+ people on waiting lists have to be rich. Three economists have estimated the cost of buying an organ in a free market at a price well within most people's budgets.

Donors could collect the money while living, in exchange for permission to remove the organ after their death. They could also authorize an organ transplant from a family member already dead.

The trump card of the left is always "the poor." But, if our real concern is the poor, the money to pay for them to receive organ transplants can be paid by others, whether the government or philanthropic individuals or organizations.

Here as in numerous other cases, what it would cost to take care of the poor is a small fraction of what it costs to finance huge programs that cover—and restrict—everybody.

It is not just the political left that stands in the way of allowing more organs to be made available through the free market to those who are dying. An article in the neo-conservative quarterly *The Public Interest* argued that non-profit organizations alone should be allowed to handle any financial transactions if organ sales are permitted.

The fact that some organizations call the money they

make "profits" and others do not seems to impress some people. But one of the biggest non-profit organizations dealing in organ donations today spends no more than half the money it takes in on actual organ donations, according to *Forbes* magazine. This non-profit paragon has even stonewalled the federal government on what they are spending the rest of the money for.

Like other bureaucracies, the organ donation bureaucracy produces arbitrary rules. These rules have kept people from getting organ transplants that were available because they were not available in the particular regions where they happened to live.

The fundamental problem is not simply how to ration the existing shortage of organs. The problem is how to reduce the shortage by getting more organs by lifting the ban on sales.

People who think that they should be the arbiters of other people's destinies are bad enough when they want to choose winners and losers in industry and commerce. But when they want to choose who lives and who dies, that is a little much.

The High Cost of Busybodies: Part II

A reader wrote recently about his father, who has been a farmer, but is now ready to retire. His father figured on selling his land to get some money for his golden retirement years. But he found that he cannot get anywhere near the land's market value because busybodies have passed laws that destroy most of that value by restricting the sale of farmland.

The rationale for such laws is "preserving farmland." Think about it. Two of our biggest problems today are obesity and agricultural surpluses. The last thing we need to do is keep farmland from being sold to those who want to use it to build housing, businesses or other things.

Even if we accept, for the sake of argument, the notion that farmland needs to be preserved in order to serve some great national interest, the Constitution of the United States says that private property cannot be taken by the government without just compensation.

When the government destroys half the value of someone's property, that is the same thing economically as taking half of that property. But, because the farmer is left owning all his land, judges have let politicians get away with essentially confiscating much of its value without having to pay any compensation at all.

People who lead crusades to preserve farmland usually know little about farming and less about economics. Yet they think that they have a right to prevent other people from making mutually agreeable transactions, when that goes against the fetishes of third parties.

Busybodies may flatter themselves that they are wiser or nobler than others—which is perhaps the biggest benefit from being a busybody—but the Constitution of the United States says that all citizens are entitled to the equal protection of the laws.

In other words, people who want to wring their hands about farmlands or wetlands, or about some obscure toad or snake, have no more rights than people who don't care two cents about such things. It is hard for those who have presumptions of being the morally anointed to accept that, but that is what the Constitution says.

Unfortunately, too many judges are ready to fudge or fake what the Constitution says because they too share the vision of the anointed. So they downgrade property rights and let third parties impose their pet notions on others, using the power of government to violate the rights of those who do not agree with them.

What makes a lot of the talk about "preserving" or "saving" farmland or other things as phony as a three-dollar bill is that the real agenda is often very different—namely, keeping out people who do not have the income or the inclination to share the lifestyle of the anointed.

The real reason for preventing farmland from being sold to those who might build housing on it is that the people who live in that housing might not be as upscale as those already living nearby. Developers—heaven forbid—might build apartments or townhouses in a community where people live in single-family homes.

In other words, developers might build some of that "affordable housing" that some people talk so much about and do so much to prevent.

The rationale for laws forbidding farmers from selling their land to whoever wants to buy it is that existing residents have a right to "preserve the character" of "our community." But these lofty words are lying words.

Only sloppy thinking allows sloppy words to pass muster. There is no such thing as "our community." Nobody owns the whole community. Each individual owns his or her own property—and other individuals have the same right to own or sell their own property.

If the busybodies want to put their money where their mouth is, they can buy up the farmland themselves and then they can legitimately prevent anybody from building anything on it. But verbal sleight-of-hand is no justification for denying others the same rights that they claim for themselves.

If there were some way to add up all the costs imposed by busybodies—on everyone from farmers to people wanting organ transplants—it would probably be greater than the national debt.

The High Cost of Busybodies:
Part III

One of the staples of liberal hand-wringing is a need for "affordable housing." Last year, the standard liberal solution—more government spending—was proposed in a televised speech at the National Press Club in Washington, in a report billed as a "new vision."

This year, supply and demand made front-page news in the *New York Times* of November 29, 2003: "Apartment Glut Forces Owners to Cut Rents in Much of U.S." As apartment vacancy rates reached an all-time high of 10 percent nationwide, landlords have been cutting rents, both directly and by such gimmicks as giving gift certificates and allowing so many rent-free months for new tenants.

Buried deep inside the second section of the newspaper are facts that completely undermine the liberal notion that high housing costs are a "national crisis" calling for a "national solution" by the federal government.

Far from being a national crisis of affordable housing, outrageous rents and astronomical home prices are largely confined to a relatively few places along the east and west coasts. Rent per square foot of apartment space in San Francisco is more than double what it is in Denver, Dallas, or Kansas City, and nearly three times as high as in Memphis. Home prices show even greater disparities.

The *Times* story notes that the difference between apartment rents in coastal California and those in the rest of the country is widening. It also refers to cities "where land is abundant but building regulations are not," where "housing costs were already among the least expensive of the country's urban areas."

Wait a minute. Vacant land is at least as abundant in coastal California as in places with far lower rents and home prices. More than half the land in huge San Mateo County, adjacent to San Francisco, is vacant and is kept that way by law.

The difference is not in the land but in the politics. The long-time dominance of liberal Democrats from San Francisco to Silicon Valley has meant that restrictions on land use have proliferated and the costs of building anything have skyrocketed as a result of environmental red tape, bureaucratic delays, and legal harassment by activists of various sorts.

The *New York Times* story refers gingerly to "many cities on the coasts, where new construction is more difficult" than in the rest of the country. To put it more bluntly, liberals have driven housing prices sky high by forbidding, restricting, and harassing the building of housing.

In turn, this has meant driving people of modest incomes out of the communities where they work. Nurses, teachers and policemen, for example, typically live far away from places like San Francisco or Silicon Valley, and have to commute long distances to and from work.

All the while, liberals wring their hands about a lack of affordable housing, about urban sprawl, and about congested highways. In their puzzlement about the causes of all these things, they never think to look in the mirror.

While the *Times* story noted in passing "the growing gap between the cost of living in the Northeast and parts of California and the cost of living almost anywhere else," it does not take the next fatal step of connecting the dots.

It is precisely in the places that have been most

dominated by liberals for the longest times that housing costs and other costs of living have been driven up to levels that force many people out of town and even out of state. New York and California are losing more of their native-born populations than any other states and only influxes of immigrants help conceal that fact in gross statistics on population.

It was not always like this. Prior to the 1970s, home prices in California were comparable to those in the rest of the country. Today they are more than three times as high.

What happened during the 1970s was the beginning of the drastic restrictions on building pushed by liberal Democrats in general and environmental extremists in particular.

The High Cost of Busybodies:
Part IV

During the gasoline shortage that began in 1979, motorists were often waiting in long lines of cars at filling stations—sometimes for hours—in hopes of reaching the pump before the gas ran out. The ways that Ted Kennedy and Ronald Reagan proposed to deal with this situation speak volumes about the difference between the left and the right.

Senator Kennedy said: "We must adopt a system of gasoline rationing without delay," in "a way that demands a fair sacrifice from all Americans."

Ronald Reagan said that we must get rid of price controls on petroleum, so that there won't be a shortage in the first place. One of his first acts after becoming president was to end federal price controls. Lines at filling stations disappeared.

Despite angry outcries from liberals that gas prices would skyrocket as Big Oil "gouged" the public, in reality prices came down within months and continued falling for years. More taxes were piled onto gasoline by the government but the real cost of the gas itself hit a new low by 1993.

"Fairness" is one of the great mantras of the left. Since everyone has his own definition of fairness, that word is a blank check for the expansion of government power. What "fairness" means in practice is that third parties—busybodies—can prevent mutual accommodations by others.

Busybodies not only prevent farmers from selling their land to people who would build housing on it, they prevent people on waiting lists for organ transplants from paying someone to donate a kidney or a liver that can be the difference between life and death.

Like Ted Kennedy, the organ donation bureaucracy is preoccupied with imposing their notions of fairness on people who are on waiting lists. And, like Senator Kennedy, they have no interest in freeing people to reduce or eliminate the shortage, which could make fairness in rationing a moot issue.

Such thinking—or lack of thinking—is not new. Back in the 18th century, Adam Smith wrote of politicians who devote "a most unnecessary attention" to things that would work themselves out better in a free market.

What is conventionally called "the free market" is in reality free people making their own mutual accommodations with other free people. It is one of the many tactical mistakes of conservatives to use an impersonal phrase to describe very personal choices and actions by people when they are not hamstrung by third parties.

When the issue is posed as "the free market" versus "compassion for the poor," which do you think is likely to win out? Our bloated and ever-growing welfare state—from which the poor get a very small share, by the way—answers that question.

The fatal attraction of government is that it allows busybodies to impose decisions on others without paying any price themselves. That enables them to act as if there were no price, even when there are ruinous prices—paid by others.

Millions of people's lives are made worse in innumerable ways, in order that a relative handful of busybodies can feel important and superior. Artificially high land prices in those places where busybodies reign politically, based on land use restrictions, make housing costs a crushing burden on people of average incomes.

Some of the busybodies imagine that they are preventing "over-crowding" or "traffic congestion." But what they are really doing is moving the crowding somewhere else, since people have to live somewhere, regardless.

As for traffic congestion, that is made needlessly worse because of long-distance commuting by those people whose incomes will not permit them to live in the artificially more expensive communities where they work. It is not uncommon in liberal California communities for many commuters to spend 3 or 4 hours a day in their cars, fighting traffic—all for the greater glory of those with the mantra of "open space."

Because of the innumerable problems caused by busybodies who devote "a most unnecessary attention" to things that would be better without them, the rest of us should devote some very necessary attention to these busybodies and their sloppy arguments.

"Partial Truth" Abortion

Now that a federal judge has ruled that the law banning "partial birth abortion" is unconstitutional, there is certain to be much media coverage of the issue as it makes its way up the appellate chain to the Supreme Court of the United States. How that will turn out legally is anybody's guess but the process will reveal at least as much about the media as it does about the law.

Many in the media resent any suggestion that they are either politically biased or that journalists' personal views stop them from doing a good professional job of accurately reporting the news. The way the issue of partial birth abortion has been reported—or not reported—gives the lie to such protests.

Whether you or they are for or against abortion in general or this specific procedure in particular, if the much proclaimed "public's right to know" means anything, it should mean that the readers and viewers should be told what a partial birth abortion is. Much of the liberal media fails that simple test completely.

Some in the media use only the opaque expression "late-term abortion," while others refer to the fact that some people call it a late-term abortion and others call it a partial birth abortion. But all this reporting about semantics is not telling the public just what it is that is being discussed in the first place.

Neither the defenders nor the critics are talking about semantics. They are talking about what is actually done—

and that is what a major part of the mainstream media refuses to tell us.

Even a quality news program like *The News Hour with Jim Lehrer* featured a debate earlier this year, with both sides represented—at the end of which the viewer still had no way to learn just what is a partial birth abortion or a "late-term abortion," as the liberals prefer to call it.

What happens is that a baby who is in the process of being born, with part of his body outside his mother's body and part still inside, is deliberately killed. One of the methods of doing this is to have his brains sucked out of his head by a device.

Although this is called an abortion, the late Senator Daniel Patrick Moynihan said that it seemed too much like infanticide to him. What keeps it from being murder, as far as the law is concerned, is that part of the baby's body is still inside the mother, so that this procedure can be classified as an abortion.

The American Medical Association some years ago said that there is no medical necessity for such an unusual procedure. Its purpose is not medical but legal: to keep the doctor and the mother from being indicted for killing a newborn baby.

Whether you are for or against this, you ought to know what you are for or against. But there are newspapers, TV programs, and whole networks that you could watch for years without ever finding out.

They have decided what you can be allowed to know. That is the real problem of media bias. If they report the news straight and let you make up your own mind, then what the journalists themselves do in the voting booth on election day is their own business.

The partial birth abortion issue is just one of those issues in which major parts of the media filter out facts that might lead you to take a position different from the one the journalists have.

When a white racist commits an atrocity against some black person, that is headline news across the country. But when a black racist does exactly the same thing to some white person, that is not likely to get the same publicity, if it is reported at all.

The liberal view that white racism is a major problem and a major explanation for other social problems is not allowed to be undermined by news which might suggest that racism is a curse of the whole human species. You cannot even assess where this racism is worse when only one kind of it is reported by much of the media.

Similarly, atrocities committed against homosexuals are big news but atrocities committed by homosexuals, including atrocities against children, are unlikely to see the light of day in much of the media. Neither is any statistical information on how homosexuals differ from the general population in life span, diseases or costs to the taxpayers for dealing with their diseases.

Filtering and spinning are not reporting. The public has a right to know that, but that right is too often aborted.

Lying about Yosemite

Yosemite National Park is one of the beauties of nature that has brought me back every year for more than 20 consecutive years. But, in recent years especially, there seem to be two Yosemites—the one discussed in the media and the one I see with my own eyes.

On the first day of my visit this year—June 6, 2004—there appeared one of the standard propaganda pieces on Yosemite in the *San Francisco Chronicle*, illustrated with the standard propaganda photographs.

They say the camera doesn't lie but it can do some serious misleading. A standard lie of the environmental extremists is that Yosemite is "over-crowded" and choked with bumper-to-bumper traffic. True to form, the *San Francisco Chronicle* shows a line of cars and a couple of pedestrians scooting between them.

The pedestrians ought to give a clue as to what is wrong with this picture. The cars are not moving along a street or highway. They are stopped and lining up. Cars get stopped at the entrance to the park to pay a fee to get in and they get stopped by road construction delays inside the park.

My wife and I were among those stopped for about 15 minutes at a road repair site. When traffic is stopped dead in its tracks for 15 minutes, you can collect quite a backup almost anywhere. In Yosemite, you can also collect misleading photographs to be used to advance the political agendas of environmental extremists.

Once past the construction site, the traffic in Yosemite

flowed far more smoothly than it does in San Francisco and parking spaces were far easier to find. For three days in a row, we had lunch at the popular Ahwahnee Hotel in Yosemite Valley and each time we had our choice of parking spaces in the main parking lot.

If anything, the traffic was somewhat lighter than it has been in some past years. We also had no trouble finding parking spaces at Glacier Point, Curry Village or any other place in the park where we decided to stop.

Why then the campaign of lies?

Groups like the Sierra Club and other environmental zealots have for years been trying to reduce the number of people visiting our national parks. They seem to think that our national parks are their own private property, and that it would be best if the unwashed masses are kept out as much as possible, leaving the backpackers to enjoy these parks in seclusion.

Like other special interest groups, the environmental extremists have a disproportionate influence on government officials, including in this case those who run the National Park Service. One of their coups has been to get the gas station in Yosemite Valley removed. The next nearest gas station is 13 miles outside the park and it charges more than $3 a gallon.

Was the gas station in Yosemite Valley spoiling some natural scenery? Far from it. It was part of a built-up area that included motel buildings, restaurants, and a gigantic parking lot. That parking lot remains, with something like a hundred cars on it and next to it is a very unattractive tent city.

Esthetics had nothing to do with removing the gas station. The environmental zealots know that the automobile is the key to ordinary people having access to the national parks. The more hassles are created for people driving automobiles, the more people will be discouraged from coming, advancing the goal of reserving the national parks for environmentalists and for those who live the lifestyle that the environmentalists approve of.

The essence of bigotry is denying other people the same free choices you have. Many of those who call themselves environmentalists could more accurately be called green bigots.

The automobile allows people to see Yosemite in their own ways and at their own pace, which is especially important for the elderly and for families with small children. But the park bureaucrats and the green bigots want to force people out of their cars and regiment them into buses, to be taken when, where and how the bureaucrats decide.

The restrictionists love to talk about the "fragile" environment and "saving" it for "future generations." No definition of "fragile" is offered. What this amounts to is saying that future generations of green bigots can keep out future generations of ordinary citizens and taxpayers.

Growing Old

Random thoughts about growing old:

Despite the problems that come with aging, I would not be a teenager again for $1,000 a day plus expenses.

I never really felt old until my younger brother retired.

This is the period of life that Disraeli referred to as "anecdotage."

Nothing is more ridiculous than discounts for senior citizens, when people in their sixties have far more wealth than people in their thirties.

These are my declining years. I decline all sorts of invitations and opportunities.

People who talk about "earlier and simpler times" are usually too young to remember those times—and how complicated they were.

An old body is like an old automobile, where the brakes need repairing today, the steering wheel next month and the transmission after that.

Looking at old photographs makes it hard for me to believe that I was ever that thin physically. And remembering some of the things I did in those days makes it hard to believe that I was ever that thin mentally.

You would think that young people, with decades of life ahead of them, would look further ahead and plan for the future more so than older people. But it is just the opposite. The young tend to be oriented to right now, while old timers think about the future of their children and grandchildren, and worry about where the country is heading in the years ahead.

They say you can't teach an old dog new tricks. But maybe the old dog already knows about tricks that only seem new to the young—and doesn't think much of those tricks.

When I was young, age forty seemed so ancient that I couldn't imagine what it would be like to be forty. Now I can barely remember what it was like to be forty.

Age gives you an excuse for not being very good at things that you were not very good at when you were young.

An old saying is that we are once a man and twice a child. The difference is that we more or less automatically have parents to look after us the first time, but whether we will have someone to show us the same love and care when we are at the other end of life is another story.

It is amazing—and appalling—how many people who are walking with the elderly try to pull them along faster than they want to go, or perhaps faster than they are able to go. What does this accomplish, except to create needless tension and stress? And how urgent is it to save a few seconds here and there?

When someone had to tell me that I was on a topless beach, I knew I was getting old.

Like so many people who are getting on in years, I am fine—so long as I remember that I am not fine.

The old are not really smarter than the young. It is just that we have already made the mistakes that the young are about to make, so we already know that these are mistakes and what the consequences are.

Some people age like fine wine and others just turn into vinegar.

Someone asked a man in his seventies at what age he

started to lose interest in women. "I don't know," he said. "But when it happens, I will tell you."

I urge my fellow old-timers to write their memoirs, just so that "revisionist" historians will not be able to get away with lying about the past.

More than once, after I woke up some morning feeling like I was twenty again, I did something that ended up with me on crutches or otherwise being reminded emphatically by my body that I was definitely not twenty again. Women may lie about their age to other people but men lie about their age to themselves.

When old-time Dodger pitching ace Don Newcombe was near the end of his career, someone asked him if he could still throw as hard as ever. "Yes, I throw the ball as hard as ever," he said. "But it just takes longer to get to the plate."

Oliver Wendell Holmes said it best: "If I could think that I had sent a spark to those who come after I should be ready to say Goodbye."

April Fools' Party

"This is your eyewitness news team, reporting from the big, posh April Fools' Day party at the Dewdrop Inn out at Moot Point, overlooking Dyer Straits. Everybody who is anybody is here.

"There's the karate expert Marshall Artz, timber heiress Lotta Wood, famous meteorologist Cole Winter, the British boxing sensation Battler Hastings, and the gossip columnist N.U. Endo. There's insurance magnate Justin Case, the famous efficiency expert Ben Dunn Wright, and Ivy University's dean of students, N. 'Loco' Prentiss.

"Let's talk with one of the guests. Excuse me, sir, what is your name?"

"Chester Mann."

"Are you related to that famous social justice advocate?"

"N.V. Mann? Yes."

"What kind of work do you do?"

"I run an automobile junk yard."

"What's the name of it? You might as well give it a free plug."

"Oedipus Wrecks."

"How are you enjoying the party?"

"Frankly, I am here only because my wife dragged me here."

"You don't like the party?"

"As Robinson Crusoe said, 'I don't like this atoll.'"

"As Napoleon said, 'What's your beef, Wellington?'"

"Oh, just the food, the drinks, and the people."

"Well, let me move along. Here's the famous author I. Wright, whose latest best-seller is a steamy novel about India titled *Whose Sari Now?* Incidentally, you look great in those long, flowing robes. Were you born in India?"

"No, Brooklyn."

"But I'll bet you did a lot of research in India?"

"Yes, mostly in the Punjab."

"What is it like to live in a country completely different from the Western world?"

"Actually Indians are not cut off from the Western world. For example, a friend of mine in the Punjab is obsessed with Western classical music."

"Likes his Beethoven and Bach, does he?"

"He's really obsessed with Haydn. He's a Haydn Sikh."

"Thank you. Let's go on to talk with some more guests. Here's the famous psychiatrist N.D. Nile, that sweet-looking actress Candy Barr and her sister Minnie who, I believe, is involved in hotels."

"Yes, I am. I have also had some hostel takeovers."

"Not everyone has been successful, of course. Over there is the well-known architect whose firm just went bankrupt— Frank Lloyd Wrong. Let's go over and see what he has to say.

"Sir, this is your eyewitness news team, checking up on how you are doing."

"Terrible! I am suffering from hardening of the arteries, curvature of the spine, cirrhosis of the liver. . ."

"Rumpole of the Bailey?"

"Absolutely."

"I understand that you are also an artist."

"Well, architecture is itself an art, as well as a science. But I also paint pictures, if that is what you mean."

"Yes, I remember a famous painting of yours showing a Rolex sitting on a half-eaten piece of watermelon."

"Yes, I called it 'Watch on the Rind.'"

"You are really on the cutting edge. Are all the people in your set like that?"

"No, actually. My uncle's wife, for example, is the most conservative person I know."

"Really?"

"Yes, I call her my status quo auntie."

"How conservative is she?"

"Once I asked her if she believed in gun control and she said: 'Yes! You've got to control those things or else the shot will go wild and miss the guy you are trying to blast!'"

"Over here is the famous weatherman, Cole Winter. He's usually pretty well informed, since he is on the same program as the news. Cole, what's the latest news?"

"A leopard was spotted in midtown Manhattan today!"

"That's not news. Leopards are spotted everywhere. Anyhow, it is time to return you to the studio. Happy April Fools' Day!"

PART VI

EDUCATION ISSUES

Choosing a College

When a student at New York University committed suicide recently, it was the 6th suicide at that same institution this year. The suicide of someone in the prime of life, and getting an education that promises a bright future, should be much rarer than it is. But NYU is not unique by any means.

Back when I taught at UCLA, one morning on my way to my office I saw an attractive and well-dressed young woman lying quietly in the bushes next to the building, apparently asleep. But the presence of police nearby alerted me to the fact that something was wrong. She had jumped from the roof of the building to her death.

When I taught at Cornell, it averaged a suicide a year.

Selecting a college for a young man or young woman to attend is more than a matter of looking up the rankings and seeing where the chances of admission look good. How the atmosphere of the college matches the personality of the individual can mean far more than anything in the college catalogue or the pretty brochures.

Some young people are not yet ready for coed living arrangements and the pressures and dangers that can lead to. Some are at risk on a campus with widespread drug usage. Some students can get very lonely when they just don't fit in.

Sometimes there is no one to turn to and sometimes the adults they turn to on campus have nothing but psychobabble to offer.

Late adolescence and early adulthood are among the most dangerous times in people's lives, when one foolish decision can destroy everything for which parents and children have invested time and efforts and hopes for years.

Too many know-it-alls in the high schools and colleges urge or warn parents to get out of the picture and let the child decide where to go and what to do. A high school counselor once told me that I would be "kept informed" of the decisions that she and my daughter were making as to which colleges to apply to.

Apparently there are enough sheep-like parents these days to let "experts" take control of their children at a critical juncture in their lives. But these "experts" suffer no consequences if their bright ideas lead some young person into disaster. It is the parents who will be left to pick up the pieces.

Too often parents are pushed to the sideline in the name of the child's need for freedom and autonomy. But what is presented to parents as a need to set their children free as young adults is too often in fact abandoning those children to the control of others. The stakes are too high to let that happen.

From the moment a student sets foot on a college campus, a whole apparatus of indoctrination can go into motion, in the name of "orientation," so as to mold each young mind to politically correct attitudes on everything from sex to "social justice."

Colleges used to say that their job was to teach the student how to think, not what to think. Today, most colleges are in the business of teaching the student what to think or "feel."

Many colleges—even many of the most prestigious—lack any real curriculum, but they seldom lack an ideological agenda. Too often they use students as guinea pigs for fashionable notions about how to live their own lives.

As for education, students can go through many colleges selecting courses cafeteria-style, and graduate in complete ignorance of history, science, economics, and many other subjects, even while clutching a costly diploma with a big name on it.

Students who make more astute choices from the cafeteria of courses can still get a good education at the same colleges where their classmates get mush. But seldom is there any curriculum that ensures a good education, even at prestigious colleges.

Parents need to stay involved in the process of choosing a college. They need to visit college campuses before making application decisions—and remember to take their skepticism with them. They also need to ask blunt questions and not take smooth generalities for an answer.

An indispensable guide to the atmosphere on various college campuses, and the presence or absence of a real curriculum, is a 971-page book titled *Choosing the Right College*. It is head-and-shoulders above all the other college guides.

Among other things, it tells you which colleges have a real curriculum, rather than a cafeteria of courses, as well as the kind of atmosphere each campus has. The latter is always important and sometimes can even be a matter of life and death.

The Idiocy of "Relevance"

One of the many fashionable idiocies that cause American schools to produce results inferior to those in other countries is the notion that education must be "relevant" to the students—and especially to minority students with a different subculture.

It is absurd to imagine that students can determine in advance what will turn out to be relevant to their progress as adults. Relevance is not something you can predict. It is something you discover after the fact—and after you have left school and are out in the real world.

When I was in high school, I was puzzled when a girl I knew told me that she was studying economics, because I had no idea what that was. It never occurred to me to take economics, so it was certainly not something that seemed relevant to me at the time.

Had someone told me then that I would someday spend more than 20 years as an economist at a think tank, I wouldn't have known what they were talking about, because I had no idea what a think tank was either.

When students are going through medical school, they may not see the relevance of all the things they are taught there. But someday they may have a patient at death's door, whose life may depend on how well the doctor remembers something he was taught in medical school—and whose relevance may not have been all that clear to him at the time.

People who have already been out in the real world,

practicing for years whatever their particular specialty might be, have some basis for determining which things are relevant enough to go into a curriculum to teach those who follow. The idea that students can determine relevance in advance is one of the many counterproductive notions to come out of the 1960s.

The fetish of "relevance" has been particularly destructive in the education of minority students at all levels. If the students do not see immediately how what they are studying applies to their lives in the ghetto, then it is supposed to be irrelevant.

How are these students ever going to get out of the poverty of the ghetto unless they learn to function in ways that are more economically productive? Even if they spend all their lives in the ghetto, if they are to spend them in such roles as doctors or engineers, then they are going to have to study things that are not peculiar ("relevant") to the ghetto.

Worst of all, those teachers who teach minority students things like math and science, whose relevance the students do not see, may encounter resistance and resentment, while those teachers who pander to minority students by turning their courses into rap sessions and ethnic navel-gazing exercises capture their interest and allegiance.

Some educators embrace relevance out of expediency, rather than conviction or confusion. It is the path of least resistance, though that path seldom leads upward. By the time minority students get out into the real world and discover the uselessness of what they were taught in "relevant" courses, it is too late for them—but they are no longer the teachers' responsibility.

Even as a graduate student in economics, I did not see the relevance of a little article by Friedrich Hayek, titled "The Use of Knowledge in Society," that was assigned reading in Milton Friedman's course at the University of Chicago. A few years later, however, I was beginning my own teaching career and had to teach a course on the Soviet economy—about which I knew nothing.

As I read through many studies of the Soviet economy in preparation for teaching my course, and was puzzled by all the strange and counterproductive economic practices in the Soviet Union, it then began to dawn on me that what Hayek had said applied to these otherwise inexplicable Soviet actions. For the first time, years later, I saw the relevance of what he had written.

Fast forward another 15 years. I was now writing a book that would be a landmark in my career. It was titled *Knowledge and Decisions*—a 400-page book building on what Hayek had said in a little essay.

Just a few years ago, I was stopped on the streets of San Francisco by a young black man who shook my hand and told me that reading *Knowledge and Decisions* had changed his life. He had seen the relevance of these ideas—at a younger age than I had.

Julian Stanley and
Bright Children

Bright children and their parents have lost a much-needed friend with the death of Professor Julian Stanley of Johns Hopkins University. For decades he not only researched and ran programs for intellectually gifted students, he became their leading advocate in books and articles.

His efforts were very much needed. Unusually bright children are too often treated like stepchildren by the American educational system.

While all sorts of special classes and special schools are created for various categories of students, there is resistance and even hostility to the idea of creating special classes or schools for intellectually gifted students.

Not only are such elite public schools as New York's Stuyvesant High School and the Bronx High School of Science rare, they are under political pressure to admit students on other bases besides pure academic achievement. So is San Francisco's Lowell High School, where ethnic "balance" affects admissions decisions.

While it is well known that the average American student does poorly on international tests, what is not so well known is that gifted American students lag particularly far behind their foreign counterparts.

Professor Julian Stanley pointed out that the performance level of gifted American students "is well below both the level of their own potential and the achievement levels of previous U.S. generations." In other words, our brightest kids have been going downhill even faster than our average kids.

Part of the reason is undoubtedly the general dumbing down of American education since the 1960s but what has also been happening since the 1960s has been a preoccupation with the "self-esteem" of mediocre students and a general hostility to anything that might be construed as intellectual elitism.

Even classes in so-called "gifted and talented" programs are too often just more of the same level of work as other students do, or trendy projects, but not work at a greater intellectual depth.

Sometimes, as Professor Stanley has pointed out, it is just busy work, in order to keep bright students from being bored and restless when classes are being taught at a pace far too slow for very intelligent youngsters.

It is not at all uncommon for the brightest students to become problem students in their boredom and frustration, to develop negative attitudes towards education and society—and to fail to develop their inborn talents.

Julian Stanley did not just criticize existing practices. He created special programs for unusually bright high school students on weekends and during the summer at Johns Hopkins University. The success of these programs has inspired similar programs at Purdue University and elsewhere.

Such programs have not only produced academic benefits, the gifted students in such programs have expressed an almost pathetic gratitude for finally being in a setting where they are comfortable with their peers and are viewed positively by their teachers.

In regular public school classrooms, these gifted students have been too often resented by their classmates and their teachers alike. Some teachers have seemed glad to be able to catch them in occasional mistakes.

Given the low academic records of most public school teachers, it is hard to imagine their being enthusiastic about kids so obviously brighter than they were—and often brighter than they are. No small part of the gross neglect of gifted students in our public schools is the old story of the dog in the manger.

Julian Stanley made a unique contribution to the development of gifted children, both directly through his program at Johns Hopkins and indirectly through his research and advocacy. Fortunately, he is survived by collaborators in these efforts, such as Professors Camilla Persson Benbow and David Lubinski of Vanderbilt University.

The effort must go on, both to stop the great waste of gifted students, whose talents are much needed in the larger society, and for the humane purpose of relieving the frustration and alienation of youngsters whose only crime is being born with more intellectual potential than most of those around them.

For What Purpose?

It has been said that, when Ronald Reagan was governor of California, someone told him that admitting students to the University of California on individual performance alone could mean that all the students at Berkeley might be Asian Americans.

"So what?" was the Gipper's response.

Like many other Reagan remarks, it cut through mountains of nonsense and knocked over numerous houses of cards that keep the intelligentsia wringing their hands. A classic example is a recent *New York Times* story that said: "Asians gain when affirmative action ends. Other minorities don't. What's fair?"

Let's go back to square one. Why do universities exist in the first place? Is it to parcel out benefits to different racial or ethnic groups? If so, why not just give them money? Do universities exist to be fair—whatever that means? If fair means equal chances or proportional representation, then why not make admissions a lottery?

All too many people in college admissions offices talk and act as if their job is to hand out goodies to those who seem most deserving, in terms of how well they used whatever particular opportunities they happen to have had.

In other words, if student *A* went to a top-notch high school and scored 1500 on the SATs, while student *B* went to a mediocre high school and scored 1300, then student *B* may be admitted and student *A* denied admission if the little tin gods in the admissions office decide that *B* made better use of his limited opportunities.

You couldn't make up anything as silly as this. Educational institutions do not exist to reward people for their past but to prepare them for the future. The taxpayers and donors who are supporting these institutions with their hard-earned money are doing so to benefit the society that these graduates will be serving, not to allow bureaucrats to hand out pork barrel benefits to individuals or groups.

In all the swirl of words around the issue of affirmative action in college and university admissions—including the endlessly repeated mantra of "diversity"—there is seldom a single word about serving the public by admitting those who have the academic skills to put the educational resources to the best use.

If a disproportionate number of those who can master the skills that educational institutions provide are Asian Americans, then as the Gipper said, "So what?"

Do you want to fly in planes flown by the best qualified pilots available or in planes flown by quota pilots or by pilots whose life stories were most appealing to those on admissions committees? If you are going to have heart surgery, do you want the best surgeon you can get or do you want a surgeon who had to overcome a lot of handicaps just to make it through medical school?

Would you be offended to have your life saved by someone who had easily become the best surgeon around because he was born in the lap of privilege and always had the finest education available, regardless of how much it cost? Would it bother you if he was Asian American or even—heaven help us—a WASP?

Institutions and occupations exist for a purpose—and that purpose is not to provide a statistical picture that is pleasing for those people who are preoccupied with statistical pictures. Food and shelter, housing and health, life and death, are among the many things that depend on how well institutions function and how well people do their jobs.

These things are too important to sacrifice so that busybodies can feel important directing other people's lives. Indeed, the freedom of those other people is too important to be sacrificed for the sake of third parties' vanity.

Anyone who is serious about wanting to help minority young people must know that the place to start is at precisely the other end of the educational process. That means beginning in the earliest grades teaching reading, math and other mental skills on which their future depends. But that would mean clashing with the teachers' unions and their own busybody agenda of propaganda and psychological manipulation in the classrooms.

The path of least resistance is to give minority youngsters a lousy education and then admit them to college by quotas. With a decent education, they wouldn't need the quotas.

School Performances

Everyone knows that black students in general do not perform as well in school as white students, much less Asian American students. But few realize how painfully large the gap is. Even fewer know that there are particular black schools, even in low-income neighborhoods, where students perform above the national average.

Discussing racial gaps in education is taboo in some quarters. But this subject is discussed deeply and thoroughly in a new book titled *No Excuses: Closing the Racial Gap in Learning* by Abigail Thernstrom of the Manhattan Institute and Stephan Thernstrom of Harvard. They are also the authors of the best book on race relations—*America in Black and White*—so there are high expectations for this new book.

No Excuses lives up to those expectations. If you read just one book about American education all year, this should be the book. It not only goes into the causes and cures of racial disparities in education, in the process it punctures many of the fads, dogmas, and pious hypocrisies of the education establishment.

First, the existing gap: Black high school students graduate an average of four years behind white students in academic skills. In other words, the high school diplomas they receive are given—not earned—for a junior high school education.

The excuses for this range across the spectrum from poverty to racism and even innate lack of ability. Yet none of these excuses stands up to the facts.

As the Thernstroms show, there are some schools where the students are equally poor and equally black, where test scores are outstanding. Moreover, such schools seldom get any more money than the schools that are failing.

Some of the most heavily financed schools are doing miserably. Even spending $17,000 per pupil, Cambridge, Massachusetts, was still left with a huge gap between the test scores of its black and white students. In fact, black students in Cambridge scored lower than other black students in nearby communities with less than half as much spending per pupil.

Those who believe that money is the answer are not going to be stopped by anything so mundane as facts. To many in politics and in the media—and to everyone in the teachers' unions—"improving" the schools means spending more money on them. But what is called "investing" in better education could more accurately be called pouring money down a bottomless pit.

Don't suburban schools with high levels of spending do better than other schools with lower levels of spending? Usually, yes. But olympic-sized swimming pools and tennis courts do not make you any smarter. Nor do generous-sized parking lots for affluent students with fancy cars.

No Excuses does not limit its comparisons to blacks and whites. In some cases, the educational performance of Asian American students exceeds that of whites by more than the performance of whites exceeds that of blacks.

There is nothing mysterious about any of these differences. Asian students put more time into study and homework and watch less television. They behave themselves in class. Their parents don't tolerate low grades—or even medium grades.

In those rare black schools where the students follow a

pattern similar to that of Asian Americans, they get educational results similar to those of Asian Americans.

What about the role of the schools in all this?

American schools waste an incredible amount of time on fads, fun and propaganda for political correctness. Those students who come from homes with highly educated parents, or parents whose values stress education, get a lot of what they need outside of school, as well as making the most of what they get within the school.

It is those children who do not come from these kinds of homes whose futures are forfeited when class time is frittered away. Low-income black students are the biggest losers when educators fail to educate and when courts create so many legal obstacles to enforcing school discipline that a handful of classroom clowns or hoodlums can prevent everyone else from getting a decent education.

More money won't cure any of this.

School Performances: Part II

My son learned fractions and decimals when he was in the first grade. He learned them from me as I drove him to school on the Los Angeles freeways, where he became curious about the signs that said things like "Wilshire Boulevard 2¼ miles."

At the private school he attended, he never went near a math class because that was optional and he found the math they taught too boring. Yet, if test scores for that school were collected, his would have helped the school look impressive in math and some might conclude that they did a great job of teaching the subject.

It is a completely different ball game for some kid in the ghetto attending a public school. If his teachers don't do a decent job of teaching math, chances are that he won't know much math.

Among the many misleading statistics on education are test scores comparing results from affluent suburban schools and poorer schools in the inner city. The results may well be valid in the sense that there really is a huge difference in educational achievement. But they may be very misleading as to why.

Schools in both places may be wasting vast amounts of time on non-academic fads and activities. But the children from homes with educated and affluent parents will learn a lot before going to school and outside of school. That will show up on the tests.

The schools in poorer neighborhoods may not be that

much worse, in themselves, but they are the only places where many poor children with poorly educated parents have any opportunity to get an education. When these particular schools waste time, they are dooming most of their students to a life of poverty.

Homes matter—and they matter especially when the schools are not doing their job of educating the children.

Too many suburban parents may be too easily satisfied that their schools are doing a good job because the students there score in the top 10 or 20 percent on standardized tests. Suburban schools may look good compared to inner city schools, but both look bad compared to their counterparts in other countries.

The fact that schools in high-income areas get better results than schools in low-income areas has allowed the education establishment to escape responsibility for their own failings by saying that it all depends on the economic and educational levels of the home. It does not.

With all the abysmal results in ghetto schools in general, there are nevertheless particular schools serving low-income minority students with test results well above the national average. What is the difference?

The biggest difference is that successful schools teach in ways that are directly the opposite from what is fashionable in the public schools in general. Successful schools spend their time on the three R's, they teach reading with phonics, they memorize multiplication tables, and—above all—they have discipline, so that a few disruptive students are not able to prevent all the others from being educated.

Despite the self-serving claim from the teachers' unions that successful schools for minorities skim the cream from the public schools, often these successful charter schools or other private schools admit students on the basis of a lottery, so that those they take in are no better than those they don't.

The students they admit are just a lot better after they have been educated where education is the top priority.

One of the schools I researched years ago that impressed me the most—in fact, moved me to the verge of tears—was a ghetto school in a run-down building, located in a neighborhood that caused a friend to say that I was "brave"—he probably meant foolhardy—to park a car on the street there.

The children in that school scored above the national average on tests. In their classrooms, they spoke the king's English, behaved like little ladies and gentlemen, and made thoughtful answers to the questions they were asked. Yet these kids came from poor homes, often broken homes, and many were on welfare.

You can't buy that quality of education for any amount of money. It has to be created by people who have their priorities straight. Don't tell me it can't be done when I have seen it done with my own eyes.

School Performances: Part III

Many of the pronouncements coming from those who run our public schools range from fallacies to frauds. The new book *No Excuses* by Abigail and Stephan Thernstrom exposes a number of these self-serving lies.

You may have heard how hard it is to find enough teachers—and therefore how necessary it is to raise salaries, in order to attract more people into this field. One example can demonstrate what is wrong with this picture, though there are innumerable other examples.

A young man who graduated *summa cum laude* from elite Williams College decided that he wanted to be a teacher. He sent letters and résumés to eight different school districts. Not one gave him even the courtesy of a reply.

Does that sound like there is a teacher shortage? Moreover, any number of other highly qualified people have had the same experience.

The joker in the deal is that, no matter how highly qualified you are, your desire to become a teacher is not likely to get off the ground unless you have jumped through the bureaucratic hoops that keep people out of this field— thereby protecting the jobs of unionized incompetents who are already in our schools.

The most important of these hoops is taking unbelievably dreary and stupid courses in education. Using these costly and time-consuming courses as a barrier, those in the education establishment "maintain low standards and high barriers at the same time," as Secretary of Education Rod Paige has aptly put it.

Factual studies show no correlation between taking these courses and successful teaching. Private schools are able to get good teachers by hiring people who never took any such courses. That is where our Williams graduate finally found a job.

The very people in the education establishment who maintain barriers to keep out teachers are the ones constantly telling us what a shortage of teachers there is— and how more money is needed. This is a scam that has worked for years and will probably work for more years to come.

Then there are the "studies prove" scams. According to the education establishment, studies prove that Head Start helps poor children's educational performance, small classes lead to higher test scores, and busing black children to white schools produces educational benefits due to "diversity."

The quality of many of these studies is as unbelievably bad as the quality of courses in education.

Here is a common pattern: If you do 20 studies comparing the effect that A has on B, you may find that in 18 of those studies there is no correlation between A and B. In one of the other two, you may find that more A is followed by more B. And in the other, more A is followed by less B. Overall, still no correlation.

Depending on what the education establishment wants, they can seize upon the one study out of 20 that showed more A leading to more B and burst into the media with it. If the conclusion of that one study fits in with the media vision of the world, then it may be trumpeted across the land as "proof."

The Head Start program is a classic example. Anyone who expresses any skepticism about claims that Head Start is a great success will be denounced as someone who doesn't "care" about the low-income and minority children that this program supposedly helps. One of the great propaganda tricks is to change questions of fact into questions of motives.

The Thernstroms show what feeble facts there are behind the Head Start program that has cost billions of dollars. Look for them to be denounced for being heartless, if not racist. But don't expect advocates of Head Start to engage in a serious discussion of facts.

It is much the same story when it comes to claims that "studies prove" that small classes lead to better education. The Thernstroms show cases where class sizes as small as 12 led to no better results when the students were tested.

Ordering students bussed from their own neighborhoods for the sake of racial balance has similarly failed to produce the much-trumpeted educational benefits.

The time is long overdue to start looking at facts instead of listening to rhetoric. Reading *No Excuses* is a good place to start.

College Admissions Voodoo

Every year about this time, high school students get letters of admission—or rejection—from colleges around the country. The saddest part of this process is not their rejections but the assumption by some students that they were rejected because they just didn't measure up to the high standards of Ivy U. or their flagship state university.

The cold fact is that objective admissions standards are seldom decisive at most colleges. The admissions process is so shot through with fads and unsubstantiated assumptions that it is more like voodoo than anything else.

A student who did not get admitted to Ivy U. may be a better student than some—or even most—of those who did. Admissions officials love to believe that they can spot all sorts of intangibles that outweigh test scores and grade-point averages.

Such notions are hardly surprising in people who pay no price for being wrong. All sorts of self-indulgences are possible when people are unaccountable, whether they be college admissions officials, parole boards, planning commissions or copy-editors.

What is amazing is that nobody puts the notions and fetishes of college admissions offices to a test. Nothing would be easier than to admit half of a college's entering class on the basis of objective standards, such as test scores, and the other half according to the voodoo of the admissions office. Then, four years later, you could compare how the two halves of the class did.

But apparently this would not be politic.

Among the many reasons given for rejecting objective admissions standards is that they are "unfair." Much is made of the fact that high test scores are correlated with high family income.

Very little is made of the statistical principle that correlation is not causation. Practically nothing is made of the fact that, however a student got to where he is academically, that is in fact where he is—and that is usually a better predictor of where he is going to go than is the psychobabble of admissions committees.

The denigration of objective standards allows admissions committees to play little tin gods, who think that their job is to reward students who are deserving, sociologically speaking, rather than to select students who can produce the most bang for the buck from the money contributed by donors and taxpayers for the purpose of turning out the best quality graduates possible.

Typical of the mindset that rejects the selection of students in the order of objective performances was a recent article in *The Chronicle of Higher Education* which said that colleges should "select randomly" from a pool of applicants who are "good enough." Nowhere in the real world, where people must face the consequences of their decisions, would such a principle be taken seriously.

Lots of pitchers are "good enough" to be in the major leagues but would you just as soon send one of those pitchers to the mound to pitch the deciding game of the World Series as you would send Randy Johnson or Roger Clemens out there with the world championship on the line?

Lots of military officers were considered to be "good enough" to be generals in World War II but troops who served under General Douglas MacArthur or General George Patton had more victories and fewer casualties. How many more lives would you be prepared to sacrifice as the price of selecting randomly among generals considered to be "good enough"?

If you or your child had to have a major operation for a life-threatening condition, would you be just as content to have the surgery done by anyone who was "good enough" to be a surgeon, as compared to someone who was a top surgeon in the relevant specialty?

The difference between first-rate and second-rate people is enormous in many fields. In a college classroom, marginally qualified students can affect the whole atmosphere and hold back the whole class.

In some professions, a large part of the time of first-rate people is spent countering the half-baked ideas of second-rate people and trying to salvage something from the wreckage of the disasters they create. "Good enough" is seldom good enough.

Summer De-Programming

Parents who are worried because their children are receiving a steady diet of politically correct propaganda in the schools and colleges often ask for suggestions of things they should get for their children to read, in hopes of de-programming them.

The summer is a good time to let young people know that what they have been told in class is not the only side of the story or the only way to look at the world.

If all that today's students seem to know about American history are its negative aspects—which is what our society shares with human societies in general—then they may think that we are a truly awful country, without asking the question, "Compared to what?"

It speaks volumes about our schools and colleges that far-left radical Howard Zinn's pretentiously titled book, *A People's History of the United States,* is widely used across the country. It is one indictment, complaint, and distortion after another.

Anyone who relies on this twisted version of American history would have no idea why millions of people from around the world are trying, sometimes desperately, to move to this country. The one virtue of Zinn's book is that it helps you identify unmistakably which teachers are using their classrooms as propaganda centers.

There are still some honest history books around. Best-selling British historian Paul Johnson has written an outstanding book titled *A History of the American People* and another excellent book on recent world history titled *Modern Times*.

If you want a thorough, accurate, and no-spin history of race relations in the United States, the best history on that subject is *America in Black and White* by Abigail and Stephan Thernstrom. For a history of American ethnic groups in general, there is my own *Ethnic America*. I cannot be unbiased about it, of course, but the fact that it has been translated into six other languages suggests that other people liked it too.

If you would like to know the fundamental basis for the Constitution of the United States under which we all live, there is no book more important to read than *The Federalist* or *The Federalist Papers*, as it is sometimes called. It is a series of popular essays written by those who helped create the Constitution, explaining to their fellow Americans why they did what they did and what they hoped to achieve—and prevent.

It is as readable today as it was two centuries ago—and just as much needed. *The Federalist* should be at or near the top of any summer reading list.

Sometimes the way to understand your own society is to find out about other societies and other economic and political systems, so that you can get some idea of the nature and magnitude of the differences. Two Soviet economists' accounts of that country's economy makes the difference between a market economy and a centrally planned economy stand out in sharp relief. That book is titled *The Turning Point* by Nikolai Shmelev and Vladimir Popov. *India Unbound* by Gurcharan Das tells the story of India's turning toward a market economy—and the benefits that followed. The best book about the Third World in general is *Equality*, *the Third World, and Economic Delusion* by the late Peter Bauer of the London School of Economics.

The appeal of socialism—the beauties of it in theory and its painful consequences in practice—are discussed in a very readable book titled *Heaven on Earth* by Joshua Muravchik. The young need not be embarrassed by finding socialism attractive. Many who were old enough to know better also fell for it.

Economic illiteracy is almost as dangerous as slanted political propaganda. A painless way to get some sense of economic realities would be by reading a popular, topical, and often humorous treatment of economic issues in John Stossel's book titled, *Give Me A Break.*

The current issue of the *Cato Journal* strongly recommends "two remarkable books" on economics as a way for voters to understand economic issues in this election year. The books are *Basic Economics* and *Applied Economics.* The former takes the reader "on an exhilarating tour" of economics, the *Cato Journal* says, and the latter is characterized by "cogent reasoning." I could not use such glowing terms myself, since I am the author of both books.

Happy de-programming this summer.

Fat in California's Budget

Whenever there is a budget deficit, politicians automatically want taxes raised. In our private lives, whenever we find ourselves running out of money, most of us think about cutting back on our spending. Not so in government.

Despite California's record budget deficit there is still a lot of fat left that has not yet been cut—and may never be cut. Every pound of fat has a constituency ready to proclaim that the world will end if that spending is toned down, much less eliminated.

Typical of such political spin is a "news" story about California in a recent issue of *The Chronicle of Higher Education*, the trade publication of the academic world. The headline says: "Preparatory programs at universities help low-performing pupils excel, but budget cuts imperil the efforts."

Wait a minute. I thought 12 years of taxpayer-provided education were supposed to prepare students for college. Now we have to have courses in college to prepare students for college?

The long, rambling story in *The Chronicle of Higher Education*, complete with photographs, at no point offers any hard evidence that these programs actually work any better than the public schools, which have obviously failed if you need such remedial programs in college.

Instead, the Mathematics Engineering Science Achievement program (MESA) is praised because it helps students become "excited" about math and science. "Exciting" is one of the big fad words in educational circles, as if getting your emotions worked up is the same as mastering skills.

In keeping with the excitement theme, students in this program are pictured making balloon-powered rockets and one of them is quoted as saying that this program "inspires" him to go to school.

One of the teachers in this program calls it "crazy" to cut the program—"as he watches another balloon-powered rocket fly across the room." But just what is this actually accomplishing?

The teacher says, "Look at this: It gets a bunch of diverse cultures into one room to build things. You always feel like a family here. It's just a good place."

But actual bottom-line results in terms of math and science? According to *The Chronicle of Higher Education*: "State leaders are often foggy on what exactly the various programs do, and it takes many years for supporters of the programs to gather tangible evidence of their long-term impact."

Apparently the state legislators have not been too foggy to spend $85 million of the taxpayers' money to bankroll this program that apparently cannot show hard evidence of serious improvement in math and science, as a result of balloons flying across the room in this "good place."

As for needing "many years" to document their success, that is a strange claim. I once ran a six-week summer program in economics for black students and documented its results simply by giving the students an economics exam at the beginning and at the end—both exams being sent away to be graded by others at the Educational Testing Service in Princeton.

Why would it take "many years" to show any tangible

improvement in math and science by the students in California's $85 million program? Or is this just a way of postponing accountability—indefinitely?

Even if we take it on faith that it really does require "many years" to produce results, the cold fact is that this program has been going on since 1970. That's more than 30 years. Is that not yet "many years"?

Because this is a program for low-income and minority students, lower expectations may be tolerated by many in the educational establishment. But the real irony is that Jaime Escalante produced hard evidence of high achievement in math by low-income Mexican American students years ago. And he didn't take 34 years to do it or require an $85 million budget.

At one time, one-fourth of all the Mexican American students who passed advanced placement calculus—in the entire country—came from the school where Jaime Escalante taught.

Incidentally, Mr. Escalante is still around. They could always ask him how he did it, if they really wanted to know. But they already know how to get millions of taxpayer dollars, which apparently is what it is all about.

A Scary Report

Most discussions of the problems of American education have an air of utter unreality because they avoid addressing the most fundamental and intractable problem of our public schools—the low quality of our teachers. There is no point expecting teachers to teach things that they themselves do not know or understand.

That becomes painfully obvious from a recently released report from the U. S. Department of Education. This report has an innocuous title on the cover—"Meeting the Highly Qualified Teachers Challenge"—and devastating facts inside.

According to this report, in 28 of the 29 states that use the same standardized test for teachers, it is not even necessary to come up to the national average in mathematics to become a teacher. In none of these states is it necessary to come up to the national average in reading. In some states, you can score in the bottom quarter in either math or reading (or both) and still meet the requirements to become a teacher.

This report is only the latest in a long series of studies of teachers, going back more than half a century, showing again and again the low standards for teaching. Those who go into teaching have consistently had test scores at or near the bottom among college students in a wide variety of fields.

Despite the title of this report, the issue is not highly qualified teachers. The problem is getting teachers who are even decently competent. It is a farce and a fraud when teachers' unions talk about a need for "certified" teachers, when certification has such low requirements and when uncertified teachers often have higher qualifications.

Secretary of Education Rod Paige put his finger on the crucial problem when he said that, in selecting teachers, states "maintain low standards and high barriers at the same time." You don't have to know much, but you do have to jump through all kinds of hoops, in order to become certified to teach in the public schools.

The biggest obstacles are the education courses which can take up years of your time and thousands of dollars of your money, but which have no demonstrated benefit on future teaching. Research shows that teachers' actual knowledge of the subject matter is what benefits students.

Emphasis on something that does not affect educational quality reflects the priorities of the teachers' union in restricting competition, not the requirements for educating children. It would be hard for anyone who has not looked into education courses to believe just how bad they are. I wouldn't believe it myself if I hadn't seen the data, the professors and the students.

People go to these institutions in order to get certified, not because they expect to find anything either interesting or useful. Education courses repel many intelligent people, who are just the sort of people needed in our schools. As Secretary of Education Rod Paige puts it, "schools of education fail to attract the best students." That is an understatement. They repel the best students.

Although many states provide alternative routes to teacher certification, these alternative routes are usually made burdensome enough to protect existing schools of education from losing their students. Indeed, these alternative routes often include many hours of education courses. The net result is that only 6 percent of certified teachers received their certificate via alternative routes. Many such programs, according to the report, "are 'alternative routes' in name only, allowing states to boast of reform while maintaining artificial restrictions on the supply of new teachers."

These artificially created shortages are then used by teachers' unions to argue for higher pay. Secretary Paige does not buy the teachers' union argument that teacher shortages are due to inadequate pay. He points out that "compensation in most private schools is lower than in public schools."

Yet private schools are able to get better qualified people, partly because most private schools do not let education course requirements screen out intelligent people. Some private schools even refuse to hire people who have been through that drivel.

It is refreshing to see a Secretary of Education who says what is wrong in plain English, instead of being a mouthpiece for the status quo in general and the teachers' unions in particular.

"Teaching to the Test"

Florida's school year has already started early, so that its students will have more preparation before the state-mandated tests that will be administered to them later in the school year. Meanwhile, there is much wringing of hands and gnashing of teeth because so much classroom time is spent "teaching to the test" as our "educators" put it.

Unfortunately, most of the people who call themselves educators have not been doing much educating over the past few decades, as shown by American students repeatedly coming in at or near the bottom on international tests. That is why some states are trying to force teachers to teach academic material by testing their students on such material, instead of relying on the inflated grades and high "self-esteem" that our schools have been producing, instead of producing knowledge and skills.

While our students spend about as much time in school as students in Europe or Asia, a higher percentage of other students' time is spent learning academic subjects, while our students' time is spent on all sorts of non-academic projects and activities.

Those who want to keep on indulging in popular educational fads that are failing to produce academic competence fight bitterly against having to "teach to the test." It will stifle "creativity," they complain. The author of a recent feature article in the *New York Times Magazine* declares that "genuinely great teaching—the sort of thing that Socrates and his spiritual descendants have delivered" will be discouraged by having to "stuff our charges with information" in order to pass tests.

If there has actually been such "genuinely great teaching," then why has there been no speck of evidence of it during all these years of low test scores and employer complaints about semi-literate young people applying for jobs? Why do American students learn so much less math between the 4th and the 8th grades than do students in other countries? Could it be because so much more time has been wasted in American schools during those four years?

Evidence is the one thing that our so-called educators want no part of. They want to be able to simply declare that there is genuinely great teaching, "creative" learning, or "critical thinking," without having to prove anything to anybody.

In states where tests have been mandated by law, the first order of business of the teachers' unions has been to introduce as much mushy subjective material as possible into these tests, in order to prevent anyone from finding out how much—or rather, how little—academic skills they are actually providing their students.

The more fundamental question is whether our educational establishment has even been trying to impart academic skills as a high priority goal. Over the past hundred years, American educators have been resisting the idea that schools exist to pass on to the next generation the basic mental skills that our culture has developed. They have said so in books, articles, speeches—and by their actions in the schools.

Since the rise of teachers' unions in the early 1960s— which coincided with the decline of student test scores—the education establishment has increasingly succeeded in deemphasizing academic skills. In that sense, our schools have not failed, they have succeeded in changing the goals and priorities of education.

Despite all-out efforts by the education establishment to blame the declining educational standards in our schools on everything imaginable except the people who teach there— on parents, students, television, or society—the cold fact is that today's students are often simply not taught enough academic material in the first place. Even if there were flawless parents, perfect students, no television, and no problems in society, students could still not be expected to learn what they were never taught.

In fact, it is a lot to expect the teachers themselves to teach what they do not know or understand. Tests have repeatedly shown, for decades on end, that college students who go into teaching score at or near the bottom among students in a wide variety of fields. No wonder they dislike tests! And no wonder that they find innumerable fads more attractive than teaching solid skills, which they themselves may not have mastered.

"Teaching to the Test":
Part II

One of the objections by the educational establishment to state-mandated tests for students is that this forces the teachers to teach directly the material that is going to be tested, instead of letting the students "discover" what they need to know through their own trial and error, under the guidance of teachers acting as "facilitators" from the sidelines.

In other words, the students should not simply be taught the ready-made rules of mathematics or science, but discover them for themselves. The fact that this approach has failed, time and again, to produce students who can hold their own in international tests with students from other countries only turns the American education establishment against tests.

"Discovery learning" is just one of the many fads in education circles today. Only someone with no real knowledge or understanding of the history of ideas could take such a fad seriously.

It took more than a century of dedicated work by highly intelligent economists to arrive at the analysis of supply and demand that is routinely taught in the first week of Economics One. How long are novices in economics supposed to flounder around trying to "discover" these same principles?

Nobody believes that the way to train pilots is to let them "discover" the principles of flight that the Wright brothers arrived at—after years of effort, trial and error. Would anyone even try to teach people how to drive an automobile by taking them out on a highway and letting them "discover" how it is done?

The issue is not what sounds plausible but what actually works. But judging one method of teaching against another by the end results that each produces is the last thing that our fad-ridden educators want. That is at the heart of their objections to having to "teach to the test" instead of engaging in "creative" teaching and "discovery learning" by students—as they arbitrarily define these terms.

The education establishment's bitter opposition to the testing of students by independent outsiders with standardized tests is perfectly understandable for people who do not want to have to put up or shut up. For decades, the ultimate test of any teaching method has been whether it was fashionable among educators.

Educational philosophies that have been put to the test in other countries—Russia in the 1920s and China in the 1960s, for example—and which have failed miserably there, as they are now failing here, continue in vogue because there are no consequences for failure here. Not so long as teachers have iron-clad tenure and get paid by seniority rather than results.

At the heart of the problem of educational failure is the low academic quality of the people who become teachers and principals. This low academic quality has been documented by empirical research so many times, over so many years, that it is incredible how this crucial fact gets overlooked again and again in discussions of the problems of our schools.

So long as teacher training courses in education schools are Mickey Mouse, they are going to repel many intelligent people who would like to teach, and we are going to be left with the dregs of the college students. When the resulting pool of "certified" teachers consists disproportionately of these dregs, do not expect them to be even intellectually oriented, much less intellectually competent.

It is impossible to understand what is happening in our schools without understanding the kind of people who run them. But, once you see the poor academic quality of those people, you can easily understand why textbooks have been dumbed down and why there is such bitter opposition by educators to letting exceptionally bright children be taught in separate classes with more advanced material. Do not expect intellectual losers to look favorably on intellectual winners.

Such teachers are the natural prey of education gurus pushing non-intellectual fads with glittering names. If you got rid of every single counterproductive fad in our schools today, but left the same people in place, this would lead only to a new infusion of different counterproductive fads tomorrow.

And there would still be the same bitter opposition to "teaching to the test," which spoils their self-indulgences.

"Teaching to the Test":
Part III

While we ought to learn from our own experiences, it is even better to learn from other people's experiences, saving ourselves the painful costs of the lessons. In the case of the dominant educational fads of our times, many have been tried out before in other countries. Their failures there should have warned us that they were likely to fail here as well.

Our education establishment's objections to "teaching to the test" are echoes of what was said and done in China during the 1950s and 1960s, when examinations were de-emphasized and non-academic criteria and social "relevance" were given more weight. In 1967, examinations were abolished.

This was an even bigger step in China than it would be in the United States, for China had had extensive examinations for more than a thousand years. Not only were there academic examinations, for centuries most Chinese civil servants were also selected by examinations.

A decade after academic examinations were abolished in China, the Ministry of Education announced that college entrance examinations "will be restored and admittance based on their results." Why? Because "the quality of education has declined sharply" in the absence of examinations and this had "retarded the development of a whole generation of young people."

Mao's successor, Deng Xiaoping, complained about "the deterioration of academic standards" and said, "schools have not paid attention to educational standards and instead overemphasized practical work; students' knowledge of theory and basic skills in their area of specialization have been disregarded."

None of these failing educational fads was unique to China. They went back to the teachings of John Dewey, whose "progressive" ideas shaped developments in American schools—and especially American schools of education, where future teachers were trained. Moreover, Dewey's ideas were tried out on a large scale in the Soviet Union in the 1920s, before they had achieved similar influence in the United States.

During a visit to the Soviet Union in 1928, Dewey reported "the marvelous development of progressive educational ideas and practice under the fostering care of the Bolshevik government." He noted that the Soviets had broken down the barriers between school and society, which he had urged others to do, and said "I can only pay my tribute to the liberating effect of active participation in social life upon the attitude of the students."

Here we see the early genesis of the current idea in today's American schools that the children there should be promoting causes, writing public figures and otherwise "participating" in the arena of social and political issues. Another progressive educator, W. H. Kilpatrick, was likewise exhilarated to find that his books were being used in Soviet teacher training programs.

Kilpatrick was also delighted to learn that the three R's were not being taught directly but were being learned "incidentally from tasks at hand." Here was the basic principle behind today's "discovery learning."

Even as visiting progressive educators from America were gushing over the use of their ideas in Soviet schools, the bad educational consequences were turning the Soviet government leadership against these fads. The commissar who had imposed progressive education on Soviet schools was removed shortly after John Dewey's visit.

When the romantic notions of progressive education didn't work, the Soviet and Chinese governments were able to get rid of them because they were not hamstrung by teachers' unions. They were able to restore "teaching to the test"—which was not very romantic, but it worked.

The "barriers between school and society," which Dewey lamented, existed for a reason. Schools are not a microcosm of society, any more than an eye is a microcosm of the body. The eye is a specialized organ which does something that no other part of the body does. That is its whole significance.

You don't use your eyes to listen to music. Specialized organs have important things to do in their own specialties. So do schools, which need to stick to their special work as well, not become social or political gadflies.

Smart "Problems"

During my first semester of teaching, many years ago, I was surprised to encounter the philosophy that the brightest students did not need much help from the teacher because "they can get it anyway" and that my efforts should be directed toward the slower or low-performing students.

This advice came from my department chairman, who said that if the brighter or more serious students "get restless" while I was directing my efforts toward the slower students, then I should "give them some extra work to do to keep them quiet."

I didn't believe that the real difference between the *A* students and the *C* students was in inborn intelligence, but thought it was usually due to differences in attitudes and priorities. In any event, my reply was that what the chairman proposed "would be treating those who came here for an education as a special problem!"

A few days later, I handed in my resignation. It turned out to be only the first in a series of my resignations from academic institutions over the years.

Unfortunately, the idea of treating the brighter or more serious students as a problem to be dealt with by keeping them busy is not uncommon, and is absolutely pervasive in the public schools. One fashionable solution for such "problem" students is to assign them to help the less able or less conscientious students who are having trouble keeping up.

In other words, make them unpaid teacher's aides!

High potential will remain only potential unless it is developed. But the very thought that high potential should be developed more fully never seems to occur to many of our educators—and some are absolutely hostile to the idea.

It violates their notions of equality or "social justice" and it threatens the "self-esteem" of other students. As a result, too often a student with the potential to become a future scientist, inventor, or a discoverer of a cure for cancer will instead have his time tied up doing busy work for the teacher.

Even so-called "gifted and talented" programs often turn out to be simply a bigger load of the same level of work that other students are doing—keeping the brighter students busy in a separate room.

My old department chairman's notion that the better students "can pretty much get it without our help" assumes that there is some "it"—some minimum competence—which is all that matters.

People like this would apparently be satisfied if Einstein had remained a competent clerk in the Swiss patent office and if Jonas Salk, instead of discovering a cure for polio, had spent his career puttering around in a laboratory and turning out an occasional research paper of moderate interest to his academic colleagues.

If developing the high potential of some students wounds the "self-esteem" of other students, one obvious answer is for them to go their separate ways in different classrooms or different schools.

There was a time when students of different ability levels or performance levels were routinely assigned to different classes in the same grade or to different schools—and no one else collapsed like a house of cards because of wounded self-esteem.

Let's face it: Most of the teachers in our public schools do not have what it takes to develop high intellectual potential in students. They cannot give students what they don't have themselves.

Test scores going back more than half a century have repeatedly shown people who are studying to be teachers to be at or near the bottom among college students studying in various fields. It is amazing how often this plain reality gets ignored in discussions of what to do about our public schools.

Lack of competence is only part of the problem. Too often there is not only a lack of appreciation of outstanding intellectual development but a hostility towards it by teachers who are preoccupied with the "self-esteem" of mediocre students, who may remind them of what they were once like as students.

Maybe the advancement of science, of the economy, and finding a cure for cancer can wait, while we take care of self-esteem.

Vouchers Vindicated

The court cases that get the most media attention are not necessarily the cases that will have the most impact on the society. Despite all the controversy surrounding the 9th Circuit Court of Appeals' decision outlawing "under God" from the pledge of allegiance or the Supreme Court's decision outlawing executions of murderers with low test scores, the decision with the greatest potential for benefitting American society is the Supreme Court's decision declaring vouchers constitutional, even if most of these vouchers end up being used at religious schools.

One of the main phony arguments against vouchers is now dead. Vouchers are no more a violation of the Constitution than the G.I. Bill that paid for the education of military veterans at Notre Dame, Holy Cross, and other religious colleges.

Opponents of vouchers have other phony arguments to fall back on, however. One is that vouchers will drain money away from the public schools, making it harder for them to provide a good education to the students remaining.

That argument is just bad arithmetic, perhaps brought on by fuzzy math. Vouchers almost invariably pay much less money than the average cost of educating students in the public schools. When students who cost $8,000 a year to educate in the public schools transfer to a private school with a $4,000 voucher, the total cost of educating all the students does not go up. It goes down.

Far from reducing per capita spending in the public

schools, the departure of voucher students leaves more money per pupil for those left behind. It is of course true that the total sum of money in the public school may decline, but if half the students depart, should the school continue to get the same money it had when there were twice as many students?

This emphasis on money is a tragic farce, in view of all the research that shows virtually no correlation between spending per pupil and educational outcomes. Districts with some of the highest per pupil expenditures have some of the lowest test results, and vice versa. Students in countries that spend less than half as much per pupil as we do outperform American students on international tests, year after year.

One of the most hypocritical objections made by opponents of vouchers is that the vouchers pay so little that they can only be used in religious schools. If that is the critics' real concern, why don't they advocate raising the amount of money per voucher?

In reality, those who are up in arms about disparities in per pupil expenditure from one public school district to another almost never advocate equalizing expenditures between voucher recipients and students in the public schools.

The truly ugly aspect of the case against vouchers is the objection that vouchers will allow private schools to "skim off" the best students from the public schools. Students are not inert objects being skimmed off by others. These students and their parents choose what they want to do—for the first time, as a result of vouchers setting them free from the public school monopoly.

When these voucher critics send their own children off to upscale private schools, do they say that Phillips Academy or Sidwell Friends School are "skimming" the best students out of the public schools? Affluent parents are simply doing what any responsible parents would do—choosing the best education they can get for their children.

Only when low-income parents are now able to do the same thing is it suddenly a question of these students being "skimmed" by other institutions. But whenever any group rises from poverty to prosperity, whether by education or otherwise, some do so before others. Why should low-income families be told that either all of them rise at the same time or none of them can rise?

If there has actually been harm done to the public schools by vouchers, there ought to be evidence of it by now. But voucher critics have none, after all these years, and rely on scary but unsubstantiated theories instead.

What we are really talking about are the teachers' unions wanting to keep a captive audience, for the sake of their members' jobs, and social engineers wanting to control low-income children and their parents, as they themselves would never want to be controlled.

Artificial Stupidity

A recent news story about a teacher who assigned her students to write anti-war letters may have seemed like just an isolated episode but teachers using students for their own little ego trips is by no means uncommon. Perhaps the worst recent example was a teacher who unleashed her venom on the children of military personnel who had gone off to fight in Iraq.

Just last week I received a bundle of letters from students who have apparently been given an assignment to write to me by a teacher in an English class in Flat Rock High School in Flat Rock, Michigan. This was occasioned by a column of mine that said some things that were not politically correct.

The first of these letters was from a girl who informed me, from her vast store of teenage wisdom, of things that I knew 30 years ago, and closed by telling me that I needed to find out about poverty. Since I spent more years in poverty than she has spent in the world, this would be funny if it were not so sad.

With American students consistently scoring at or near the bottom on international tests, you would think that our schools would have better things to do than tell kids to write letters to strangers, spouting off about things they know little or nothing about.

Flat Rock High School's envelopes, in which the students wrote their assigned letters, has the motto: "Where Tomorrow's Leaders Learn!" Sadly, they are learning not to be leaders but to be sheep-like followers, repeating politically correct notions and reacting with snotty remarks to anyone who contradicts them.

It is bad enough when someone takes the position that he has made up his mind and doesn't want to be confused by the facts. It is worse when someone else makes up his mind for him and then he dismisses any facts to the contrary by attributing bad motives to those who present those facts.

Creating mindless followers is one of the most dangerous things that our public schools are doing. Young people who know only how to vent their emotions, and not how to weigh opposing arguments through logic and evidence, are sitting ducks for the next talented demagogue who comes along in some cult or movement, including movements like those that put the Nazis in power in Germany.

At one time, the educator's creed was: "We are here to teach you how to think, not what to think." Today, schools across the country are teaching students what to think— whether about the environment, the war, social policy, or whatever.

Even if what they teach were true, that would be of little use to these young people in later life. Issues and conditions change so much over time that even the truth about today's issues becomes irrelevant when confronted with the future's new challenges.

If students haven't been taught to think, then they are at the mercy of events, as well as being at the mercy of those who know how to take advantage of their ignorance and their emotions.

Classroom brainwashing is not new. I wrote about it a decade ago in my book *Inside American Education*. Hearings at the Department of Education brought out the same things a decade before that.

When will the voting public get the message? Where are

the parents of these children? Do parents in Flat Rock, Michigan, want their children's time in school wasted on their teachers' ideological hobby horses, instead of being used to prepare an intellectual foundation for their further education?

In the long run, the greatest weapon of mass destruction is stupidity. In an age of artificial intelligence, too many of our schools are producing artificial stupidity, in the sense of ideas and attitudes far more foolish than young people would have arrived at on their own. I doubt whether the youngsters in Flat Rock, Michigan, were brought up by their parents to say and do the silly things their teachers have assigned them to do.

Weapons of mass destruction in the hands of an avowed enemy can destroy many Americans, but they cannot destroy America, because we are too strong and too capable of counterattack. Only Americans can destroy America. But too many of our schools have for years been quietly undermining the values and abilities that are needed to preserve any society—and especially a free society.

"Good" Teachers

The next time someone receives an award as an outstanding teacher, take a close look at the reasons given for selecting that particular person. Seldom is it because his or her students did higher quality work in math or spoke better English or in fact had any tangible accomplishments that were better than those of other students of teachers who did not get an award.

A "good" teacher is not defined as a teacher whose students learn more. A "good" teacher is someone who exemplifies the prevailing dogmas of the educational establishment. The general public probably thinks of good teachers as people like Marva Collins or Jaime Escalante, whose minority students met and exceeded national standards. But such bottom line criteria have long since disappeared from most public schools.

If your criterion for judging teachers is how much their students learn, then you can end up with a wholly different list of who are the best teachers. Some of the most unimpressive-looking teachers have consistently turned out students who know their subject far better than teachers who cut a more dashing figure in the classroom and receive more lavish praise from their students or attention from the media.

My own teaching career began at Douglass College, a small women's college in New Jersey, replacing a retiring professor of economics who was so revered that I made it a point never to say that I was "replacing" him, which would have been considered sacrilege. But it turned out that his worshipful students were a mass of confusion when it came to economics.

It was much the same story at my next teaching post, Howard University in Washington. One of the men in our department was so popular with students that the big problem every semester was to find a room big enough to hold all the students who wanted to enroll in his classes. Meanwhile, another economist in that department was so unpopular that the very mention of his name caused students to roll their eyes or even have an outburst of hostility.

Yet when I compared the grades that students in my upper level economics class were making, I discovered that none of the students who had taken introductory economics under Mr. Popularity had gotten as high as a *B* in my class, while virtually all the students who had studied under Mr. Pariah were doing at least *B* work. "By their fruits ye shall know them."

My own experience as an undergraduate student at Harvard was completely consistent with what I later learned as a teacher. One of my teachers—Professor Arthur Smithies—was a highly respected scholar but was widely regarded as a terrible teacher. Yet what he taught me has stayed with me for more than 40 years and his class determined the course of my future career.

Nobody observing Professor Smithies in class was likely to be impressed by his performance. He sort of drifted into the room, almost as if he had arrived there by accident. During talks—lectures would be too strong a word—he often paused to look out the window and seemingly became fascinated by the traffic in Harvard Square.

But Smithies not only taught us particular things. He got

us to think—often by questioning us in a way that forced us to follow out the logic of what we were saying to its ultimate conclusion. Often some policy that sounded wonderful, if you looked only at the immediate results, would turn out to be counterproductive if you followed your own logic beyond stage one.

In later years, I would realize that many disastrous policies had been created by thinking no further than stage one. Getting students to think systematically beyond stage one was a lifetime contribution to their understanding.

Another lifetime contribution was a reading list that introduced us to the writings of top-notch minds. It takes one to know one and Smithies had a top-notch mind himself. One of the articles on that reading list—by Professor George Stigler of Columbia University—was so impressive that I went to graduate school at Columbia expressly to study under him. After discovering, upon arrival, that Stigler had just left for the University of Chicago, I decided to go to the University of Chicago the next year and study under him there.

Arthur Smithies would never get a teaching award by the standards of the education establishment today. But he rates a top award by a much older standard: By their fruits ye shall know them.

A Sign of the Times

They say a picture is worth a thousand words. That was certainly true of a recent photo of a little seven-year-old boy holding a sign demanding more money for the schools and holding his fist in the air.

He was part of a demonstration organized by his teachers, and including parents and other students, all of whom were transported to California's state capital in Sacramento to protest budget constraints brought on by the state's huge deficit.

There was a time when taking children out of classes to fight the political battles of adults would have been considered a shameless neglect of duty. But that was long ago.

The little boy with the sign and his fist raised in the air is just one of the millions of victims of a shameless education establishment. It is not just that he is not in class learning the things he will need for his own mental development. He is out in the streets learning dangerous lessons for the future.

The most dangerous lesson of all is that he doesn't need to know what he is talking about, that what matters is venting his feelings and being an activist.

He is also learning to let himself be manipulated by others, setting him up for all sorts of pied pipers he is likely to encounter in later years, who may lead him into anything from personal degeneracy to movements like the Taliban or the cult that Jim Jones led to their doom at Jonestown.

What can a seven-year-old boy know about the issues that he is carrying a sign for or shaking his fist about? Has he even heard—much less understood—any other side of the issue he is being used for?

Can he have read any of the many empirical studies which show that there is very little correlation between the amount of money that schools spend and the quality of the education that the children receive? Per pupil spending in Washington, D.C. schools is among the highest in the nation but test results there are among the lowest.

American school children have more money spent on them than the children in countries that regularly finish higher on international tests than we do.

When confronted with the undeniable fact that American high school students repeatedly finish at or near the bottom on international tests, there is a standard teachers' union party line. Supposedly only the elite finish high school in other countries, the spin goes, so it is unfair to compare other countries' elite students with our average students.

If there was ever any validity to this argument, it is long past. Countries with a higher percentage of their youngsters finishing high school still have their students outperform American students.

Sometimes the education establishment tries to use the fact that American students don't do badly in the lower grades. That is true: Our children are not stupid. It is just that the longer they stay in our school system, the further they fall behind the rest of the world.

This is not accidental. Far too many public schools have far too many other agendas than providing children with intellectual skills. Political propaganda is just one. Using the children as guinea pigs for fashionable notions is another.

And, at the top of the agenda is protecting the jobs of teachers, even those who are grossly incompetent.

Those who engineered this educational disaster have lots of glib excuses. One of the most popular is that students and parents are flawed. The great non sequitur seems to be that, if there is anything wrong with parents or students, there can't be anything wrong with the schools.

But, if the current crop of "educators" had better students, better parents, and more money, all that it would amount to would be smaller classes in nicer surroundings having their time wasted on the fads and fetishes that take the place of education in our classrooms.

We would have more expensive incompetence. And we would have more children being prepared to be led by pied pipers, like the little boy with his sign and his fist in the air.

Suspicious Stats

One of the latest in the seemingly endless rounds of alarming statistics is that one out of 12 American children has some form of disability. With all the things that are supposedly getting worse, you have to wonder how our life expectancy keeps increasing. A cynic might even wonder if the increasing availability of money from the government has anything to do with the increasing number of "problems" that need to be "solved" by government programs.

One way of telling whether a given statistic is a fact or an artifact is to ask whether the definition used fits the thing that is being defined. Buried in the news story about the children with disabilities is the fact that the definition of "disability" has been expanding over the years.

A child who is likely to be diagnosed as autistic today might not have been some years ago. Yet that is seldom mentioned in alarming statistics about the escalating number of cases of autism. As the author of a couple of books about late-talking children, I hear regularly from parents who tell me that they are being asked to allow their children to be labeled "autistic," in order to get either the government or their insurance company to pay for speech therapy.

It is amazing that, with something as serious—indeed, catastrophic—as autism, statistics are thrown around without mentioning the variation in what is being diagnosed as autism. In something much less serious, such as sales receipts at Wal-Mart, a comparison of how much money was taken in this year, compared to last year, will almost certainly make a distinction between sales receipts at the same stores as last year versus sales receipts that include new stores opened since last year.

In other words, they notify you of changing definitions behind the numbers. Otherwise, the statistics could mean almost anything. If it is important enough to do this for Wal-Mart sales, it certainly ought to be important enough to do it for autism.

Regardless of whether the old or the new criterion for autism is better, they are different criteria. Statistics should tell us whether or by how much autism has risen by any consistent standard. Moreover, those who diagnose autism range from highly trained specialists to people who never set foot in a medical school or had any comparable training elsewhere.

Another set of statistics whose definition is at least questionable are statistics about the incomes of high school dropouts versus those who have more education. Since most high school dropouts resume their education at some later time, are these statistics really counting all—or even most—dropouts? Or just the minority of dropouts who never enter a classroom again?

Although I dropped out of high school more than half a century ago, and still do not have a high school diploma, I do have a couple of postgraduate degrees. Is my income counted when they add up the incomes of dropouts? Not bloody likely.

This is not just a fine point. All sorts of efforts are being made to prevent kids from dropping out of high school, as if dropping out means the end of their education. Since it usually means only an interruption, leading eventually to a resumption of their education after some experience in the real world, the urgency of preventing them from encountering the real world is by no means obvious. They may become more serious students afterwards.

One of the most brazen uses of statistics which do not fit the definition was in a much-praised book that attempted to show that black students admitted to colleges under affirmative action do just fine. The book was titled *The Shape of the River*, written by William Bowen and Derek Bok, former presidents of Princeton and Harvard, respectively.

Although this book is crammed full of statistics, not one of those statistics is about black students admitted under affirmative action. Black students admitted under the same standards as white students are lumped together with black students admitted under lower standards. Yet, from this the authors conclude that affirmative action is a good thing—to the applause of those who apparently wanted to see that conclusion more than they wanted to see meaningful statistics.

Advocates of campaign finance reform often speak of the corrupting influence of money. But they seldom include the corrupting influence of the government's money on what statistical "facts" are fed to the public.

Peers and Pied Pipers

Some years ago, while walking across the campus of Stanford University, I happened to encounter the late Glen Campbell, then head of the Hoover Institution, where I work. Glen was also a regent of the University of California and the regents had just made some horrible decision that had me upset.

After I explained to Glen why I thought the regents' decision was so terrible, he said with a wry smile, "They know all that, Tom." That stopped me in my tracks.

"Why did they do it, then?" I asked.

"They want to be liked," he replied. "If they voted the way you wanted them to vote, they wouldn't be liked." Glen could never be accused of courting popularity and he had voted the other way.

Cynics say that every man has his price, but it is amazing how low some people's price is. Being a regent is not a career or even a stepping stone to a career.

Many of the regents were already independently wealthy—or rather, they were wealthy enough to be independent, if they were not concerned about their popularity.

Popularity may not be the right word, if it means being liked by the public at large. Many things are done—by regents, by judges, and by the intelligentsia—that are very unpopular with the public. But these things enhance their status with their peers.

The very fact that the public doesn't like what they do

may only solidify their sense of being one of the special people who are wiser, nobler or more daring. Some things are believed, without evidence, because such beliefs are a mark of belonging.

Once I asked a federal judge why some of his fellow judges made some of the incredibly bad rulings that they had made. His answer was not very different from that of Glen Campbell—except that he specified that it was the opinions of the liberal media and the elite law school professors that was the gallery to whom these judges were playing.

"You mean they care what Linda Greenhouse of the *New York Times* writes about them?" I asked, incredulous.

"Yes," he replied.

That certainly gave new meaning to the term "the Greenhouse effect."

It was even more baffling to hear, within the past year, professors at two of the top law schools in the country tell me that (1) they found the arguments used to justify affirmative action were just a crock and (2) they supported affirmative action anyway. One said he didn't want to offend donors to his law school.

We usually think of peer pressure as something that kids succumb to. But not only is such pressure effective with people who have long since passed childhood, not all the peer pressure on children is spontaneous.

Schools across the country promote using peers as guides. There are even "trust-building" exercises designed to get students to rely on their classmates. At the same time, these same schools try to put distance between students and their parents.

"Many parents wonder why they lose their children to a whole new value system," a parent once said plaintively. It is not accidental. There are not only individual pied pipers in the schools but whole nationwide educational efforts to detach children from their parents, as a way of promoting "social change."

It is not just parents, but the whole moral structure of society that must be undermined through such misnamed programs as "values clarification" and its sequels—if the fashionable brand of "change" is to be imposed.

That the pathetically under-educated people who staff our public schools should take upon themselves the task of shaping a whole society is staggering. What is even more staggering is that the rest of us let them get away with it— for the most part, because so few even know that it is happening.

There is no way to quantify just how much we are all paying so that a relative handful of people can feel important as part of some elite peer group. But we are paying, not only economically, but in everything from social disintegration to violent crime. Whole societies have come apart when the things that hold them together have been dissolved.

PART VII

RACIAL ISSUES

Older Budweiser

Back in the days of the Hapsburg Empire, there was a town in Bohemia called Budweis. The people in that town were called Budweisers and the town had a brewery which produced beer with the same name—but different from the American Budweiser.

Like many communities in Bohemia during that era, Budweis had people of both Czech and German ancestries, speaking different languages, though many were also bilingual. They got along pretty well and most people there thought of themselves as Budweisers, rather than as Czechs or Germans. But that would later change—for the worse— not only in Budweis, but throughout Bohemia.

The mayor of Budweis spoke both Czech and German but refused to be classified as a member of either group. His point was that we are all Budweisers.

As with virtually all groups in virtually all countries and in virtually all eras, there were differences between the Germans and the Czechs in Budweis. Germans were more educated, more prosperous, and more prominent in business and the professions.

The German language at that point had a much wider and richer literature, the Slavic languages having acquired written versions centuries later than the languages of Western Europe. Educated Bohemians of whatever ethnicity were usually educated in German.

Those Czechs who wished to rise into the upper echelons, whether in business, the military, or the professions, had to master the German language and culture, in order to fit in with those already at the higher levels.

People on both sides learned to live with this situation and Czechs were welcomed into the German cultural enclaves in Bohemia when they mastered that culture. In Budweis, they could all be Budweisers.

As in so many other countries and in so many other times, the rise of a newly educated intellectual class in the 19th century polarized the society with ethnic identity politics. All over Bohemia, the new Czech intelligentsia urged Czechs to think of themselves as Czechs, not Bohemians or Budweisers or anything else that would transcend their ethnic identity.

Demands were made that street signs in Prague, which had been in both Czech and German before, now be exclusively in Czech. Quotas were demanded for a certain percentage of Czech music to be played by the Budweiser orchestra.

If such demands seem petty, their consequences were not small. People of German ancestry resisted ethnic classifications but the Czech intelligentsia insisted and Czech politicians went along with the trend on many issues, large and small.

Eventually, Germans as well began in self-defense to think of themselves as Germans, rather than as Bohemians or Budweisers, and to defend their interests as Germans. This ethnic polarization in the 19th century was a fateful step whose full consequences have not yet ended completely, even in the 21st century.

A crucial turning point was the creation of the new nation of Czechoslovakia when the Hapsburg Empire was broken up after the First World War. Czech leaders declared the new nation's mission to include a correction of "social injustice" so as to "put right the historic wrongs of the seventeenth century."

What were those wrongs? Czech nobles who revolted against the Hapsburg Empire back in the 17th century were defeated and had their lands confiscated and turned over to Germans. Presumably no one from the 17th century was still alive when Czechoslovakia was created in the 20th century, but Czech nationalists kept the grievance alive—as ethnic identity ideologues have done in countries around the world.

Government policies designed to undo history with preferential treatment for Czechs polarized the existing generation of Germans and Czechs. Bitter German reactions led eventually to demands that the part of the country where they lived be united with neighboring Germany. From this came the Munich crisis of 1938 that dismembered Czechoslovakia on the eve of World War II.

When the Nazis conquered the whole country, the Germans now lorded it over the Czechs. After the war, the Czech reaction led to mass expulsions of Germans under brutal conditions that cost many lives. Today refugees in Germany are still demanding restitution.

If only the grievances of past centuries had been left in the past! If only they had all remained Budweisers or Bohemians.

Rosa Parks and History

The death of Rosa Parks has reminded us of her place in history, as the black woman whose refusal to give up her seat on a bus to a white man, in accordance with the Jim Crow laws of Alabama, became the spark that ignited the civil rights movement of the 1950s and 1960s.

Most people do not know the rest of the story, however. Why was there racially segregated seating on public transportation in the first place? "Racism" some will say—and there was certainly plenty of racism in the South, going back for centuries. But racially segregated seating on streetcars and buses in the South did not go back for centuries.

Far from existing from time immemorial, as many have assumed, racially segregated seating in public transportation began in the South in the late 19th and early 20th centuries.

Those who see government as the solution to social problems may be surprised to learn that it was government which created this problem. Many, if not most, municipal transit systems were privately owned in the 19th century and the private owners of these systems had no incentive to segregate the races.

These owners may have been racists themselves but they were in business to make a profit—and you don't make a profit by alienating a lot of your customers. There was not enough market demand for Jim Crow seating on municipal transit to bring it about.

It was politics that segregated the races because the

incentives of the political process are different from the incentives of the economic process. Both blacks and whites spent money to ride the buses but, after the disenfranchisement of black voters in the late 19th and early 20th century, only whites counted in the political process.

It was not necessary for an overwhelming majority of the white voters to demand racial segregation. If some did and the others didn't care, that was sufficient politically, because what blacks wanted did not count politically after they lost the vote.

The incentives of the economic system and the incentives of the political system were not only different, they clashed.

Private owners of streetcar, bus, and railroad companies in the South lobbied against the Jim Crow laws while these laws were being written, challenged them in the courts after the laws were passed, and then dragged their feet in enforcing those laws after they were upheld by the courts.

These tactics delayed the enforcement of Jim Crow seating laws for years in some places. Then company employees began to be arrested for not enforcing such laws and at least one president of a streetcar company was threatened with jail if he didn't comply.

None of this resistance was based on a desire for civil rights for blacks. It was based on a fear of losing money if racial segregation caused black customers to use public transportation less often than they would have in the absence of this affront.

Just as it was not necessary for an overwhelming majority of whites to demand racial segregation through the political system to bring it about, so it was not necessary for an overwhelming majority of blacks to stop riding the streetcars, buses and trains in order to provide incentives for the owners of these transportation systems to feel the loss of money if some blacks used public transportation less than they would have otherwise.

People who decry the fact that businesses are in business "just to make money" seldom understand the implications of what they are saying. You make money by doing what other people want, not what you want.

Black people's money was just as good as white people's money, even though that was not the case when it came to votes.

Initially, segregation meant that whites could not sit in the black section of a bus any more than blacks could sit in the white section. But whites who were forced to stand when there were still empty seats in the black section objected. That's when the rule was imposed that blacks had to give up their seats to whites.

Legal sophistries by judges "interpreted" the 14th Amendment's requirement of equal treatment out of existence. Judicial activism can go in any direction.

That's when Rosa Parks came in, after more than half a century of political chicanery and judicial fraud.

Those who think that politicians and judges are the answer to our racial problems, and who regard free markets or a strict construction of the Constitution as antithetical to progress, have profoundly misunderstood both history and the country they live in today.

A free market was antithetical to Jim Crow seating and a strict construction of the 14th Amendment would never have permitted laws that asked black women to give up their seats to white men.

"Friends" of Blacks

Who was it who said, "if the Negro cannot stand on his own legs, let him fall"?

Ronald Reagan? Newt Gingrich? Charles Murray?

Not even close. It was Frederick Douglass!

This was part of a speech in which Douglass also said: "Everybody has asked the question, . . . 'What shall we do with the Negro?' I have had but one answer from the beginning. Do nothing with us! Your doing with us has already played the mischief with us. Do nothing with us!"

Frederick Douglass had achieved a deeper understanding in the 19th century than any of the black "leaders" of today. Those whites who feel a need to do something with blacks and for blacks have been some of the most dangerous "friends" of blacks.

Academia is the home of many such "friends," which is why there are not only double standards of admissions to colleges but also in some places double standards in grading. The late David Riesman called it "affirmative grading."

A professor at one of California's state universities where black students are allowed to graduate on the basis of easier standards put it bluntly: "We are just lying to these black students when we give them degrees." That lie is particularly deadly when the degree is a medical degree, authorizing someone to treat sick people or perform surgery on children.

For years, Dr. Patrick Chavis was held up as a shining

example of the success of affirmative action, for he was admitted to medical school as a result of minority preferences and went back to the black community to practice medicine. In fact, he was publicly praised by the Lawyers Committee for Civil Rights—just two weeks before his license was suspended, after his patients died under conditions that brought the matter to the attention of the Medical Board of California.

An administrative law judge referred to Chavis' "inability to perform some of the most basic duties required of a physician." A year later, after a fuller investigation, his license was revoked.

Those who had for years been using Chavis as a shining example of the success of affirmative action suddenly changed tactics and claimed that an isolated example of failure proved nothing. Sadly, Chavis was not an isolated example.

When a professor at the Harvard Medical School declared publicly, back in the 1970s, that black students were being allowed to graduate from that institution without meeting the same standards as others, he was denounced as a "racist" for saying that it was cruel to "allow trusting patients to pay for our irresponsibility"—trusting black patients, in many cases.

Why do supposedly responsible people create such dangerous double standards? Some imagine that they are being friends to blacks by lowering the standards for them. Some don't think that blacks have what it takes to meet real standards, and that colleges and universities will lose their "diversity"—and perhaps federal money with it—if they don't lower the standards, in order to get an acceptable racial body count.

My own experience as a teacher was that black students

would meet higher standards if you refused to lower the standards for them. This was not the royal road to popularity, either with the students themselves or with the "friends" of blacks on the faculty and in the administration. But, when the dust finally settled, the students met the standards.

We have gotten so used to abysmal performances from black students, beginning in failing ghetto schools, that it is hard for some to believe that black students once did a lot better than they do today, at least in places and times with good schools. As far back as the First World War, black soldiers from New York, Pennsylvania, Illinois, and Ohio scored higher on mental tests than white soldiers from Georgia, Arkansas, Kentucky, and Mississippi.

During the 1940s, black students in Harlem schools had test scores very similar to those of white working class students on the lower east side of New York. Sometimes the Harlem scores were a little higher or a little lower, but they were never miles behind, the way they are today in many ghetto schools.

If blacks could do better back when their opportunities were worse, why can't today's ghetto students do better? Perhaps blacks have too many "friends" today.

"Friends" of Blacks: Part II

In a commercial that ran during the Christmas-New Year's holidays a few years ago, the husband was trying to keep an old car patched up, while the wife wanted him to get a new one. At the end, the wife asked: "Should old acquaintance be forgot?" And she answered emphatically: "Yes!"

No group is more in need of forgetting old political ties and making some new ones than blacks. The black vote has been almost an automatic monopoly of the Democratic Party for years. Yet the dominant forces among the Democrats have agendas that are directly contrary to the interests of blacks.

This is not due to racism but to the fact that single-issue zealots have more clout within the Democratic Party than blacks do. These single-issue groups will vote for whoever serves their purposes, so the Democrats have to earn their votes, while blacks vote for Democrats automatically.

Nothing is more important to the future advancement of blacks than the quality of their children's education. But any attempt to give black parents real options as to where they can send their children to school runs into a brick wall because the teachers' unions are the 800-pound gorillas of the Democratic Party.

Controlling millions of votes and millions of dollars in campaign contributions, the teachers' unions' interests prevail, even when that sacrifices the future of a whole generation of young blacks. But, despite polls which show that blacks favor vouchers more than any other group, black votes continue to go to Democrats who sacrifice their children on the altar to the teachers' unions.

Black 4th graders scored higher on tests in Texas than in any other state. But 92 percent of black votes went against the Republican governor of Texas in the 2000 presidential election. Democrats had rhetoric, symbolism, and inertia going for them.

Housing is another key area where the interests of blacks get trumped by the interests of another crucial constituency of the Democratic Party—the environmentalist cult. Most blacks cannot afford the exorbitant costs of homes and apartments in those places where the environmentalists are politically dominant.

Name a place where liberal Democrats and environmentalists have been in control for many years and you are almost certain to find a place where housing costs are far higher than housing costs in the rest of the country. That is because sky-high prices for housing are due to sky-high prices for land. These extravagant land prices are in turn due to "open space" laws and other land use restrictions which the environmentalists push, heedless of the cost to others.

But here, as in education, symbolism trumps reality, and black votes go overwhelmingly to support politicians whose policies drive up housing prices by catering to the environmental movement.

Another great problem for blacks is crime. Liberal Democrats have long resisted efforts to crack down on criminals. Instead, the great liberal dogma is that we need to seek out the "root causes" of crime and set up government social programs to solve the problem by "prevention" of crime.

Beginning in the 1960s, massive and ever-expanding

welfare state programs co-existed for decades with ever-increasing crime rates, while liberal judges kept finding new reasons to turn criminals loose. Eventually, however, tougher new laws in the 1980s began to put more criminals behind bars for longer times.

Liberal Democrats loudly protested this increased locking up of criminals. Then, when the crime rate began to fall for the first time in decades, the liberals were baffled as to why this was happening.

Since a higher percentage of blacks than whites are victims of criminals, blacks have far more at stake than others when it comes to controlling crime. But Democrats have been working against the interests of law-abiding blacks because Democrats are more responsive to liberal ideologues like the American Civil Liberties Union.

The issues on which Democrats cater to blacks are largely symbolic issues, such as naming streets for Martin Luther King or throwing money at the pet projects of various community "leaders." So long as Democrats can get the votes of blacks by promoting symbolism, and the support of other groups by substantive policies, they are in good shape on election day. But blacks are not, because symbolism does nothing about education, housing or crime.

Recycled "Racism"

One of the things that happens when you get old is that what seems like news to others can look like a re-run of something you have already seen before. It is like watching an old movie for the fifth or sixth time.

A headline in the September 14, 2005 issue of the *New York Times* says: "Blacks Hit Hardest By Costlier Mortgages." Thirteen years earlier, virtually the identical story appeared in the *Wall Street Journal* under the title, "Federal Reserve Details Pervasive Racial Gap in Mortgage Lending."

Both stories were based on statistical studies by the Federal Reserve showing that blacks and whites have different experiences when applying for mortgage loans— and both stories imply that racial discrimination is the reason.

The earlier study showed that blacks were turned down for mortgage loans a higher percentage of the time than whites were and the later story shows that blacks resorted to high-priced "subprime" loans more often than whites when they financed the purchase of a home.

Both amount to the same thing—less credit being extended to blacks on the same terms as credit extended to whites.

Both studies also say that this is true even when black and white loan applicants have the same income. The first time around, back in 1992, this seemed like a pretty good case for those who blamed the differences on racial discrimination.

However, both research and old age tend to produce skepticism about things that look plausible on the surface. Just scratching the surface a little often makes a plausible case collapse like a house of cards.

For example, neither study took credit histories into account. People with lower credit ratings tend to get turned down for loans more often than people with higher credit ratings, or else they have to go where loans have higher interest rates. This is not rocket science. It is Economics 1.

Blacks in the earlier study turned out to have poor credit histories more often than whites. But the more recent news story did not even look into that.

Anyone who has ever taken out a mortgage loan knows that the lenders not only want to know what your current income is, they also want to know what your net worth is. Census data show that blacks with the same income as whites average less net worth.

That is not rocket science either. Not many blacks have affluent parents or rich uncles from whom they could inherit wealth.

The earlier study showed that whites were turned down for mortgage loans more frequently than Asian Americans and the more recent study shows that Asian Americans are less likely than whites to take out high-cost "subprime" loans to buy a house.

Does that mean that whites were being discriminated against? Or are statistics taken seriously only when they back up some preconception that is politically correct?

These are what could be called "Aha!" statistics. If you start out with a preconception and find numbers that fit that preconception, you say, "Aha!" But when the numbers don't fit any preconception—when no one believes that banks are discriminating against whites and in favor of Asian Americans—then there is no "Aha!"

Both this year's study and the one 13 years ago provoked an outburst of accusations of racism from people who are in the business of making such accusations. Moreover, where there is a "problem" proclaimed in the media there will almost invariably be a "solution" proposed in politics.

Often the solution is worse than the problem.

The older study showed that most blacks and most whites who applied for mortgage loans got them—72 percent of blacks and 89 percent of whites. So it is not as if most blacks can't get loans.

Apparently the gap has narrowed since then, for the *New York Times* reports that lenders have developed "high-cost subprime mortgages for people who would have been simply rejected outright in the past on the basis of poor credit or insufficient income."

Of course, the government can always step in and put a stop to these high-cost loans, which will probably mean that people with lower credit ratings can't buy a home at all.

Dangerous Democracy?

One of the cornerstones of the war on terrorism is the premise that promoting democracy is a long-run goal for creating a better world, one which will not breed so many terrorists. But a new book, *World on Fire* by Professor Amy Chua of the Yale law school, argues persuasively that democracy can be positively dangerous for some non-Western countries, especially when combined with a free market economy.

While democracy and free markets have been an extremely productive combination for many European and European offshoot societies, such as the United States and Australia, Professor Chua sees these two things as being like an explosive mixture in certain non-Western nations. More specifically, this combination is seen as dangerous in those countries where some ethnic minority is dominant in a free market economy, while the majority population dominates politics through their votes.

If this thesis sounds strange, try to make a list of countries that are non-Western and which enjoy the freedoms we speak of as democracy, as well as having a free market in which some minority group is dominant.

Merely making a list of countries that are both non-Western and democratic is enough of a challenge, and adding a free market proviso shrinks that already short list. Now add the key proviso that some ethnic minority dominates the economy.

The Chinese minority is dominant in the economies of

Indonesia and Malaysia, the Indian minority is dominant in Fiji, the Lebanese have been dominant in West Africa, and other groups in other places around the world. But these have seldom been democratic countries.

Perhaps Malaysia might be considered a democracy, since it has an elected government, but the glaring absence of free speech on racial issues in Malaysia keeps it from being a free society, which is what most people mean by democracy, even though that is not the original meaning of the word. It is doubtful whether Malaysia could survive if racial demagogues were free to stir up the Malay majority against the Chinese minority that is still a dominant force in that economy.

The absence of free speech on racial matters in Malaysia means that there can be no careers like those of Jesse Jackson or Al Sharpton in the United States. Maybe the U.S. is secure enough to be able to afford to let irresponsible rabble-rousers run loose—or maybe someday we will discover that we are not—but Malaysia certainly is not.

Sri Lanka started coming apart within a decade of receiving its independence as a free, democratic nation in 1948. The Tamil minority was not as dominant in its economy as the Chinese minority in Malaysia and other Southeast Asian countries, but still Tamils were over-represented at the top in business, in the professions, and in education. That was enough to allow the Sinhalese majority to be mobilized politically against them by ambitious politicians.

Even though there had never been a single race riot between the Sinhalese majority and the Tamil minority during the first half of the 20th century, there were many in the second half, punctuated by unspeakable atrocities. Eventually Sri Lanka descended into outright civil war, in which this small island nation has suffered more deaths than the United States suffered during the Vietnam war.

Similarly, according to Professor Chua, an authority on ethnic conflicts around the world, there were no major outbreaks of violence between the Hutu and Tutsi in Rwanda in the first half of the 20th century. Then majority rule brought ethnic polarization and horrifying massacres.

What about counter-examples of free, democratic, free-market, non-Western societies where an ethnic minority is blatantly more successful in the economy than the majority population, but where the people live at peace with one another? You supply those examples. I can't think of any.

Professor Chua's thesis is especially important in an era when American foreign policy sometimes seems to be pressing our allies and others to become democracies with free markets—whether or not each country's social conditions or cultural traditions provide the prerequisites for letting that particular combination be a blessing rather than a curse.

Are Cops Racist?

In much of the liberal media, large-scale confrontations between police and people who are breaking the law are usually reported in one of two ways. Either the police used "excessive force" or they "let the situation get out of hand."

Any force sufficient to prevent the situation from getting out of hand will be called "excessive." And if the police arrive in large enough numbers to squelch disorder without the need for using any force at all, then sending in so many cops will be called "over-reacting." After all, with so little resistance to the police, why were so many cops necessary? Such is the mindset of the media.

Add the volatile factor of race and the media will have a field day. If an incident involves a white cop and a black criminal, you don't need to know the specific facts to know how liberals in the media will react. You can predict the words and the music.

Heather Mac Donald of the Manhattan Institute does have the facts, however, in her new book, *Are Cops Racist?* Unfortunately, those who most need to read this book are the least likely to do so. They have made up their minds and don't want to be confused by facts.

For the rest of us, this is a very enlightening and very readable little book. Ms. Mac Donald first tackles the issue of "racial profiling" by the police and shows what shoddy and even silly statistical methods were used to gin up hysteria. Then she moves on to police shootings and other law-enforcement issues.

Suppose I were to tell you that, despite the fact that blacks are just 11 percent of the American population, more than half the men fined for misconduct while playing professional basketball are black—and concluded that this shows the NBA to be racist. What would your reaction be?

"Wait a minute!" you might say. "More than half the players in the NBA are black. So that 11 percent statistic is irrelevant."

That is exactly what is wrong with "racial profiling" statistics. It is based on blacks as a percentage of the population, rather than blacks as a percentage of the people who do the kinds of things that cause police to stop people and question them.

A professor of statistics who pointed this out was—all too predictably—denounced as a "racist." Other statisticians kept quiet for fear of being smeared the same way. We have now reached the dangerous point where ignorance can silence knowledge and where facts get squelched by beliefs.

Heather Mac Donald also goes into facts involving police shootings, especially when the cops are white and the suspect is black. Here again, an education awaits those who are willing to be educated.

People in the media are forever expressing surprise at how many bullets were fired in some of these police shootings. As someone who once taught pistol shooting in the Marine Corps, I am not the least bit surprised.

What surprises me is how many people whose ignorance of shooting is obvious do not let their ignorance stand in the way of reaching sweeping conclusions about situations that they have never faced. To some, it is just a question of taking sides. If it is a white cop and a black suspect, then that is all they feel a need to know.

The greatest contribution of this book is in making

painfully clear the actual consequences of cop-bashing in the media and in politics. The police respond to incentives, like everyone else.

If carrying out their duties in the way that gets the job done best is going to bring down on their heads a chorus of media outrage that can threaten their whole careers, many cops tend to back off. And who pays the price of their backing off? Mainly those blacks who are victims of the criminals in their midst.

Drug dealers and other violent criminals have been the beneficiaries of reduced police activity and of liberal judges throwing out their convictions because of "racial profiling." These criminals go back to the black community—not the affluent, suburban and often gated communities where journalists, judges, and politicians live.

The subtitle of *Are Cops Racist?* is: "How the War Against the Police Harms Black Americans."

Rattling the Chains

The president of Brown University has appointed a committee to look into the history of the connections of that institution to the slave trade. This is to be no academic exercise of scholarly research. There is obviously supposed to be a pot of gold at the end of this rainbow.

Brown University president Ruth J. Simmons was coy on the one hand but clear on the other. According to the *New York Times,* "Dr. Simmons said she would not reveal her opinion on reparations so as not to influence the committee."

"Here's the one thing I'll say," she stated. "If the committee comes back and says, 'Oh it's been lovely and we've learned a lot,' but there's nothing in particular that they think Brown can or should do, I will be very disappointed."

How is that for not influencing the committee? If there is anything worse than race hustling, it is being coy about race hustling. At least Al Sharpton and Jesse Jackson are up front.

Dr. Simmons said that the idea of appointing a committee to look into Brown University's past came to her because she is a descendant of slaves and the building in which she works was built with the help of slaves. Unfortunately, there are descendants of slaves all over the world, and they are every color of the rainbow.

Slavery was an ugly, dirty business but people of virtually every race, color, and creed engaged in it on every inhabited continent. And the people they enslaved were also of virtually every race, color, and creed.

A recently published book titled *Christian Slaves, Muslim Masters* by Robert Davis shows that a million Europeans were enslaved by North Africans between 1500 and 1800. Nor were they the only Europeans enslaved.

Europeans enslaved other Europeans for centuries before the drying up of that supply led them to turn to Africa as a source of slaves for the Western Hemisphere. Julius Caesar marched in triumph through Rome in a procession that included British slaves he had captured. There were white slaves still being sold in Egypt two decades after blacks were freed in the United States.

It was the same story in Asia, Africa, and among the Polynesians and the indigenous peoples of the Western Hemisphere. No race, country, or civilization had clean hands.

What makes the current reparations movement a fraud, whether at Brown University or in the country at large, is the attempt to depict slavery as something uniquely done to blacks by whites. Reparations advocates are doing this for the same reason that Willie Sutton robbed banks: That's where the money is.

No one expects Kaddafi to pay reparations to the descendants of Europeans whom his ancestors captured on the Mediterranean coast or Western Europeans to pay reparations to Slavs who were enslaved on such a scale that the very word slave derived from their name.

Still less does anyone expect Africans to pay reparations to black Americans whose ancestors they sold to white men who took them across the Atlantic. Only in America can guilt be turned into cash.

Who is supposed to benefit from all this?

Are young blacks, who have a lot of educational lags to make up, supposed to be helped by this distraction or to become more employable with a chip on their shoulders? Are they to be helped by being led to believe that the way to get ahead is to hustle white people?

White guilt is too much of a declining asset to depend on. More and more white people are feeling less and less guilty. Ruth Simmons may squeeze a few bucks out of Brown University but it is doubtful whether whatever good that does will balance the resentments and polarization it creates.

The only clear winners in the reparations movement, whether at Brown or elsewhere, are the people who engage in it. At a minimum, they get publicity and ego gratification.

Dr. Simmons' standing has no doubt risen in politically correct circles, which would include not only the academic world but the foundation world and the world of liberal politics. If she ever wants to make a career move in any of these directions, she is now well set.

But at what price?

Roasting Walter Williams

At George Mason University, they are giving a "roast"—that peculiarly American combination of praise and ridicule—to Walter Williams, professor of economics and columnist extraordinaire. Although I cannot be there, let me participate vicariously with a few observations about Walter.

I first met Walter Williams back in 1969, when I was teaching summer school at UCLA and he was a student working toward his Ph.D. in economics there. Contrary to some accounts in the media, Walter was never a student of mine. Nor did he get his ideas from me.

The very reason Walter Williams dropped by my office that summer was that someone had told him that there was another black man who was expressing the same kinds of ideas that he had been expressing before I got there. To both our surprise, we discovered that we had in fact reached similar conclusions on a wide range of issues, especially those involving race.

In the years ahead these ideas would be called "black conservatism" in the media, though it is hard to imagine two less conservative guys. In the military, each of us was indicted for a court martial—Walter in the Army and I in the Marine Corps—because we did not conform. It should not be surprising that we did not conform to the racial orthodoxy of the 1960s.

Because Walter was tied up writing his doctoral dissertation, I was the first to go into print with ideas that we both had. One of Walter's earliest writings was an article explaining why "the poor pay more" in stores in low-income neighborhoods.

Some sociologists had written a book with that title but their explanations overlooked the economic factors behind high prices in ghettos and barrios. After Walter explained the economics behind these high prices, those who were now deprived of their all-purpose explanation—racial discrimination—reacted bitterly by denouncing Walter as a "white racist."

After Walter went on television, liberals had to come up with some new derogatory labels—and they did. But these labels were like water off a duck's back to Walter Williams.

Walter was as undaunted by apartheid in South Africa as he was by lockstep racial rhetoric in the United States. Many economists have said that how much discrimination there will be depends on how much it costs to discriminate in the marketplace. But Walter was the only one to put it to a test by living in a neighborhood that the apartheid government had designated as "white only."

Not very conservative.

Out of this experience came a book titled *South Africa's War Against Capitalism.* Over the years, I have used examples from that book in my own writings. This is as good a time as any to acknowledge my debt—especially since our flawed legal system will not enable Walter to collect.

Another very enlightening book by Walter Williams is *The State Against Blacks.* This goes into the many American government policies and practices which have had a major negative economic impact on blacks.

These include minimum wage laws, occupational licensing laws, and regulation of railroads and trucking. None of these is explicitly racial in intent but their actual consequences have included restrictions of employment opportunities for blacks, as Walter demonstrates with hard facts and figures.

Both these books are written in plain English, by the way, a rarity among the writings of economists. The ability to speak this rare dialect has also helped Walter during his appearances on TV programs and as an occasional fill-in host for Rush Limbaugh.

Walter Williams is the only debater to leave Jesse Jackson speechless. On another occasion, he flabbergasted Ted Koppel when a woman on welfare said that she didn't have enough money to take care of all her children and Walter replied: "Did you ever consider that you might have had too many children for the money?"

Although Walter often comes across as hard-boiled on social issues—he once said that the government has no right to take a dime of his money to spend on someone else—the fact is that he has been very generous using his own money and his own time to help others. He just doesn't want politicians doing it and messing things up.

This is a long overdue tribute to a great guy.

"Diversity" in India

If facts carried some weight with those who are politically correct, the recent outbreak of savage and lethal violence in India's state of Gujarat might cause some reassessments of both India and "diversity."

This is only the latest round in a cycle of violence and revenge between the Hindus and the Muslims in that country. The death toll has reached 489 people in a few days. That includes the Hindu activists who were firebombed while on a train returning from the site of a razed mosque, where they planned to build a Hindu temple, and many Muslims then slaughtered by Indian mobs in retaliation.

These mobs have burned Muslim women and children alive in their homes. Nor is such savagery new in India or limited to clashes between Hindus and Muslims. At other times and places, it has been one caste against another, locals versus outsiders, or the storm trooper organization Shiv Sena against anybody who gets in their way. In some places, thugs resentful of Western influence attack shops that sell Valentine cards.

None of this fits the pious picture of peaceful and spiritual India that so captivates many Americans. India has served as one of the foreign Edens to which those Americans turn, in order to show their disdain for the United States.

At one time, the Soviet Union played that role, then China, then Cuba, and for some, India. What happens in the real India doesn't matter. It is the symbolic India of their dreams to which they impute all the virtues they declare to be lacking in the USA.

It is not India's fault that we have some fatuous Americans who want to put Indians up on a pedestal, in order to score points against their fellow Americans. But we need to be aware of the truth as well.

Those who are constantly gushing about the supposed benefits of "diversity" never want to put their beliefs to the test of looking at the facts about countries where people are divided by language, culture, religion, and in other ways, such as caste in India. Such countries are all too often riddled with strife and violence.

India is one of the most diverse nations on earth. No more than one-third of its people speak any given language and the population is divided innumerable ways by caste, ethnicity, religion and numerous localisms. Lethal riots have marked its history from the beginning.

When India gained its independence in 1947, the number of Hindus and Muslims who killed each other in one year exceeded the total number of blacks lynched in the entire history of the United States. Yet we are told that we should be like those gentle people, as if India were a nation of Gandhis. In reality, Gandhi was assassinated for trying to stop internecine strife in India.

If there is no need to impute wholly unrealistic sainthood to India, there is also no need to single it out for demonization. Many other countries with the much-touted "diversity" have likewise been racked by internal slaughters and atrocities.

Only about 20 miles away from India, the island nation of Sri Lanka has suffered more deaths among its majority and minority populations, as a result of internal strife and civil war, than the much larger United States suffered during the Vietnam war. Other such "diverse" countries as Rwanda and those in the Balkans have a similar catalogue of horrors.

"Diversity" is not just a matter of demographics. It is also a matter of "identity" and identity politics. Sri Lanka was one of the most peaceful nations on earth before demagogues began hyping identity and demanding group preferences and quotas back in the 1950s.

Demographically, the United States has always been diverse, having received immigrants from all over the world. However, until recent times, it was understood by all that they came here to become Americans—not to remain foreign. By the second generation, most were speaking English, and by the third generation they were speaking only English.

Today, however, our citizen-of-the-world types are doing all they can to keep foreigners foreign and domestic minorities riled up over grievances, past and present, real and imaginary. Above all, they want group identity and group preferences and quotas.

In short, they want all the things that have brought on the kinds of disasters from which India and other such "diverse" countries have suffered grievously.

Race and IQ

Years ago, while doing research on education and IQ, I happened to be in the principal's office at a black school in Cincinnati, as he was preparing to open a large brown envelope containing the results of IQ tests that his students had taken. Before he opened the envelope, I offered to bet him that a large majority of the students with IQs over 110 would be girls.

He was too smart to take the bet. Studies had shown that females predominated among high-IQ blacks. One study of blacks whose IQs were 140 and up found that there were more than five times as many females as males at these levels.

This is hard to explain by either heredity or environment, as those terms are usually defined, since black males and black females have the same ancestors and grow up in the same homes. Meanwhile, white males and white females have the same average IQs, with slightly more males at both the highest and lowest IQs.

This is just one of many unsolved mysteries that is likely to remain unsolved, because doing research on race and IQ has become taboo in many places. My own research was financed in part by a grant from a foundation that told me to remove any mention of IQ research from the activities listed in my project's application.

They didn't care if I used their money for that purpose but they did not want it on the record that they had financed research into race and intelligence. Many schools and boards of education also did not want it on the record that they had cooperated by supplying data for any such research. Only when assured of complete anonymity would they let me into their records.

A well-known black "social scientist" urged me not to do any such research. His stated reason was that it would "dignify" Professor Arthur Jensen's thesis of a genetic basis for black-white differences in IQ scores. But my own suspicion was that he was afraid that the research would prove Jensen right.

As it turned out, the research showed that the average IQ difference between black and white Americans—15 points—was nothing unusual. Similar IQ differences could be found between various culturally isolated white communities and the general society, both in the United States and in Britain. Among various groups in India, mental test differences were slightly greater than those between blacks and whites in the United States.

In recent years, research by Professor James R. Flynn, an American expatriate living in New Zealand, has shaken up the whole IQ controversy by discovering what has been called "the Flynn effect." In various countries around the world, people have been answering significantly more IQ test questions correctly than in the past.

This important fact has been inadvertently concealed by the practice of changing the norms on IQ tests, so that the average number of correctly answered questions remains by definition an IQ of 100. Only by painstakingly going back and recalculating IQs, based on the initial norms, was Professor Flynn able to discover that whole nations had, in effect, had their IQs rising over the decades by about 20 points.

Since the black-white difference in IQ is 15 points, this

means that an even larger IQ difference has existed between different generations of the same race, making it no longer necessary to attribute IQ differences of this magnitude to genetics. In the half century between 1945 and 1995, black Americans' raw test scores rose by the equivalent of 16 IQ points.

In other words, black Americans' test score results in 1995 would have given them an average IQ just over 100 in 1945. Only the repeated renorming of IQ tests upward created the illusion that blacks had made no progress, but were stuck at an IQ of 85. But we would never have known this if some researchers had not defied the taboo on studying race and IQ imposed by black "leaders" and white "friends."

Incidentally, Professor Jensen pointed out back in 1969 that black children's IQ scores rose by 8 to 10 points after he met with them informally in a play room and then tested them again after they were more relaxed around him. He did this because "I felt these children were really brighter than their IQ would indicate." What a shame that others seem to have less confidence in black children than Professor Jensen has had.

Race and IQ: Part II

Professor John McWhorter, a black faculty member at the University of California at Berkeley, has made a suggestion that is explosive in itself and directly the opposite of what is being said by those who are seeking to promote lower college admissions standards for blacks through affirmative action.

One of the reasons given for wanting more black students on a given campus, even if that means lowering admissions standards, is the claim that a certain number of blacks—a "critical mass"—on campus is necessary, in order for these students to feel comfortable enough to relax and do their best work. It sounds plausible, but lots of things have sounded plausible.

Professor McWhorter says just the opposite in his book *Losing the Race*. According to McWhorter, anti-intellectualism in the black culture keeps many black youngsters from doing their best. If he is right, then creating a critical mass is creating a bigger handicap for black students.

There have been many media stories about hard-working black school children being ostracized, or even threatened with or subjected to violence, for "acting white" by trying to succeed academically. Creating a critical mass with that attitude is unlikely to help anyone.

More direct factual evidence is available, however. A study of the effect of an increased proportion of black students in a racially integrated school found little effect of this on the academic performances of most other students—

except for high-ability black students, whose performances declined.

Another study, about the effects of ability-grouping, found that high-ability students performed better when put into classes with other high-ability students—and that this was especially so with high-ability minority students. In other words, a critical mass of students sorted by high ability did more for bright minority students than a critical mass of students sorted by race.

If Professor McWhorter is right, then his thesis might also help explain another puzzling phenomenon. A study of black orphans adopted by white families found their test scores to be higher than those of black youngsters raised by their own biological families. However, this initial finding eroded away when these same students were tested again in later years.

One of the things that can change as black kids grow older is that they become more conscious of race as they go into adolescence—and more responsive to peer pressure. If Professor McWhorter is right, then an anti-intellectual culture would be more likely to handicap them in the later period.

In an earlier era, when there were seldom enough blacks on most elite white college campuses to form a "critical mass," did those students not do as well as in the post-affirmative action era, when blacks became more numerous on such campuses?

It is significant that no such evidence has been sought by those promoting the critical mass theory. However, students who graduated from an academically outstanding black high school in Washington between 1892 and 1954 left an impressive academic record at Amherst College during that era, even though there were seldom more than a handful of black students on that campus at that time.

About three-quarters of these black students graduated from Amherst and more than one-fifth of these graduates were Phi Beta Kappas. This was long before the era of grade inflation or affirmative action.

None of this is definitive proof. But those with the critical mass theory offer no evidence at all and none is asked. Their views prevail by default—and dogmatism.

The time is long overdue to judge beliefs and the policies based on them by what actually works, not by what sounds good or what makes people feel good.

Having opposed the racial inferiority thesis in various writings over the years, I have in my own teaching held black students to the same standards as white students, though not all black students appreciated this kind of equality. Many of those who promote double standards for blacks seem convinced that blacks cannot achieve what whites have achieved. That is part of the ugly secret behind affirmative action.

Race and IQ: Part III

I happened to run into Charles Murray in Dulles Airport while he and Richard Herrnstein were writing *The Bell Curve*. When I asked him what he was working on and he summarized what he was writing, he could tell that I was concerned about him, so I told him why: "Charles, no matter what you say, people will hear what they want to hear."

That is one prediction that I wish had not come true, but it has. There are people who have never read a single word of *The Bell Curve* but who are convinced that they not only know what it says but also know what the motivation was for saying it.

Partly this is because there are increasing numbers of people for whom indignation is a way of life. But that is not the sole reason. Historically, blacks have been among the many peoples accused of being innately inferior, especially in intelligence.

Back in the days of the Roman Empire, Cicero warned his fellow Romans not to buy British slaves, because he found them hard to teach anything. A 10th century Muslim scholar noted that Europeans grew more pale the farther north they were and that the "farther they are to the north the more stupid, gross, and brutish they are."

With our love of labels today, we might dismiss both these statements as "racism." In reality, both statements were probably true, as of the time they were made. At the very least, the people who said these things were eyewitnesses, which we cannot possibly be.

Britain was a primitive, illiterate, tribal land at a time when the Roman Empire was in its glory as one of the most advanced civilizations on earth. A Briton transplanted to Rome in captivity must have found this complex civilization completely baffling and was probably none too quick to understand instructions on what to do and how to do it in such a wholly unfamiliar setting.

As of the 10th century, the Islamic world was more advanced than Europe in general and far more advanced than the northern regions of Europe, which had for centuries lagged behind Mediterranean Europe. The relative development of these different regions of Europe, especially in economic terms, would be reversed in later centuries, but what the Muslim scholar said in the 10th century was probably still true then.

The point here is that there have always been gaps between the development of one people and another, even if their relative positions did not remain the same permanently, and even if their genes had nothing to do with it. In the case of blacks in the United States, there was a special reason for particularly negative pronouncements.

Although slavery existed all over the world for thousands of years, among people of every race, it was considered a "peculiar institution" in the United States because it was in complete contradiction to the principles on which the country was founded. Slavery was controversial among Americans when it was still accepted as just another fact of life in other countries.

Nowhere else in the world was such a literature of justification of slavery produced as in the antebellum South, because nowhere else was slavery under such sustained attack. An especially virulent racism arose to try to justify slavery, and this racism lasted long after slavery itself was gone.

That history and its painful consequences are undeniable. But, in a world where whole nations have in effect raised their IQs by 20 points in one generation, it is time for black "leaders" and white "friends" to stop trying to discredit the tests and get on with the job of improving the skills that the tests measure.

A number of black schools, even in rundown ghettos, have already reached or exceeded national norms on tests, so there is no question that it can be done. The question is whether it will in fact be done, on a large enough scale to change the abysmal educational results in too many predominantly black schools.

So long as demagogues are concentrating on demonizing anyone who points out the problem, do not expect the kind of general improvement that is needed. This demonization has made *The Bell Curve* one of the most misrepresented books of our time. But such demagoguery has not helped one black child to get a better education.

An Old War and a New One

Back in 1939, when Senator Daniel Inouye was a teenager, he attended a Japanese language school in Hawaii. He was appalled to discover that it was also a center for political propaganda, urging young Japanese Americans like himself to remember that they were Japanese first and owed an overriding loyalty to Japan—in peace or in war. They also ridiculed Christianity.

When young Daniel Inouye objected, he was thrown bodily out of the school. Later, during World War II, he proved his loyalty to America as a soldier in battle, where he lost an arm.

Inouye was one of many Japanese Americans who proved themselves in battle, many winning combat medals for valor. It is also true that there were some other Japanese Americans who went to Japan and joined their military forces to fight against America.

In short, there were both loyal Japanese Americans and disloyal Japanese Americans, including among the latter some who cooperated with Japan's espionage and subversion networks within the United States before and during the war. This was recognized at the time, even within the Japanese American community.

They could hardly have failed to recognize the disloyal among them, for some loyal Japanese Americans were bullied or beaten by those who were loyal to Japan.

The passage of time has, however, caused much of this to fade into the background. Thus steps taken during the war to deal with the dangers of espionage and subversion have later been widely attributed to sheer racism, an ever-popular explanation in some quarters.

A new book by Michelle Malkin, titled *In Defense of Internment*, challenges the widespread condemnation of the relocation of Japanese Americans away from the militarily vulnerable west coast. She brings out many facts and arguments that have long been ignored by those who prefer simpler explanations that enable them to condemn America.

As if inconvenient facts were not enough to guarantee that she would be viciously attacked and demonized, Ms. Malkin argues that what is called "racial profiling" was valid then, with the country in grave danger, and is valid again today when it comes to people from the Middle East living in the United States.

Michelle Malkin does not say that all Arabs or Muslims in America today should be rounded up and interned. Nor does she claim that all or most Japanese Americans were disloyal during World War II. Her argument is much more sober and thoughtful than that, and a brief summary here cannot do it justice.

Ms. Malkin's book begins with the essential task of trying to re-create for today's generation of Americans the circumstances and dangers faced by the United States in early 1942, when the relocation of Japanese Americans began.

The term "relocation" is more accurate than the term "internment" that has become more popular. Japanese American citizens in the west coast military zone were allowed to move anywhere else in the country without going into internment camps, and thousands did.

Relocation was the policy but internment became the

reality for most, because at that time many were still citizens of Japan and thus enemy aliens in wartime. Internment on the mainland was an alternative to putting the whole west coast population—of whatever race or citizenship—under martial law, as happened in Hawaii.

The times were grim and the choices stark, even if later second-guessers would grandly dismiss as "hysteria" the weighty concerns of that time. Japan launched many stunning attacks in the wake of its bombing of Pearl Harbor, including the sinking of American ships off the California coast and the shelling of that coast itself. No one knew where Japan would strike next.

In Defense of Internment is a carefully researched and carefully analyzed history but it is also a warning for our own times. Too many American lives are at risk today from people already inside this country to be paralyzed by the politically correct rhetoric of those who decry "racial profiling."

"It is entirely appropriate to take into account nationality when deciding which foreigners present the highest risks," Michelle Malkin says. Agree or disagree with her book, it makes us think—and political correctness is no substitute for thought.

Silly Letters

Most of the letters and e-mails I receive are a pleasure to read and my only regret is that I cannot answer even one-tenth of them. However, there are certain e-mails and letters that repeat the same fallacies again and again. Let me try to answer one of those fallacies now, once and for all.

One of the silly things that gets said repeatedly is that I should not be against affirmative action because I have myself benefitted from it.

Think about it: I am more than 70 years old. There was no affirmative action when I went to college—or to graduate school, for that matter. There wasn't even a Civil Rights Act of 1964 when I began my academic career in 1962.

Moreover, there is nothing that I have accomplished in my education or my career that wasn't accomplished by other blacks before me—and therefore long before affirmative action.

Getting a degree from Harvard? The first black man graduated from Harvard in 1870.

Becoming a black economist? There was a black economist teaching at the University of Chicago when I first arrived there as a graduate student in 1959.

Writing a newspaper column? George Schuyler wrote newspaper columns, magazine articles, and books before I was born.

A recent silly e-mail declared that I wouldn't even be able to vote in this year's California election if there hadn't been a Voting Rights Act of 1965. I have been voting ever since I was 21 years old—in 1951.

The Civil Rights Act of 1964 and the Voting Rights Act of 1965 were necessary for some people in some places. But making these things the cause of the rise of most blacks only betrays an ignorance of history.

The most dramatic rise of blacks out of poverty occurred before the civil rights movement of the 1960s. That's right—before. But politicians, activists and the intelligentsia have spread so much propaganda that many Americans, black and white, are unaware of the facts.

There is a lot of political mileage to be gotten by convincing blacks that they owe everything to the government and could not make it in this world otherwise. Dependency plus paranoia equals votes. But blacks made it in this world before the government paid them any attention.

Nor has the economic rise of blacks been speeded up by civil rights legislation. More blacks rose into professional ranks in the years immediately *preceding* the Civil Rights Act of 1964 than in the years right after its passage.

What moved blacks up was a rapid increase in education. There was certainly discrimination but, in many fields that demanded higher levels of education, there were not that many blacks to discriminate against in the first place.

Moreover, even if certain laws and policies may once have served a purpose, that does not mean that these laws and policies should last forever, in total disregard of their counterproductive effects today. For a California election in 2003 to be held up by the federal government because of what happened in Mississippi decades ago is ludicrous.

Finally, the argument that anyone who has benefitted from affirmative action should never oppose it is as illogical as it is ignorant of the facts. I certainly benefitted from the Korean war, which led to my being in the military and therefore getting the G.I. Bill that enabled me to go to college.

Does that mean that I should never be against any war? Was it wrong of me to be against the Vietnam war after I had personally benefitted from the Korean war? Are the duties of a citizen, not to mention the duty to be honest and truthful, to be overridden by what happened to benefit me personally?

Some of the things I advocate would ruin me personally if my recommendations were followed. For example, I am totally opposed to the environmentalist extremism that has made it an ordeal to try to build any kind of housing—much less "affordable housing"—on the San Francisco peninsula. But if such restrictive policies were repealed, the inflated value of my home would be cut at least in half when more housing began to be built in the area.

Is myopic selfishness supposed to be a moral obligation?

Black History Month

What is called Black History Month might more accurately be called "the sins of white people" month. The sins of any branch of the human race are virtually inexhaustible, but the history of blacks in America includes a lot more than the sins of white people, which are put front and center each February.

Obviously, there is current political mileage to be gotten from historic grievances. At a minimum, politicians and activists get the media attention that is the lifeblood of their careers. Then there are racial quotas, money for special minority programs and hopes for reparations for slavery. If nothing else, some people get excuses for their own shortcomings—and excuses are very important.

One of the many penetrating insights of the late Eric Hoffer was that, for many people, an excuse is better than an achievement. That is because an achievement, no matter how great, leaves you having to prove yourself again in the future. But an excuse can last for life.

Those black achievements which did not involve fighting the sins of white people get little attention during Black History Month. Indeed, many of those achievements undermine the blanket excuse that white sins are what prevent blacks from accomplishing more. How many people have heard of Paul Williams, who became a prominent black architect long before the civil rights revolution, or about successful black writers in the 19th century?

There was also an outstanding black high school in

Washington, D. C., which had remarkable achievements from 1870 to 1955. For example, most of its graduates during that period went on to college, even though most white high school graduates did not make it to college during that era. As far back as 1899, this school's students scored higher on standardized tests than two of the three white academic high schools in the District of Columbia.

Given the terrible educational performances of so many ghetto schools, you might think that there would be great interest in how this particular school succeeded when so many others failed. But you would be wrong. Where there was any reaction at all from the black establishment to an article I wrote about the history of this school, that reaction was hostility.

Dunbar High School was an achievement but it destroyed a thousand excuses. The prevailing dogma is that all the failures of black schools were due to the sins of white people, including inadequate funding and racial segregation. But Dunbar was inadequately funded—its class sizes were sometimes 40 or more—and it was racially segregated for more than 80 years. Its history of success was therefore not welcomed by black "leaders."

Another big problem with Black History Month is its narrowness. You cannot understand even your own history if that is the only history you know. Some explanations of what has happened in your history might sound plausible within the framework of just one people's history, but these explanations can collapse like a house of cards if you look at the same factors in the histories of other groups, other countries, and other eras.

Shelby Steele has pointed out that whites are desperate to escape guilt and blacks are desperate to escape implications of inferiority. But, viewed against the background of world history, neither group of Americans is unique. Nor are the differences between them. Both their anxieties are overblown.

Black-white differences in income, IQ, lifestyle or anything else you care to name are exceeded by differences between innumerable other groups around the world today and throughout history—even when none of the factors that we blame for the differences in America were present.

For example, when the Romans invaded Britain, they came from an empire with magnificent art, architecture, literature, political organization and military might. But the Britons were an illiterate tribal people. There was not a building on the island and no Briton's name had ever been recorded in the pages of history.

The Britons didn't build London. The Romans built London. And when the Romans left, four centuries later, the country fragmented into tribal domains again, the economy collapsed, and buildings and roads decayed. No one would have dreamed at that point that someday there would be a British Empire to exceed anything the Romans had ever achieved.

Maybe we need a British History Month.

Bravo for Bill Cosby

Bill Cosby has provided a lot of laughs for millions of Americans over the years but black "leaders" were not laughing after he lashed out at those black parents who buy their children expensive sneakers instead of something educational. He also denounced both those children and those adults in the black community who refuse to speak the king's English.

"Everybody knows it's important to speak English except these knuckleheads," Cosby said. "You can't be a doctor with that kind of crap coming out of your mouth." He also mocked those who referred to "the incarcerated" as "political prisoners."

At this gathering on the 50th anniversary of *Brown v. Board of Education*, some in the audience laughed and applauded but the pillars of the black "leadership" establishment—the head of the NAACP, the head of the NAACP Legal Defense Fund, and the president of Howard University—were "stone-faced," according to the *Washington Post*.

Theodore Shaw of the Legal Defense Fund then "told the crowd that most people on welfare are not African Americans, and many of the problems his organization has addressed in the black community were not self-inflicted."

Other groups are not perfect—but is that an excuse for doing self-destructive things?

Bill Cosby and the black "leadership" represent two long-standing differences about how to deal with the problems of the black community. The "leaders" are concerned with protecting the image of blacks, while Cosby is trying to protect the future of blacks, especially those of the younger generation.

Far from just bashing blacks, Cosby has given generously to promote black education. But he is still old-fashioned enough to think that others need to take some responsibility for using the opportunities that were gained for them by "people who marched and were hit in the face with rocks to get an education."

Now, in too many black communities, dedicating yourself to getting an education is called "acting white."

These are painful realities and they do not become any less real or any less painful by hushing them up. Nobody enjoys being made to look bad in public. But too many in the black community are preoccupied with how things will look to white people, with what in private life would be concern about "what will the neighbors think?"

When your children are dying, you don't worry about what the neighbors think. When the whole future of a race is jeopardized by self-destructive fads, you put public relations on the back burner.

There are still whites out there who think that blacks are innately incapable of achievement—and some of them support affirmative action for that reason. But there is plenty of evidence that innate ability, or even developed mental skills, are not the big problem.

Not only blacks with low test scores, but even blacks with high test scores, do not do as well academically as whites with the same test scores. Among Asian Americans, it is just the opposite. They do better than whites with the same test scores, whether in educational institutions or in economic activities.

Years ago, Cosby urged a group of young blacks to put more effort into their studies, the way Asian students do. "Do you know why they are called Asians?" he asked. "Because they always get A's."

The differences among all these groups are in one four-letter word that you are still not supposed to say: work.

Anyone who has taught black, white, and Asian students will know that they do not work equally. Studies show it but you don't need studies. Just go into a university library on a Saturday night and see who is there and who is not there.

In some places, you might think it was an all-Asian university, judging by the students in the library on Saturday night.

How surprised should you be when you go into a classroom on Monday morning and find out who is on top of the work and who is struggling to keep up?

What Bill Cosby said was no laughing matter. It is closer to being something to cry about.

Quota "Logic"

Old-timers may remember a radio program about a crime-fighting hero called The Shadow, who had "the power to cloud men's minds, so that they cannot see him." Affirmative action has that same power today. Some of the murkiest thinking of our times has come from those defending group preferences and quotas.

Professor James M. McPherson of Princeton University has launched a recent defense of affirmative action that is classic. For example, affirmative action is redefined to include such things as the fact that he and other white males of his generation "received a great deal of support from faculty and families to aspire to a career" and to hope to reach the top, while minorities and women did not.

This was, Professor McPherson says, "a more powerful form of affirmative action than anything we have more recently experienced in the opposite direction." Moreover, he was first hired to teach at Princeton on the recommendation of his faculty adviser at Johns Hopkins, part of "the infamous 'old-boy network,' surely the most powerful instrument of affirmative action ever devised."

As if this were not enough special privilege, James McPherson was also part of a generation born "during the trough of the Depression-era birth rate," so that he entered the job market just when the baby boom generation was being educated, at a time when there were relatively few people from the previous generation around to educate them. Therefore he was spared the exhausting job searches of today.

"The jobs sought us, not vice versa," he says. This too constituted—you guessed it—affirmative action. Professor McPherson calls it "a sort of demographic affirmative action."

Even if we accept all of Professor McPherson's arguments and redefinitions, what is the conclusion that he reaches? Is he going to resign his professorship at Princeton and his presidency of the American Historical Association as undeserved windfalls? Not on your life!

Instead, McPherson is prepared to sacrifice other people to his vision of undeserved good fortune. "Having benefitted in so many ways from these older forms of affirmative action that favored white males," he says, he cannot condemn the newer version that "seems to disadvantage this same category."

In short, older white males of Professor McPherson's generation benefitted unfairly, so reparations are owed to minorities and women—not from those who benefitted, but from white males of this generation, including those too young to have had anything to do with the advantages and disadvantages he describes.

And we thought The Shadow could cloud men's minds!

This is classic academic self-indulgence in the name of noblesse oblige. Professor McPherson can get credit for noblesse and force someone else to pay the cost of oblige.

This argument is also classic academic thinking in another sense—talking about people in the abstract, as members of "the same category." As Professor McPherson knows full well from his scholarly work, the 14th Amendment mandates equal treatment for flesh-and-blood individuals, not for abstract categories.

One of the many differences between abstract people and flesh-and-blood human beings is that real people are born, live and die—taking their sins and their sufferings to the grave with them. Only by focusing on abstract categories that live on can redressing the wrongs of history be made to seem even plausible.

Professor McPherson's argument also confuses gratitude and guilt. He should indeed be grateful for the support and encouragement that he received from family and mentors. But neither he nor they should feel guilty because others did not receive similar support and encouragement.

Anyone who is serious about extending the same benefits to others must become serious about developing the same abilities in others—that is, raising them up to the same standards, not bringing the standards down to them.

Finally, the notion that demographic trends constitute social injustices to be lamented shows the unreality of this jerry-built argument. But confusing the vagaries of fate with the sins of man is also part of the argument for affirmative action—and betrays how lacking it is in real arguments.

Quota "Logic": Part II

Princeton professor James M. McPherson's recent arguments for affirmative action, in a newsletter to members of the American Historical Association, make many sweeping assertions and implicit assumptions that need not even be challenged to show the shakiness of his arguments. However, since we both belong to an organization devoted to history, let me make a few corrections of the history that Professor McPherson offers.

First of all, he mentions that his academic career began in 1962 at Princeton, as a result of what he now calls "the infamous 'old boy network,'" which he characterizes as affirmative action for white males. Despite being black, my own academic career also began that very same year, 1962, just a few miles up the road from where McPherson's career began, at Douglass College, Rutgers University.

I too received my appointment via the old boy network, being recommended by my mentors at the University of Chicago, just as McPherson was recommended by his mentor at Johns Hopkins. Women were hired the same way, out of the same "old boy network," which was also an old girls' network.

I was hired despite the fact that Douglass College was a college for young women and almost all these women were white. I was even hired despite having challenged and antagonized one of the senior members of the department during the job interview.

Incidentally, during my first semester of teaching, I

received an unexpected offer of another appointment, at the University of California at La Jolla. A signed contract arrived in the mail, requiring only my signature to make it official. So the idea that there were no academic opportunities for blacks in 1962 is not easy to sell to someone who was there. Save that one for guilty whites.

McPherson makes much of the fact that "virtually none" of his fellow students in graduate school were minorities or women. That was my experience as well, but Professor McPherson leaves the impression that absence means exclusion. Otherwise, why is that fact relevant to his discussion of affirmative action?

We need not rely on personal anecdotes, either his or mine. My research, using data from the American Council on Education, showed that black faculty members with the same degrees and publications as white faculty members were receiving higher pay than their white counterparts, as far back as 1969.

The real problem was that there were not nearly enough black faculty members with the same qualifications. There are still not enough. In some years, the total number of blacks in the entire country who receive Ph.D.s in mathematics is in single digits.

With women, the problem was different: Women became mothers and that was by no means the same as men becoming fathers, no matter what politically correct parallels we create today with words, such as "an expectant couple."

Those academic women who never married—which, back in those days, had some relationship to becoming a mother—had higher incomes than academic men who never married. Apparently Professor McPherson's "infamous 'old boy network'" was either not as powerful or not as sinister as he depicts.

The fact that recommendations from established scholars in a field carry weight when hiring an unknown graduate student to become a faculty member has been made to seem like some exclusionary plot, if you believe defenders of affirmative action. Indeed, any reliance on any criterion of quality—test scores, publications, whatever—can be depicted as an exclusionary bias by those who want quotas.

White guilt may be fashionable in some quarters but the only people it helps are those whites who want to become saints on the cheap and those blacks who have learned to hustle guilty whites. What most blacks need is—first of all— the kind and quality of education that they do not get in most ghetto schools. Least of all do they get this education from those teachers who spend precious class time dredging up the past instead of preparing students for the future.

Professor McPherson's defense of affirmative action to members of the American Historical Association invited comments via e-mail (jmcphers@princeton.edu). He did not say whether that included comments from people in the real world beyond the ivied walls.

PART VIII

RANDOM THOUGHTS

Random Thoughts

Random thoughts on the passing scene:

One of the sad signs of our times is that we have demonized those who produce, subsidized those who refuse to produce, and canonized those who complain.

Everything is relative. In much of coastal California, Ted Kennedy would be politically middle of the road—and, in San Francisco, right of center.

My computer operating system is so out of date that people don't even write viruses for it any more.

Politics is the art of making your selfish desires seem like the national interest.

If navel-gazing, hand-wringing or self-dramatization helped with racial issues, we would have achieved Utopia long ago.

People who cannot be bothered to learn both sides of the issues should not bother to vote.

Impractical men especially need to get married. The problem is that practical women may have better sense than to marry them.

The old adage about giving a man a fish versus teaching him how to fish has been updated by a reader: Give a man a fish and he will ask for tartar sauce and French fries! Moreover, some politician who wants his vote will declare all these things to be among his "basic rights."

There are people who can neither find happiness in their own lives nor permit those around them to be happy. The best you can do is get such people out of your life.

What is called an educated person is often someone who has had a dangerously superficial exposure to a wide spectrum of subjects.

If the battle for civilization comes down to the wimps versus the barbarians, the barbarians are going to win.

I am going to stop procrastinating—one of these days.

Thanksgiving may be our most old-fashioned holiday. Gratitude itself seems out of date at a time when so many people feel "entitled" to whatever they get—and indignant that they didn't get more.

When this column predicted that a discredited study would continue to be cited by gun control advocates, I had no idea that it would happen the next week in the 9th Circuit Court of Appeals.

It is a little much when people come to this country preaching hatred against others and demanding tolerance for themselves.

It may be expecting too much to expect most intellectuals to have common sense, when their whole life is based on their being uncommon—that is, saying things that are different from what everyone else is saying. There is only so much genuine originality in anyone. After that, being uncommon means indulging in pointless eccentricities or clever attempts to mock or shock.

As I try to clear out the paper jungle in my office, my wife has suggested using dynamite. But I am saving that as Plan B.

Those who want to take our money and gain power over us have discovered the magic formula: Get us envious or angry at others and we will surrender, in installments, not only our money but our freedom. The most successful dictators of the 20th century—Hitler, Lenin, Stalin, Mao—all used this formula and now class warfare politicians here are doing the same.

Everyone is for "due process" in our courts. But the very concept of due process implies that there can be such a thing as undue process. Unfortunately, undue process is also found in our courts—perhaps more often than due process.

As a black man, I am offended when white people take the likes of Al Sharpton seriously—or pretend to.

The scariest thing about politics today is not any particular policy or leaders, but the utter gullibility with which the public accepts notions for which there is not a speck of evidence, such as the benefits of "diversity," the dangers of "overpopulation," and innumerable other fashionable dogmas.

People who are very aware that they have more knowledge than the average person are often very unaware that they do not have one-tenth of the knowledge of all of the average persons put together.

Immigration has become one of a growing number of issues that can no longer be discussed rationally, but must be discussed only in pious shibboleths.

Watching CNN after watching Fox News Network is like drinking skim milk after you have gotten used to egg nog.

A lot of what is called "public service" consists of making hoops for other people to jump through. It is a great career for those who cannot feel fulfilled unless they are telling other people what to do.

The Empire State Building was built in less time than has already been spent debating what to build on the site of the World Trade Center.

One of these days the 9th Circuit Court of Appeals may declare the Constitution unconstitutional.

Everything depends on what you are used to. There is a story about a man from Los Angeles who went up to a mountaintop, took a deep breath of the clear fresh air and said: "What's that funny smell?"

The end of the Cold War now reveals that many on the far left who were thought of as pro-Communist were in fact anti-American—as they have remained, even as our enemies have changed.

I hate to think that someday Americans will be looking at the radioactive ruins of their cities and saying that this happened because their leaders were afraid of the word "unilateral."

There is no excuse for sending grossly abused children back

to their abusive parents, when there are plenty of people who want to adopt a child—and who are being put through the wringer by the same social workers who want to give terrible parents second, third, and fourth chances.

People who enjoy meetings should not be in charge of anything.

My favorite New Year's resolution was to stop trying to reason with unreasonable people. This has reduced both my correspondence and my blood pressure.

E-mail from the mother of a late-talking child: "We didn't know Ryan could read letters and numbers until one day when he was two-and-a-half years old and I held up a number 9 and asked him what it was. He turned his back to me, bent over, looked between his legs and said, '6.' Then he stood up, faced me and said, '9'!"

Activism is a way for useless people to feel important, even if the consequences of their activism are counterproductive for those they claim to be helping and damaging to the fabric of society as a whole.

It is amazing that people who think we cannot afford to pay for doctors, hospitals, and medications somehow think that we can afford to pay for doctors, hospitals, medications and a government bureaucracy to administer "universal health care."

No matter how much people on the left talk about compassion, they have no compassion for the taxpayers.

Intellectuals may like to think of themselves as people who

"speak truth to power" but too often they are people who speak lies to gain power.

Why do actors—people whose main talent is faking emotions—think that their opinions should be directing the course of political events in the real world? Yet it is a mistake that they have been making as far back as John Wilkes Booth.

Although rank-and-file terrorists are sent out on suicide missions, many of the leaders who send them out have been captured alive. I wonder if this will cause some second thoughts—or perhaps first thoughts—among their followers.

Much of what is promoted as "critical thinking" in our public schools is in fact uncritical negativism towards the history and institutions of America and an uncritical praise of the cultures of foreign countries and domestic minorities.

Too many critics of missile defense start the argument in the middle, with enemy missiles already in the air. But, if a missile defense system simply creates enough serious doubt in an enemy's mind as to whether his missiles will get through, then it has done its job.

People who send me letters or e-mails containing belligerent personal attacks probably have no idea how reassuring their messages are, for they show that critics seldom have any rational arguments to offer.

France has never gotten over the fact that it was once a great power and is now just a great nuisance.

Sometimes life seems like Italian opera music—beautiful but heart-breaking.

Considering how often throughout history even intelligent people have been proved to be wrong, it is amazing that there are still people who are convinced that the only reason anyone could possibly say something different from what they believe is stupidity or dishonesty.

While it is true that you learn with age, the down side is that what you learn is often what a damn fool you were before.

Ask anyone who is suffering the agonies of some terrible disease whether he believes that there is such a thing as reality, or whether he thinks it is all just a matter of "perceptions." The pompous but silly notion that it is all a matter of how you choose to look at things is an indulgence for those who are insulated from suffering, from accountability, and from reality.

A reader has suggested that elections be held on April 16th—the day after we pay our income taxes. That is one of the few things that might discourage politicians from being big spenders.

A reader writes: "I want to live in the country I grew up in. Where is it?"

If you talk to yourself, at least carry a cell phone, so that people won't think you are crazy.

Judges should ask themselves: Are we turning the law into a trap for honest people and a bonanza for charlatans?

When youngsters say that "everybody" does this or that, it probably never occurs to them that what they call "everybody" is probably less than one percent of the human race.

Some full professors could more accurately be described as empty professors.

Why is there so much hand-wringing about how to keep track of violent sex offenders after they have been released from prison? If it is so dangerous to release them, then why are they being released, when laws can be rewritten to keep them behind bars?

Both the Sicilian mafia and the criminal tongs in China began as movements to defend the oppressed, so perhaps we should not be so painfully surprised that venerable American civil rights organizations have begun to degenerate into extortion rackets.

The next time you hear an alarming speech about "global warming" on Earth Day, just remember that the first Earth Day featured alarms about the danger of a new ice age.

Too often what are called "educated" people are simply people who have been sheltered from reality for years in ivy-covered buildings. Those whose whole careers have been spent in ivy-covered buildings, insulated by tenure, can remain adolescents on into their golden retirement years.

Some ideas sound so plausible that they can fail nine times in a row and still be believed the tenth time. Other ideas sound so implausible that they can succeed nine times in a row and still not be believed the tenth time. Government controls in the economy are among the first kinds of ideas and the operations of a free market are among the second kind.

It is amazing how many people seem to think that the government exists to turn their prejudices into laws.

One of the sad signs of our times are the twisted metal "sculptures" put in front of public buildings at the taxpayers' expense—obviously never intended to please the public, and in fact constituting a thumbing of the artist's nose at the public.

"Tell all" autobiographies sometimes tell more than all.

Would you prefer to have a "compulsory" health care system imposed on you and your doctor or to have "universal" health care? Or do you realize that they are the same thing in different words?

You can fail to achieve any of the things you planned and still live a happy and fulfilled life, because of opportunities that come along that you never planned for. But these opportunities can be missed if you stick doggedly to your preconceived blueprint.

Being slick is what keeps some people from being intelligent.

People have a right to their own cultures—even Americans. Those who come here and say that they cannot follow some of our laws that conflict with their culture are free to leave.

Much of what are called "social problems" consists of the fact that intellectuals have theories that do not fit the real world. From this they conclude that it is the real world which is wrong and needs changing.

Some of the questions on the California High School Exit Exam are the kinds of questions whose answers you would have been expected to know before you got into high school in past generations.

Although my wife and I live a modest life, I am amazed at the bills that come in each month—and I can't help wondering how people who live it up manage to make ends meet.

Tony Snow of Fox News seems to be the only one in the media who has pointed out what a farce it is for people to be talking about a tax cut in terms of so many billions of dollars. Government can only change the tax rates. How much the tax revenue will change—and in which direction—will be known only after the fact.

Thank heaven human beings are born with an ability to laugh at absurdity. Otherwise, we might go stark raving mad from all the absurd things we encounter in life.

The best thing about buying a house is that it puts an end to the exhausting process of house-hunting.

Although Ronald Reagan was the only actor to become President, he was one of the few politicians who was not acting.

A recently reprinted memoir by Frederick Douglass has footnotes explaining what words like "arraigned," "curried" and "exculpate" meant, and explaining who Job was. In other words, this man who was born a slave and never went to school educated himself to the point where his words now have to be explained to today's expensively under-educated generation.

Too many in the media act as if decency is a violation of the First Amendment.

People sometimes ask if I have tried to convince black

"leaders" to take a different view on racial issues. Of course not. I wouldn't spend my time trying to persuade the mafia to give up crime. Why should I spend time trying to convince race hustlers to give up victimhood? It's their bread and butter.

Egalitarians create the most dangerous inequality of all—inequality of power. Allowing politicians to determine what all other human beings will be allowed to earn is one of the most reckless gambles imaginable. Like the income tax, it may start off being applied only to the rich but it will inevitably reach us all.

To too many teachers, social workers and others in occupations with pretensions of being "professional," what being a professional means is not having to listen to common sense from ordinary people, much less develop any of their own.

Great Predictions Department: "I do not mind saying I think they are taking a gamble." That was Red Sox owner Harry Frazee after selling Babe Ruth to the Yankees.

Those who are preoccupied with "making a statement" usually don't have any statements worth making.

A magician was asked what had happened to the lady he used to saw in half in his act. "Oh, she's retired," he said. "Now she lives in Chicago—and Denver."

Despite the rhetoric of the "haves" and the "have-nots" that is so dear to the heart of the political left, a more accurate description of most Americans today would be the "have-lots" and the "have-lots-more."

The people I feel sorry for are those who do 90 percent of what it takes to succeed.

Trust is one of those things that is much easier to maintain than it is to repair.

It is self-destructive for any society to create a situation where a baby who is born into the world today automatically has pre-existing grievances against another baby born at the same time, because of what their ancestors did centuries ago. It is hard enough to solve our own problems, without trying to solve our ancestors' problems.

Don't you love it when the intelligentsia condemn the United States for responding "unilaterally" after we are attacked, instead of waiting for the approval of that confusion of voices known as "world opinion"?

Have you ever heard a single hard fact to back up all the sweeping claims for the benefits of "diversity"?

Ask ten people what "fairness" means and you can get eleven different definitions. Expecting government to promote "fairness" is just giving politicians more arbitrary power.

We seem to be getting closer and closer to a situation where nobody is responsible for what they did but we are all responsible for what somebody else did.

As long as human beings are imperfect, there will always be arguments for extending the power of government to deal with these imperfections. The only logical stopping place is totalitarianism—unless we realize that tolerating imperfections is the price of freedom.

The people I feel sorry for are those who insist on continuing to do what they have always done but want the results to be different from what they have always been.

Alaska is much larger than France and Germany—combined. Yet its population is less than one-tenth that of New York City. Keep that in mind the next time you hear some environmentalist hysteria about the danger of "spoiling" Alaska by drilling for oil in an area smaller than Dulles Airport.

Of all ignorance, the ignorance of the educated is the most dangerous. Not only are educated people likely to have more influence, they are the last people to suspect that they don't know what they are talking about when they go outside their narrow fields.

One of the many problems with envy is that you have no real way of knowing that someone is more fortunate than you until you are both at the end of your lives—and then it is too late to matter.

Bad credit affects many things, including your chances of getting a job that requires responsibility. On the other hand, if your credit is too good, you get inundated with junk mail.

The harm that divorce does to children is not limited to the children of parents who get divorced. Children whose parents never divorce nevertheless see their friends' and classmates' parents getting divorced and have something to worry about whenever their own parents have a disagreement.

People used to say, "Ignorance is no excuse." Today, ignorance is no problem. Our schools promote so much self-esteem that people confidently spout off about all sorts of things that they know nothing about.

I am so old that I can remember when other people's achievements were considered to be an inspiration, rather than a grievance.

Imagine that a genie magically appeared and offered to grant you one wish—and, being a decent sort, you wished that everyone's income would be doubled. That could bring down on you the wrath of the political left, because it would mean that the gap between the rich and the poor had widened. That is basically their complaint against the American economy.

What "multiculturalism" boils down to is that you can praise any culture in the world except Western culture—and you cannot blame any culture in the world except Western culture.

One of the sure signs of full employment is bad service.

You know you have a lot of junk when there is not enough room to park one car in a three-car garage.

Some bad policies are just good policies that have been carried too far.

It always seems to come as a big surprise to the media when the stock market goes up and down—even though stocks have been going up and down for centuries.

If you have a right to respect, that means other people don't have a right to their own opinions.

Liberals seem to believe that blacks should be represented

proportionally everywhere—except in conservative organizations.

If there is anything worse than outliving your money, it is outliving all your loved ones.

Considering that we all enter the world the same way and leave in the same condition, we spend an awful lot of time in between trying to show that we are so different from other people.

No matter how old I get or how sophisticated I think I have become, I still find it hard to deal with betrayal.

What are bond issues on the ballot except taxes on future taxpayers who cannot vote yet? It is taxation without representation.

The spectacular success of some people with no college degree, such as Bill Gates and Rush Limbaugh, may give college education a bad name—justifiably, in many cases.

Every time you watch Congress on C-SPAN, you are seeing millions of dollars worth of free advertising for incumbents, while those same incumbents vote restrictions on their potential rivals' ability to raise money to pay for advertising, using the pretty phrase "campaign finance reform."

The first time I flew into London, I was stirred by the thought that, in these skies during World War II, a thousand men of the Royal Air Force saved Western civilization. Today, I wonder how many of our young people have any idea what that was all about, given how little time our schools devote to history, except as a source of grievances, whining, and excuses.

The phrase "glass ceiling" is an insult to our intelligence. What does glass mean, except that we cannot see it? In other words, in the absence of evidence, we are expected to go along with what is said because it is said in accusatory and self-righteous tones and we will be denounced if we don't accept it.

A careful definition of words would destroy half the agenda of the political left and scrutinizing evidence would destroy the other half.

Can one person make a difference? I hate to think where we would be if James Q. Wilson had not written about crime or if Milton Friedman had not written about markets, much less where we would be if Winston Churchill had not been prime minister when Britain faced seemingly hopeless odds against the Nazis.

How anyone can argue in favor of being non-judgmental is beyond me. To say that being non-judgmental is better than being judgmental is itself a judgment, and therefore a violation of the principle.

As a rule of thumb, Congressional legislation that is bipartisan is usually twice as bad as legislation that is partisan.

At one time, I could tear a Washington phone book in half. Not only was I a lot younger, the Washington phone book was a lot smaller.

How many other species' members kill each other to the same extent as human beings?

Time and again, over the centuries, price controls have

produced three things: shortages, quality deterioration and black markets. Why would anyone want any of those things with pharmaceutical drugs?

Don't you get tired of seeing so many "non-conformists" with the same non-conformist look?

Everyone is presumed to be innocent until proven guilty—in a court of law. But we cannot just mindlessly repeat words outside the context in which they apply. If you discovered that your spouse had been secretly checking into motels with someone else, would you presume innocence until proven guilty?

Automobiles are getting to look so much alike that it is hard to tell some cars apart, even when they are made by different manufacturers or even made in different countries. Recently, I was embarrassed to realize that I was trying to get into someone else's German-made car on a parking lot, thinking it was my own Japanese-made car.

Nolan Ryan's baseball career was so long that he struck out seven guys whose fathers he had also struck out. (Barry Bonds and Bobby Bonds, for example.)

Why do some people use a fancy mathematical term like "parameters" when all that they really mean is boundaries?

Flattery makes the most effective chains. Hitler told the Germans that they were a master race—and came very close to making them slaves.

One of the dumbest things you can do is have taxpayers supporting idle adolescents who have nothing but time on their hands to get into trouble. The money it costs is the least of the problems.

Neither the depth of despondency nor the height of euphoria tells you how long either will last.

Sign on a monument to people who served in the military: "All gave some. Some gave all."